# INVESTING
# FOR INCOME

www.legalfish.com

start-up business of Restaurant
NYC

# INVESTING FOR INCOME

## A Bond Mutual Fund Approach to High-Return, Low-Risk Profits

*"A Sensible Way to Maximize Your Income for the New Millennium"*

**RALPH G. NORTON**

**McGraw-Hill**

New York   San Francisco   Washington, D.C.   Auckland   Bogotá
Caracas   Lisbon   London   Madrid   Mexico City   Milan
Montreal   New Delhi   San Juan   Singapore
Sydney   Tokyo   Toronto

**Library of Congress Cataloging-in-Publication Data**

Norton, Ralph G.
    Investing for income : a bond mutual fund approach to high-return,
low-risk profits / by Ralph G. Norton.
        p.   cm.
    "A sensible way to maximize your income for the new millennium."
    ISBN 0-07-134295-8
    1. Mutual funds.   2. Investments.   I. Title.
HG4530.N67   1999
332.63'27—dc21                                                98-48173
                                                                        CIP

# McGraw-Hill

*A Division of The **McGraw·Hill** Companies*

1 2 3 4 5 6 7 8 9 0 DOC/DOC 9 0 4 3 2 1 0 9

ISBN 0-07-134295-8

The sponsoring editor for this book was Stephen Isaacs, the editing supervisor was
Donna Muscatello, and the production supervisor was Suzanne W. B. Rapcavage.
It was set in Palatino by North Market Street Graphics.

Printed and bound by R. R. Donnelley & Sons Company.

This publication is designed to provide accurate and authoritative information
in regard to the subject matter covered. It is sold with the understanding that
neither the author or the publisher is engaged in rendering legal, accounting,
or other professional service. If legal advice or other expert assistance is required,
the services of a competent professional person should be sought.

*—From a Declaration of Principles jointly adopted by a Committee
of the American Bar Association and a Committee of Publishers.*

McGraw-Hill books are available at special quantity discounts to use as premiums
and sales promotions, or for use in corporate training programs. For more information, please write to the Director of Special Sales, McGraw-Hill, 11 West 19th
Street, New York, NY 10011. Or contact your local bookstore.

 This book is printed on recycled, acid-free paper containing a minimum
of 50% recycled de-inked fiber

*To Donna, Rebecca,*
*Mom, and Dad,*
*for their support and patience*

# CONTENTS

**Chapter 3**

# Fund Yields   27

**Chapter 7**

# Fund Types   55

**Chapter 10**

## Keeping Track of Your Investments and the Market    135

**Appendix A**

## 26 Key Questions to Ask Before You Invest in an Income Fund    141

**Appendix B**

## Tables of Top Funds by Category    145

**Appendix C**

**Internet Resources    191**

Investing for income is now more complicated and difficult than ever. With the decline in interest rates over the last several years, the days of double-digit CD and money fund yields are over. Ironically, things are getting harder just at a time when they need to be easier.

When I started in the mutual fund business in 1982, the hottest mutual fund investments were money markets. At the time, rates on many of these funds were in excess of 15%, and they were selling faster than prospectuses could be mailed. By the mid-1980s, bond funds became the hot sellers within an environment of declining rates and huge total returns. During that time, I spoke to thousands of income fund investors. What I found was that most knew very little about the risks or returns inherent in these funds. Many were used to buying individual bonds and did not even know that a bond or money fund actually never matures. There was a need for information then, and there is even more of a need today.

Currently, about half of all money invested in mutual funds is in bond and/or money market accounts. There are more than 4300 funds in about 50 different categories, ranging from 100% U.S. Treasury money funds to highly aggressive zero coupon bond funds. However, very little information is available to help individual investors understand and adequately select the best income fund choices for their particular needs. It's my hope that this book will lay the foundation for good income fund selection and sensible income-generating strategies.

As we move into the 21st century, the need for information in this part of the market will grow tremendously. Baby boom investors will start to shift their investment pattern from one of saving to one of distribution. Indeed, there are many economists who suggest that sometime around the year 2010, money that has flowed into stocks and stock funds will begin to flow out and will be the catalyst of a protracted bear market. The thinking is that baby boomers will move into retirement and want to live off the hard-earned savings of the previous 20 to 30 years. To do this, they will shift money from the more aggressive equity allocation in their portfolios to securities that provide higher levels of income, such as high dividend stock funds, bond funds, and money markets. As this happens, the need for objective information on how to select and maintain an income portfolio will be immense.

*Investing for Income* is set up in 10 chapters. Each chapter can leverage the information in the others but is not required reading to understand the concepts in any other. In this way you can go right to the topic you are interested in without having to read everything that has come before.

1. **Start with Yourself** is set up to help you evaluate your income investing needs and your risk tolerance. It also helps you examine your long-term objectives, which in turn define your investment plan and allocations.

2. **The Basics** will take you through the basics of income investing, including the relationship between interest rates and income fund value. It also reviews the risks that all income investors face, whether they invest in individual securities or funds.

3. **Fund Yields** is designed to unravel the complexity of understanding how to measure your income. There are lots of terms to describe yield. Each is a bit different, but all are valuable in your investment tool chest.

4. **Assessing the Fund and the Fund Manager** helps you learn about who is managing your money, a vital concern. Do they have the experience? Do they have the resources? This section of the book helps you develop a framework to assess the people behind a fund investment.

5. **Fees and Loads** proves there are no free lunches on Wall Street. Mutual fund companies are in the business of making money. Knowing just what you are being charged is key in any investment process. This section of the book reviews the key expenses and charges associated with income funds.

6. **Understanding Fund Returns and Risk** shows you how to properly measure both return and risk, which is vital in assessing the value of any mutual fund. This section of the book takes you through the most common and important measures and how they relate to your investment.

7. **Fund Types** explains the major types of income funds, with easy-to-understand examples of risk and return. Each section also identifies who may be most suitable for each category of fund.

8. **Selecting Income Funds** starts with the important point that buying the "right" fund is a function of your objectives. Some investors buy for total return; others select funds for yield. This

chapter offers several different methods for identifying superior funds.

9. **Income Portfolio Strategies** offers income investing strategies designed to meet a wide variety of objectives, from conservative yield to aggressive total return and income. Each portfolio description includes allocation percentages and suggested funds.

10. **Keeping Track of Your Investments and the Market**—The investing process just begins when funds are purchased. This chapter shows you how to track your fund's progress and what factors will influence your income returns over time.

   **Appendix A: 26 Key Questions to Ask Before You Buy**—In this section of the book, you are provided with a list of 26 key questions to ask yourself and the fund family before you invest. These questions will help you determine if the fund is really suitable for you.

   **Appendix B: Tables of Top Funds by Category**—In this section you are provided a list of top funds selected by the author for each fund category discussed in the book. In addition, to the fund names, you are given key data that will help you find the right fund for your strategy.

   **Appendix C: Internet Resources**—In this last section of the book, we have provided you with a comprehensive list of on-line Internet resources to help you on your investment journey. They range from daily fund information to resources to help you with your taxes.

**Good Investing!**
**Chip Norton**

# ACKNOWLEDGMENTS

I would like to thank all those who have supported me in this project over the last year, including the folks at Standard & Poor's, Shauna Morrison, Susan Pevear, and Jim Forest. I'd also like to thank Tom Lydon and Doug Fabian for helping me develop my first bond fund publication. Thanks to McGraw-Hill Professional Publishing for providing me with the opportunity to write this book and to *Research* magazine for allowing me to use information that appeared in my monthly column. I'd also like to thank the following organizations for their kind approval of the use of mutual fund information throughout the book: S&P Micropal, IBC Financial Data, Morningstar, and the Investment Company Institute.

# CHAPTER 1

# Start with Yourself

## WHY INCOME WILL BE IMPORTANT
## IN THE COMING YEARS

**T**oday, huge numbers of retired individuals need supplemental income to maintain their lifestyles. Many of these investors turn to bond and money market funds for income generation and a conservative investment approach. Of the 8300 mutual funds now available to the individual investor, about 4300 are income funds. These funds total over $2.5 trillion in assets under management, about half of all mutual fund assets. Income funds occupy all sorts of portfolios. They act as anchors in volatile markets in diversified portfolios as well as primary income sources for retirement portfolios. Almost every 401k, 403b, and other retirement account offers an income fund choice. This will not change in the future. In fact, these funds will become more important.

The baby boom generation is getting older. Currently, most boomers are trying to figure out how to pay for their childrens' education and their own retirement. Most of their mutual fund money is in equity funds, as it should be. But as time marches on, the investment objectives and goals of this investing generation will change. As they do, boomers will begin to shift their investments from growth to a more conservative balance. This shift will channel large sums into income funds. (See Figure 1-1.)

For investors seeking finally to live off of what they have earned, income funds provide a superior way to generate income, preserve principal, and accumulate value. To many, the preservation of principal and cap-

**FIGURE 1-1**

How Mutual Fund Assets Are Invested

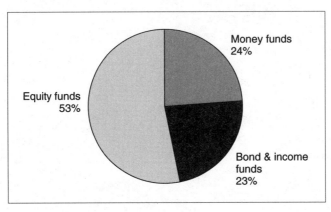

Source: Investment Company Institute

ital appreciation are mutually exclusive. The stereotype of fixed income funds has been one of boring, low-returning funds. High-income bond funds averaged 14% between 1995 and 1997 and 11% over the last five years, which rivals the long-term average return for the S&P 500. Yet this fund group did it with about one quarter of the risk. Convertible bond funds averaged a 20% return in 1997 and currently sport a three-year return of 18%. There are many other fixed income stories like these. The bottom line is that income funds can produce excellent returns and income.

## Income Fund Growth

As mentioned, there are currently over 4300 funds and $2.5 trillion in income funds. These numbers didn't materialize overnight. Indeed, the growth of the income fund sector has been steady for many years. According to the Investment Company Institute, the mutual fund trade group, bond and income funds totaled $54 billion in 1984. By the end of 1997, assets had swelled to just over $1 trillion, an 1800% increase. During that period, shareholder accounts increased by 27.6 million, from 4.4 million in 1984 to 32 million in 1997. The number of funds went from 345 to 2751 in the same period. This growth trend is illustrated in Figure 1–2.

The growth in the money market sector is equally impressive. In 1984, total money fund assets were $232 billion. By 1997, assets had moved to $1.05 trillion, a 352% rise. Shareholder accounts rose from 13.9 million to 35.7 million, while the number of funds increased from 373 to 1013. Assets of all mutual funds increased 1113% in the same period.

**FIGURE 1-2**

Income Fund Asset Growth 1984–1997

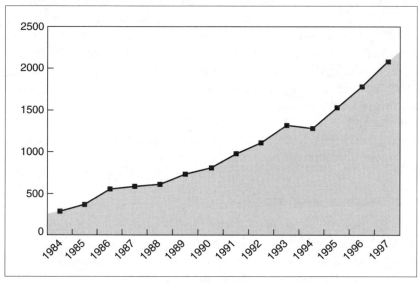

Source: Investment Company Institute

## WHO ARE INCOME INVESTORS? ARE YOU ONE?

Over the years I have talked with many income fund investors and have heard numerous reasons for the purchase of income funds. Two major themes continue to dominate consideration, income and total return. There is a big difference between the two.

### True-Blue Income

True income investors are typically those who are using the income generated by the fund to supplement their personal income needs. This means a distribution to the investor of the fund's monthly income. These investors often are looking for the absolute best yields and are usually willing to accept a bit of risk to get it. Preservation of principal and capital growth of the fund are secondary considerations. It is this type of investor who would most likely buy a high municipal bond fund or a high-income "junk" bond fund. However, I've also seen a type of investor who is ultraconservative and is looking for yields in excess of bank CD rates or Treasury bills. This type of investor may find a high-quality, safe money market, or a short-term bond fund suitable for their needs. Often, it is the "income need" that drives the investment.

By "income need," I mean the amount of cash flow an individual requires to meet his or her expenses. For example, let's say the investor has $500,000 to invest. The investor calculates that living expenses and other discretionary spending will require about $2000 per month. To achieve the $2000 per month, the investor needs to get a yield of about 5% on the $500,000, or $25,000 annually. The next step for this investor is to find a fund that delivers 5%. In this case, a good top-yielding money fund will do the trick. However, if expenses dictate higher yields, a move away from the money funds might be necessary to achieve the desired monthly cash flow.

When evaluating a fund, the "true blue" income investor will clearly be focusing on actual yield distributions for the fund rather than looking at a total return figure that takes into account yield and price gain or loss.

## Total Return Income Investor

The other type of investor often seen is the "total return" income investor. This investor does not require the income for expenses or to supplement other cash flow needs. This investor typically reinvests all the income each month and leverages the power of compound interest. The goal of this investor is to build capital in the fund by both income and price appreciation. Total return income investors may have a significant portion of their accounts in equities and are only using the income portion as a stabilizer to balance the risk of the overall portfolio. This type of investor will often use funds that generate high total returns, such as long-term municipal or corporate funds, convertible and international funds, as well as specialty funds like strategic income or zero coupon bond funds.

When total return investors evaluate a fund's return, they often focus on the total return of the portfolio rather than just the yield. While yield is an important component of return, some of the funds mentioned get much of their return boost from an appreciation in price. If this sounds a bit complicated, don't worry. We'll get to fund performance measures and how they work in coming chapters.

## Someplace in Between

While these are the two most common types of income investors, there are many more who fall somewhere between true income investors and total return investors. For in-between investors a combination of strategies can be used to effectively generate both income and total return. In the chapters on income strategies, we'll look at combining various types of funds to achieve specific goals of yield, total return, or a mix of both. You'll find that you don't have to take on huge amounts of risk to increase your returns or yields.

## DEFINE YOUR PLAN

There's an old saying: "If you don't know where you are going, any road will get you there." The point is that without a plan, you can't develop an investment strategy and won't end up selecting funds that are consistent with your objectives. The planning process does not have to be complex. All it requires is a review of your needs, expectations for return, and your tolerance for risk.

### Income Needs

The amount of income you'll need is a function of your lifestyle. Some investors rely solely on their investments for income, whereas others use their investments to supplement other income sources such as Social Security or corporate pension plans. In either case, you need to define just how much income you will need to support your lifestyle and then work backwards to define how much income will be required to meet the goal. I say backwards because you are trying to fit the amount of income required to an investment yield. Typically, we look at it from the other direction. For example, if you have $100,000 and an interest rate of 5%, you know the annual income will be $5000. From a planning perspective, the question is how much income you need to meet your needs. Let's say you want to live on an income of $50,000 from your investments. If you can only get a 5% return, then you would need $1,000,000 in the investment ($1,000,000 × 5% = $50,000). As you can see, it's a question of both income need *and* return.

The optimal scenario is to find an investment that provides enough income for your needs with the smallest amount of money in the fund portfolio. For example, if you were able to increase the yield on the investment to 10%, you would only need half as much money—$500,000—in your account to meet the same income target. As you can see, increasing your return can go a long way toward achieving your goals. On the lifestyle end of the scenario, the difference between 5% and 10% of course doubles your income. If you had that same million to invest at 10%, your annual income would be $100,000. That extra $50,000 would go a long way in improving your lifestyle, or making it that much more secure.

The lesson here is that you must take some time to identify both your expenses and your investment scenario before you even start to consider which funds or allocation is right for your situation.

## Time Horizon

The investment time horizon is simply the amount of time you expect to hold the securities you are considering for purchase. The time horizon can be as short as a few weeks or as long as the rest of your life. It is critical to define the time horizon before you buy a fund because it is key to have consistency between your time horizon and your goals. For example, if you absolutely must have your investment money in six months to buy a new home, your investment time horizon will be six months. Would you want to invest in the most speculative, volatile investment for those six months? Probably not, because there would be a greater probability that at the end of the six months, you would not have achieved your investment goals. Indeed, you might have lost a significant portion of your money. In this case, you might want to consider a more conservative, stable investment that provides a reasonable return and keeps your principal secure. Conversely, if you have 30 years to invest and your goal is to achieve the highest return and you are willing to accept lots of risk, a fund such as a money fund would be the last investment you'd want. More likely, you'd be focusing on long-term growth stock funds in such a case.

*As a rule, a longer time horizon is needed for more volatile investments.*

## Return Expectations

As you develop your investment plan, you need to consider the amount of return you want from your investment. If you are looking for high levels of return, you focus on certain types of funds and portfolios. If you don't mind conservative returns, you focus on other funds. Each fund or allocation selection will be a function of your income needs and time horizon, both previously discussed.

For example, if you have five years to meet a particular goal and you know how much you must end up with at the end of those five years, you can calculate the return you will need to achieve the goal. Once you do this, you can target funds or allocations that have been able to consistently achieve that level of return. Lets say you have $10,000 to invest and you need to accumulate about $25,000 in five years. To do this, you need an annualized return of 20%. This tells you a 5% money fund won't help, but an aggressive equity fund might get you a lot closer to your goal. Keep in mind, however, that there are no guarantees in the investment world. This is why it is crucial to understand the risks associated with various investment strategies. A time horizon of five years is fairly short for an aggressive fund, and there is a good chance that the 20% return might not be achieved. Conversely, if you had that same $10,000 but only needed about $13,000 in five years, a money fund would be a good alternative, with far less volatility along the way. The same rules apply with income investing. Funds with the highest yields will pose more risk, while those that are safer will have lower yields.

*As a rule, the greater the expected return, the more aggressive the fund must be to achieve the return.*

## Reality of Risk

Another element in the investment equation is risk. To achieve higher return or yields, you are forced to accept higher levels of risk. The trick is to balance risk and return. You don't want to take on extraordinary risk if you have goals for moderate or low returns. The goal is to match return expectations with the risk inherent in the investment and your time horizon.

You can manage risk in many ways, including the selection of the proper funds and by mixing funds in various allocations. We'll talk about risk and how to measure it in many of the upcoming chapters.

*As a rule, risk will be proportionate to return or yield. You should be willing to accept reasonable risk for reasonable return.*

## TAKE SOME TIME—DON'T BE SURPRISED

Taking just a short amount of time to review your income needs, time horizon, return expectations, and risk will help you define your ultimate investing goals and lead you to fund or portfolio selections that are consistent with those goals. This process is not a one-time affair. You should review these factors at least once each year. As we get older, our goals and expectations for our investments can and do change. Your portfolio should reflect these changes. You don't want to wake up one day and be shocked by a huge decline in your portfolio. Being involved with your investments and taking an active role helps you in the investment process. Reviewing your portfolio, checking fund prices and returns, and reading about what's happening in the market are all part of being an active, profitable investor.

# CHAPTER 2

# The Basics

## THE WONDERS OF COMPOUNDING

**A**ll income investments provide interest or dividends. What is done with these gains will have a significant impact on the accumulation of value of an account over time. An investor who simply uses the income to pay current expenses will only have the original principal at work in the account. The investor who puts the income back to work, or reinvests it, takes full advantage of the powers of compounding.

Compound interest is simply the *interest earned on interest*. It has been called the eighth wonder of the world. Why? Over time, the interest on interest element can exponentially increase the value of your money. The two key items in determining just how much growth you will receive when compounding are the interest rate and the amount of time the compounding takes place. Let's look at a few examples.

Say an investor purchases $10,000 of a money fund that yields 5% annually. This will bring an annual income of $500. If the investor decided to have the income distributed to be used for expenses each year, he or she would be left with the $10,000 principal throughout the entire holding period of the investment because the price of the money fund would always be held at $1.0 per share. After 30 years the investor would have earned $15,000 ($500/yr × 30 years). The total account value would be $25,000 when you include the original $10,000 investment.

Now assume that same investor reinvests the $500 each year. At the end of the first year, the account would be worth $10,500 ($10,000 original investment plus the $500 income). Now here's where it becomes interesting. At the end of the second year, the investor will have earned 5% on an account value of $10,500. This will provide an annual income of $525 (5% × $10,500). Now, carry this forward 30 years. Since the investor reinvested the income and earned interest on interest, the total value of the account would be $43,219. This is $18,219 more than the investor who did not reinvest and is all due to the power of compounding.

*The power of compounding is maximized with both time and return.*

Let's say our hypothetical investor was able to achieve an interest rate of 10% annually rather than 5%. What would happen to the account? Even though your intuition suggests the investment should be about double, amazingly, the $10,000 would have grown to $174,500 in the 30-year period. This is a whopping four times more than the value based on the compounded 5%, and just about seven times more than the investor who did not compound. As you can see, both time and rate can produce spectacular results.

### Rule of 72

In the previous two examples I assumed a money fund that has a stable price per share. When using funds that have prices that can move higher, the impact of compounding becomes even greater. There is a simple guide called the Rule of 72 that helps you determine the approximate time it takes for an investment to double based on a certain interest rate. You simply divide 72 by the interest rate. Here's how it works:

Time it takes for an investment to double = 72/Interest Rate
$$= 72/5\% = 14.4 \text{ years}$$

### MATURITY

Bond investments are often called *fixed income securities* because certain attributes of the bond are fixed or held constant. The first and most important element is the maturity. The *maturity* of a bond describes when the issuer will make the final interest and principal payment. For example, a 10-year municipal bond due on December 31, 2008, will pay back its last coupon payment and the entire initial principal in December 2008. Between now and then, the bond will also pay a "fixed" interest payment called the *coupon*.

A bond or money market fund has no set maturity date. The fund manager attempts to buy bonds in a target maturity range, say 10 years. As old bonds get shorter in maturity, they are replaced with new, longer-term bonds. What you get is a fund that essentially has a perpetual maturity in that the fund will always have an average maturity based on the bonds in the portfolio, but will actually never mature. This is a major point that is often overlooked by fund investors.

## COUPON

Bonds usually pay their coupon twice each year. The coupon amount is fixed and is the same for the life of the bond. The amount is based on a percentage of the face or par value of the original bond. For example, an individual 10-year corporate bond may have an issuance face value of $1000 and a coupon rate of 10%. The bond holder will receive $100 per year (10% × $1000) each year for 10 years. In addition, at the end of the tenth year, the bond holder will receive the full $1000 principal amount.

Today, many bonds are held in "street name." This means that instead of being held specifically with the owner, they are held with the owner's broker-dealer. This facilitates transfer when bonds are bought and sold. If they were in registered form with the owner, which means that the bond is registered in the name of the bond owner on the books of the issuer, transactions would require physical transfer of the bond certificates. Historically, the actual bond certificate was often held physically by the owner. Attached to the certificate were coupons that were "clipped" off and redeemed for the interest payment on the appropriate date. This is where we get the term *coupon clipper* as an expression of a conservative investor in bonds. Because of changes in technology in the finance industry, a simple term like this will probably be forgotten in a few more years. The mutual fund shares are held by the fund family in "street name." The fund also handles all purchases, sales, or exchanges.

A bond fund's interest payment is derived from the income payments of all the bonds in the portfolio and is NOT fixed like an individual bond's coupon payment. Most bond and money funds pay their interest once per month. The income amount will vary depending on the interest rates being paid by each of the bonds in the portfolio. To complicate matters even further, the interest payment of a fund is actually considered a dividend payment by the IRS.

## PAYMENT METHOD

Another challenge with individual coupon bonds in a small portfolio is that the semiannual income payment can be restrictive. With the income arriving just twice a year, a good amount of planning has to be done to balance the incoming revenue with an individual's expenses. In addition, new bonds can't be purchased until enough money is accumulated to buy a new bond. In the case of municipal bonds, which come in denominations of $5000, it might take quite a few coupon payments to buy a new bond.

As mentioned above, a bond fund or money fund's income is paid each month, rather than semiannually like a bond's. A fund investor can elect to reinvest the income into new fractional shares each month. In this way, investors don't have to wait until enough money is accumulated to buy a whole bond. This option gives the investor a chance to increase the compounding effect of the investment. Investors can also elect to have the monthly distribution sent to another fund or even out to their bank account. Most money funds offer check-writing as yet another way to access your money.

## DIVERSIFICATION

For an investor with limited capital, a good amount of work is involved in buying individual bonds. A good review of the bond's current price and yield as well as its credit quality, call options, maturity structure, and other complicated factors must be performed. This takes a lot of time and effort.

Bond and money funds are pools of bonds managed by a professional money manager and can be bought for as little as $1000. Most funds have many bonds in the portfolio, which provides the investor with great diversification. If one bond has trouble, hopefully its impact on the overall portfolio will be small. Add to this the manager's ability to stay clear of troubled issues and buy only suitable bonds and you dramatically reduce this risk in the portfolio.

## BOND QUALITY

Like any investment, the quality of the underlying issuer is a key component in determining the value of the issuer's securities. In the bond world, creditworthiness is measured by a bond's rating.

Several credit agencies, including Standard & Poor's, Moody's Investor's Service, and Fitch Investor's Services, specialize in analyzing the creditworthiness of bonds. The issuer must request and pay one of these firms for a rating of its issue. Once a rating is assigned, it will be regularly reviewed by the rating agency and may be raised, lowered, or put on special alert. Each firm has its own criteria for a rating, which takes into account many factors, such as management ability, income outlook, and cash flow.

Bonds with ratings of BBB and above are considered investment-grade bonds. Many investors require this rating for purchase. If a bond falls below this grade, these firms normally are forced to sell the issue. This is why it is very important for an issuer to hold a high rating. In addition, the higher the rating, the lower the interest required by the issuer to pay bondholders. **A higher quality issue will normally have a lower yield for a given maturity than a lower quality bond.** First-time bond buyers are usually advised to purchase only those bonds with the highest quality rating. Treasury bonds, or those backed by the U.S. government, are of the highest quality ratings, usually AAA.

It is important to note that while a rating assists an investor in analyzing the creditworthiness of a bond, the rating is not a guarantee. Ratings can and do change. Bonds also may be insured. There are several private insurance firms that insure bonds. Once a bond has been insured, it normally receives the top rating by the rating agency.

Like bonds, income funds come in many varieties of quality. Treasury bond funds have the highest quality, and high income "junk" bonds usually have the lowest. Higher yields are offered on those funds that have the lowest quality rating because the investor assumes the greatest risk to his or her principal and interest.

One of the tricky parts of assessing quality in a bond fund has to do with diversification. As mentioned in the previous section, the ability of the manager to mix and match bonds in a fund's portfolio can reduce the risk of the overall portfolio. For example, the manager of a junk bond fund could pick just the "cream of the junk bond crop" for the portfolio. A manager's ability to avoid bad issues through quality, active management adds another layer of assurance (not insurance) that the fund will have limited credit quality problems. In this example, the fund may never own a bond that defaults despite investing in a sector where default rates tend to be high.

Rating Agency Symbols

| | S&P | Moody | Fitch |
|---|---|---|---|
| *Investment Grade* | | | |
| Highest Quality | AAA | Aaa | AAA |
| High Quality | AA | Aa | AA |
| Upper Quality | A | A | A |
| Medium Upper Quality | BBB | Baa | BBB |
| *Speculative Grade* | | | |
| Speculative Grade | BB | Ba | BB |
| | B | B | B |
| | CCC | Caa | CCC |
| | CC | Ca | CC |
| | C | C | C |
| Default | D | | DDD |

## INTEREST RATES AND BOND PRICES

**Interest rates and bond prices move in opposite directions. As rates increase, bond and bond fund prices will decline. Conversely, as rates decline, bond prices will increase.** This is an extremely important relationship to understand because interest rates are the driving force in the bond world.

The amount a bond or bond fund will move as rates change is a function of the bond type. Short-term bonds and funds will move less for a given change in rates, whereas bonds and funds with longer maturities and durations (more on this later) are more sensitive to rate changes. Understanding this relationship helps you select the right fund for your objectives. For example, if your objective is to be extremely conservative and you are concerned about the value of your fund, you will most likely steer clear of long-term funds because they present the most risk if rates change. On the other hand, if you feel confident that rates will fall and you have a longer-term investment time horizon, a fund with a longer maturity that offers greater price gain might be more attractive.

## YIELD IS THE PRICE OF RISK

As you may have guessed, bonds and/or funds that have more risk because of longer maturity or are more speculative should, and normally will, offer higher rates. It makes sense that investors will demand more compensation if they have to accept more risk. **Simply put, yields reflect the risk of the bond or fund.** This is why U.S. government securities, which are backed by the full faith and credit of the U.S. government, offer a lower interest rate than a comparable security issued by a small start-up company. On the other end of the yield spectrum, bond funds that focus on speculative junk bonds offer the highest yields to compensate for the potential that the issuer will not be able to make regular interest or principal payments.

## THE YIELD CURVE

A *yield curve* is a chart that graphically depicts the yields of different maturity bonds of the same credit quality and type. Yield is depicted on the vertical axis and maturity on the horizontal axis. The yield curve is also called the *term structure of interest rates.* A normal yield curve is upward sloping, with short-term rates lower than long-term rates. An inverted yield curve is downward sloping, with short-term rates higher than long-term rates. A flat yield curve occurs when short-term rates are the same as long-term rates.

Yield curves are generally normal, that is, upward sloping. Given the greater uncertainty investors face when investing over longer time horizons, long-term rates are generally higher than short-term rates. There are a number of different theories that try to explain the shape of the yield curve. One theory suggests that the yield curve is determined by investor expectations of future short-term rates. An upward sloping yield curve implies that short-term interest rates will be higher in the future. Another theory suggests that the yield curve is determined by supply and demand for different maturity securities.

The most common yield curve is the Treasury yield curve, which is shown in Figure 2–1. The Treasury yield curve is used as a benchmark rate because of its high liquidity and riskless nature. Interest rates of non-Treasury securities are typically based on the Treasury yields. For example, a high quality 10-year corporate bond may carry a yield that is ½% higher than the 10-year Treasury. The additional ½% "risk premium" compensates the buyer for the additional risk inherent in corporate issues. The risk premium incorporates such factors as the issuer's perceived credit quality, the issue's expected liquidity, and taxability of income. Another yield curve can be constructed from yields of bond or money market funds. Money funds have the shortest maturity and lie on the left side of the curve. Long-term bond funds normally have higher yields and sit at the upper right portion of the "fund" yield curve.

**FIGURE 2–1**

Treasury Yield Curve

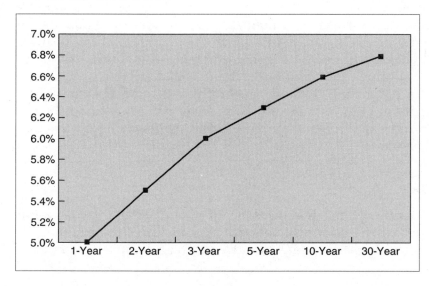

One of the most important uses of a yield curve is that it allows a quick, graphic way to see the value of income of various funds or securities. If a money fund yield as higher than a more volatile junk bond fund, the income advantage would clearly be with the money fund.

## RISK

The term *risk* can be very subjective in the investment world. Since risk is a concept that is really defined by each individual, there is no single definition for it. For example, what one person perceives as risk may be seen as opportunity by another. As a baseline, there are several types of risk in the investment world that pertain to income investing. These include interest rate risk, credit risk, income risk, inflation risk, event risk, tax risk, currency risk, and management risk. Each impacts a bond or a fund's price differently.

### Interest Rate Risk

The most important risk is interest rate risk. *Interest rate risk* is the risk that the price of a bond or a bond fund will decline due to higher interest rates. As we discussed earlier, rising rates cause bond prices to fall, and falling rates cause prices to rise. However, just how much they rise and fall depends on a number of factors, including the years to maturity and coupon yield of the bond. Generally, longer maturity bonds will have greater price swings for a given change in rates, whereas shorter maturity securities are less sensitive to changes. This is exactly why rates are normally higher on bonds with long maturities. As an investor, you must be compensated with yield and return for the potential volatility in price you accept. But maturity is not the only thing to consider when trying to determine how much the price of the bond will rise or fall. While the maturity of a bond fund tells you generally that more risk should be expected, it doesn't tell you how much. To answer this question involves looking at a more quantitative measure called *duration*. Duration is discussed in Chapter 6.

### Credit Risk

*Credit risk* describes the risk that the issuer of a bond will not pay principal and/or interest when it is due. Issuers that are considered to be high quality generally have high credit ratings and a very high ability to pay interest and principal. On the other hand, lower quality issuers, such as junk bond issuers, often have lower credit ratings and are more likely to miss a payment. An investor should be compensated with yield or return for accepting an investment that has higher credit risk. Conversely, when investing in bonds such as Treasury bonds, which have virtually no credit risk, an investor should expect lower yields and return.

### Income Risk

*Income risk* is the risk associated with the volatility of the monthly dividend paid by a fund. For example, an investor might expect a Treasury bond fund to provide stable monthly income because the bond characteristics of the portfolio would be expected to remain steady. However, a fund that invests in speculative bonds could have high income one month and low income the next. This variability in income is not an attractive attribute for an investment. Again, higher levels of yield and/or return should accompany greater uncertainty.

### Inflation Risk

*Inflation risk* is the risk that the return generated by a fund will not keep up with the rate of inflation or "cost of living." If inflation rises, say 5%, and the return on your fund advances only 3%, your buying power actually diminishes. In this case, the real rate of return (investment rate – inflation) is negative. On the other hand, if inflation is very low, say 1.5%, and your investment provides 5%, it's real rate of return is 3.5%, which exceeds the increase in the cost of living. Funds become more attractive as their real rates of return become more positive.

### Event Risk

*Event risk* is the risk that some unexpected event will occur that will impact a fund. For example, let's say a fund owns a bond from ABC Company that is highly rated and seems to be perfectly suitable. But then a flood hits the ABC Company and demolishes the plant. The company now has neither earnings power nor the ability to pay its bond obligations. Therefore, the price of this bond and of a fund that owns it would decline. Event risk differs from credit risk because event risk is driven by unexpected events, which cannot be quantified. Event risk is often associated with junk bonds, whose issuing companies are much less stable.

## Tax and Regulatory Risk

*Tax risk* describes the effects that changes in regulations or tax laws will have on a bond or fund's price. A good example of this took place in the late 1980s when it appeared that Congress would repeal the federal income tax exemption for municipal bonds. Since municipal bond prices take into account the value of tax-free income, and since it appeared that this advantage would be eliminated, virtually no bonds were priced and municipal bond prices subsequently dropped. Later, this legal action was defeated and municipal prices rebounded.

## Currency Risk

*Currency risk* is most associated with international bond funds. It is the risk that the currency relationship between the U.S. dollar and another foreign currency will change in such a way that an investment made abroad will actually be worth less when converted back to U.S. dollars. This occurs when the value of the dollar gains against a foreign currency. If the fund is not "hedged," a rising dollar is detrimental to a U.S. dollar-based fund that invests in securities of the nation whose currency is losing value.

## Management Risk

*Management risk* is the risk that key managers will leave a fund. If the fund manager is not easy to replace or investors lose confidence in the fund when management changes, massive redemptions can occur. This may force the fund to sell shares at low prices, which in turn causes fund shares to decline. You often see this kind of risk in one-fund or one-manager companies where the fund manager really *is* the fund. Fund families that have great depth in their portfolio management ranks rarely encounter this problem.

## FUNDS AND TAXES

Like any investment, sooner or later all mutual funds are hit with taxes. Taxation of mutual funds or of securities in general can be quite complex, especially when the tax code changes as it did in 1997 with the Taxpayers Relief Act. In the following section, we touch on some of the basic concepts surrounding taxes and funds. However, this is by no means a complete review of the subject. How taxes are handled in events such as capital gains can have a significant impact on the value of your accounts. We strongly advise you to consult your tax advisor on the specifics of your financial situation. In addition, most fund families now offer extensive educational material to help you deal with fund taxes. One of the best fund sources is Vanguard Group's Internet site at *www.Vanguard.com.* For further help on mutual fund calculations from the IRS, call 800/TAX-FORM and order Publication 564—Mutual Fund Distributions.

## HOW FUNDS ARE TAXED

In the case of mutual funds, a tax liability can occur in several different ways. A taxable event occurs when you sell shares (exchange or redeem), when capital gain distributions are made to you by the fund, or when the fund pays its monthly or quarterly dividend.

### Dividend Distributions

In the case of taxable "income" from equity, bond, or money funds, all distributions are considered dividends rather than interest. When dividend distributions are paid, they are considered ordinary income and are taxed based on your personal tax bracket. Examples of such distributions include the monthly income from bond and money market funds. Dividend distributions from municipal funds are exempt from federal tax. If you own a state municipal fund, your income distribution will most likely be exempt from state taxes as well. If you own a national tax-exempt fund that holds bonds in your state, you are usually exempt from state taxes on the portion that was invested in your state. Again, the fund family breaks this down for you in its special dividend form. In most states (rules can vary state to state), mutual fund dividends derived from direct obligations of the U.S. government or qualifying government agencies will be exempt from state taxes. These include a 100% Treasury bond fund or a 100% Treasury money fund.

In January, the fund company will send you a 1099-DIV. The 1099-DIV reports taxable income and capital gains distributed from the fund. Some fund families send a separate 1099-DIV for each fund, while others send one 1099-DIV with the distributions of all funds listed. If you have a tax-free bond or money fund, the dividend distribution will not be on the 1099-DIV form because it is not taxed at the federal level. The fund family will normally send you a separate form showing the amount of tax-exempt income you have earned. While this amount is not taxed, it is still reported on your IRS Form 1040.

## Capital Gains Distributions

A capital gains distribution occurs when the fund you own has traded securities throughout the year at a profit. To qualify as a registered investment company, they must distribute these gains. Capital gains do not occur on money market funds, but they are common with bond and equity funds. Usually, the capital gain is distributed once per year in November or December. When the distribution is made, the fund's NAV will drop by the amount of the distribution. This does not mean you lose money. Your value stays the same because the fund pays additional shares to your account. When capital gains distributions are paid, they are taxed at a level commensurate with how long the fund held the shares before they were sold.

The current 1099-DIV form includes two items for capital gains distributions. The first is a total capital gains distribution amount for each fund. The second is the amount of the total distribution that is subject to the maximum 28% capital gains rate.

## Don't Buy the Distribution

Since capital gains distributions are a taxable event, it is always advisable to avoid purchasing a fund just prior to the distribution. Even though you may think that getting the additional shares added to your account is a benefit, it is not. This is commonly called "buying the dividend." If you buy a fund just prior to its distribution, you will be liable for the capital gains tax even though you may have owned the fund just a few days. Your account does not increase in value because the fund's NAV drops by the amount of the gain. In addition, you will have just bought yourself an unnecessary tax liability. If you really want to own the fund, purchase it just after the distribution. Before you buy the fund, ask the fund family the exact date of the distribution and plan to buy at least a few days after.

## Capital Gains from the Sale of Shares

When you sell shares of any mutual fund, including a municipal bond fund, it results in a capital gain or loss. For example, if you buy ABC Fund at $10 and sell it at $11, you have a capital gain of $1 per share. You are also selling shares of a fund when you exchange them from one fund to another. This is often overlooked, but it is still a gain and will be reported. Your capital gain from a sale of shares is reported on IRS Form 1099-B. The form reports the gross proceeds of a sale of mutual funds. It does not show you how much you purchased the share for originally.

Under the new Taxpayer Relief Act of 1997, investors have been given a break on the amount of capital gain on which they must pay upon the sale of securities. There are now basically two rates at which capital gains are taxed. The first is based on a short-term holding period of one year or less. If you bought and sold your fund for a gain in less than one year's time, you pay capital gains based on your ordinary income tax rate. If you hold a security for at least a year before selling, your gains are taxed at a more favorable rate of 20%.

### The Cost Basis

As mentioned previously, a capital gain or loss from the sale of shares occurs when you buy and sell the fund. The difference between the cost of the shares at purchase and the value at the sale is called the "cost basis" gain or loss on the transaction. In a simple transaction, say when 10 shares are bought for $10 (no distributions are made) and then sold for $12, the gain is $2 per share or $20. The cost basis in this case is $10 and the selling price is $12. The gain is simply the difference. However, if you accumulate shares over a long period of time from the reinvestment of monthly dividends, capital gains, or the additional purchase of shares, the original cost basis becomes more difficult to calculate. This is quite evident if you sell just a small number of the total shares in your account. Determining the cost basis is important, but the IRS lets you tackle the problem in a number of ways.

### Adjusting Cost Basis by Adding Distributions

One of the most common mutual fund tax filing errors is overpaying taxes on reinvested dividends and capital gains distributions when shares are sold. When shares are sold, many investors forget that they have already paid taxes on the reinvested distributions (taxable funds) and neglect to increase their cost basis by the reinvested shares. Essentially, they end up paying taxes twice on the same investment—once when it's received and again when it's sold. Reinvested dividends and capital gains are an additional investment to your fund and should be added to your cost basis before you calculate any gains or losses.

In the simple transaction above, shares were purchased for $10 and sold for $12. However, if any distribution is made, as is typical with income funds, the original cost basis should be adjusted upward by the amount of the distribution. Let's say 10 cents per share was paid each month through-out the year and the shares were reinvested. The account accumulated $1.20 in additional shares. (This amount will be taxed as ordinary income and will be reported on the 1099-DIV.) In this case, the cost basis of the orig-inal $10 share price should be adjusted upward by $1.20 to $11.20. Now, the capital gains to be taxed is only 80 cents (the $12 selling price minus the $11.20 adjusted purchase price = .80).

There are three basic methods by which the IRS allows you to calcu-late your cost basis for a fund transaction: average share, first in/first out, and specific identification. Again, remember that each and every dividend and capital gain reinvestment is viewed as a purchase of shares and must be taken into account in the cost basis process.

### Average Share Method

This cost basis approach is the most common among the three methods. The cost basis is calculated by dividing the total dollar amount of shares you have purchased by the total number of shares you own. The result is an average price per share. When you sell shares, you would use this aver-age price as your cost basis and the redemption price as the sale price. Under this method, the assumption is made that the oldest shares are sold first in determining whether the transaction qualifies for long-term or short-term capital gains treatment.

### First In/First Out Method

In this method, the oldest (first) shares you purchased are assumed to be the first you sell. For example, if you owned 1000 shares, 500 of which were bought five years ago and 500 last month, and were to sell 500 of those shares, the cost basis would be determined by the price of the first 500-share purchase. In this example, the shares sold would qualify for long-term capital gains treatment.

### Specific Share Identification Method

This last method is the one least used by fund investors. Under this process, you designate exactly which shares you are selling based on their purchase date. This method is used to give the investor the flexibility to choose how the shares will be treated for capital gains purposes. The challenge with this method is that you must designate the shares being sold prior to the trans-action, in writing, to your fund family. Since most investors exchange by phone, it is difficult to track the transaction. Many fund families do not offer services to help facilitate this method.

### Capital Losses

Capital losses occur when you sell shares for less than you purchased them. Although nobody hopes to have losses in their funds, they do have the potential to diminish any capital gains you may have realized by selling fund shares at a profit. Here are a few items to remember when you sell at a loss.

Your first consideration should be how long you have held the fund shares. If they have been held for a year or less, it is considered a "short-term" loss. If they are held for more than a year, the loss is considered long-term. You need to know the specific timing to determine whether the loss can be used to offset ordinary income taxes or capital gains taxes. Again, you will need to review your cost basis as described previously.

Short-term capital gains are considered ordinary income and taxed accordingly. Ordinary income is usually a more burdensome tax rate for upper-income taxpayers. A short-term loss must first be applied against any long-term gains you have realized. This means that only "leftover" capital losses can be used to offset your short-term gains and the taxes on them.

What if the capital loss is still not completely used up in the calendar year? For example, someone sells at a loss but does not sell any holdings that generate profits or capital gains in the same calendar year. Fortunately, $3000 of this current-year capital loss can be applied against ordinary income, even if there are no capital gains considerations. Unfortunately, that's the limit in the current calendar year. Thereafter, $3000 of the same capital loss can be carried forward for 15 years, i.e., $3000 each year for the next 15 years.

### Municipal Bond Fund Special Case

If you sell shares of a municipal bond fund at a loss and have held those shares for six months or less, some of the loss is disallowed to the extent that you received tax-exempt income from the same fund during that period.

## THE FUND PROSPECTUS

The fund prospectus is basically the instruction book for your fund. And like any good instruction book, some "assembly" is required. Luckily, the assembly or complexity is far less than it used to be. The traditional fund prospectus was strictly a legal document that allowed the fund lawyers to cover all of their regulatory and fiduciary bases. The end result was a thick, 50-to-80-page, single-spaced document crammed with legal jargon. Much of the content was required by law so that investors had enough information to make sound investment decisions. Unfortunately, the amount and format of the information produced had the opposite effect on investors; most never read the material. This led to a lot of uninformed and angry investors when things went wrong. The prospectus was almost unusable for the average investor. Fortunately, things have changed.

As mutual funds became increasingly popular in the early 1980s, there were cries from frustrated investors and fund advocates for a change in the traditional prospectus. That change did not occur until June 1998, when the Securities and Exchange Commission finally adopted new rules which allow fund companies to present information about a fund that really gives an investor a sense of the return and risk that can be expected.

There are now five different information sources for investors. In the coming years, each document will have to be written in "plain English." The first and simplest is the **Fund Profile.** This document is usually about 5 to 8 pages and briefly covers the major topics for the fund, including a description of the fund's objectives, the historical returns, risks associated with the fund and its investments, and some information about the fund services. This document provides a great "snapshot" of fund information, perfect for those investors who don't want to take the time to read the detailed format. However, it leaves out much of the real "guts" of the fund's inner workings. In fact, a fund cannot call this document a prospectus because it is so brief. Here are the nine items covered in a Fund Profile:

1. **Fund Goals**—The investment goals section helps the investor understand what the fund is trying to accomplish and how the fund expects to reach those goals. For example, if it is a junk bond fund, the prospectus might indicate that the fund will attempt to gain maximum income for its shareholders by investing in low-quality bonds.

2. **Fund Strategies**—This section describes the types of securities the fund will purchase to meet the goals described in the goals section. For example, if it is a state municipal bond fund, it may say that the fund will invest 65% of its assets in high-quality municipal bonds issued by tax-exempt entities in the state of California. If the fund invests in more speculative or risky securities, the new prospectus is supposed to describe those securities as well.

3. **Fund Risks**—As its name implies, this part of the profile is designed to give investors a sense of the risk associated with the securities described in the strategy section. For example, if the fund buys low-rated bonds, the profile should briefly describe the credit risk associated with these securities and how it may impact the overall portfolio. Also included are 10-years' worth of annual returns and annualized returns over 1-, 5-, and 10-year periods combined with appropriate market indexes.

4. **Fund Fees (table format)**—This section is key because it describes what the fund will be charging you annually for an investment.

5. **Fund Manager and Advisor**—This portion of the document is designed to give potential shareholders an idea about who is managing their money.

6. **How to Buy Shares**—This section and Section 7 explain how to buy and sell shares and how much commission will be placed on the transaction.

7. **How to Sell Shares**—See Section 6.

8. **Distributions and Taxes**—This portion of the profile describes how distributions and taxes are handled by the fund.

9. **Shareholder Services**—This segment of the profile describes the services available to shareholders, such as checkwriting or systematic investment and withdrawal options.

The second source of information is the **Simplified Fund Prospectus.** This prospectus document provides greater detail on all the factors discussed in the Fund Profile as well as additional aspects of the fund such as financial highlights and general policies of the fund. It is written in plain English, no legalese, and can be up to 25 pages in length. In addition, this document usually has an open format and is not crammed up into single-spaced lines. You'll see lots of sidebars and open space, which makes it far easier to read than the old "edge-to-edge" format. Dreyfus made one of the first simplified prospectuses available in late June 1998 for their Large Company Value Fund. This new prospectus format is the most useful fund document that the individual investor has ever seen and will finally allow a proper review of a fund.

The next document is the traditional **Long Form Prospectus.** This contains everything associated with the traditional document, including many pages of the fine detail about the fund's inner workings. Next in order of complexity, there is the **Statement of Additional Information or SAI.** The

SAI has additional information that was deemed important but not necessary in the Long Form Prospectus.

Finally, the fund's annual and semiannual reports are available to investors. These reports detail what has happened in the fund in recent months and typically includes all of the fund's holdings. Currently, funds are only required to disclose their holdings twice each year. These are great documents to have if you are trying to get a sense of what the management strategy is given the current market environment.

# CHAPTER 3

# Fund Yields

An income investor's primary motivation is maximizing yield. This is certainly not lost on mutual fund companies, as evidenced by fund advertisements that tout yield along with total return. But not all yields are created equal. In fact, yields described by mutual funds can be vastly different, and it's also possible that a single bond fund could have several yields at one time.

As a starting point, it's important to review some yield basics. **First, yield can be viewed as the "price of risk."** The greater the risk you must take, the greater the yield must be to compensate you for accepting the risk. Clearly, nobody would buy a junk bond fund with the same yield as a money market fund. In this respect, yield can immediately tell you something about the risk of the investment. If somebody tells you the fund is perfectly safe, yet it has an abnormally high yield, something is wrong and you need to ask more questions.

## ANNUALIZED AND COMPOUNDED

In the world of interest rates and yields, two common statistical practices take place in describing yield: annualizing and compounding. When an interest rate is annualized, it is extrapolated over a 12-month period. For example, if the actual yield for a one-month period was 1%, annualizing might convert it to 12%. When an interest rate is stated as a compounded yield, it is describing a simple annualized rate that has been adjusted for reinvested dividends during the period. The compounded yield is normally higher than the annualized yield. So, you may ask, which one should I use?

The answer depends on what you want to know. For example, if you plan to buy a money market fund and reinvest your dividend each month, then a compound yield will give you the best estimate of the amount of income you'll end up with over the next 12 months. If you don't plan to reinvest, then the simple annualized yield will give you a good estimate of your monthly income in the next 12 months.

## BOND YIELDS

Now let's move on to yields on individual bonds. Since bond funds are made up of individual bonds, knowing the basics takes you a long way in understanding the funds. If you were to buy an individual bond, there would be two yields you would want to know, the coupon yield and the yield to maturity. Each gives you a different view of the value of an investment.

### Coupon Yield

*Coupon yield* is the simplest to understand of all the yields. It is the stated, fixed percentage the bond will pay against its face value (usually $1000) each year until it matures. For example, a 6.0% coupon bond will pay 6% of $1000, or $60 each year. Thus, the coupon yield tells you exactly how much money you will receive for each bond you own.

### Current Yield

*Current yield* describes the income you will receive in relation to the purchase price of the bond you buy, not the face value of the bond. For example, let's say you buy the same 6% bond described in the paragraph above. In this purchase, you will receive $60 a year for each bond you buy. But if you bought the bond for $900, the $60 coupon payment is actually 6.66% ($60/$900 = 6.66%) of the dollar value you invested. The 6.66% is the current yield.

### Yield to Maturity

*Yield to maturity* is one of the trickier yields to understand. Yield to maturity attempts to mathematically take into account both the fixed coupon rate and the price of the bond over its entire life. It's a logical corollary to coupon and current yield. For example, if you buy a bond for 50 cents on the dollar ($500 to continue our hypothetical scenario) and that bond pays its face value at maturity ($1000), you have gained $500 on your principal. In addition, you will receive the annual income based on the coupon rate. Yield to maturity accounts for the impact of both the change in principal value and the coupon income on yield.

The tricky part of yield to maturity is that it does not tell you how much money you receive each year. Instead, it tells you, theoretically, what the annualized rate of both the income and principal change would be if you held the bond until maturity. Thus, yield to maturity gives you an idea of the total value of your investment in a bond. While this measure of yield is often used, it is not particularly descriptive of the true amount of money you can expect to receive each year.

## FUND YIELDS

Money fund yields are very straightforward because they do not involve any of the price factors discussed with individual bonds. The price of a money fund always remains at $1 per share. The most common yield associated with a money fund is the 7-day SEC (Securities and Exchange Commission) yield.

This yield is a net yield, meaning it is net of all expenses of a fund. It is calculated by adding up the accrued dividends over the previous 7-day period and then annualizing them. The 7-day SEC yield on a money fund can, and usually does, change every day. For example, as rates move lower, a fund's yield, which reflects current rates, will fall as well. Unlike the coupon yield of an individual bond, which tells you exactly how much you'll receive each year, the money fund 7-day yield gives you the expected return based on what has happened in the last seven days. If the 7-day SEC yield is 5.0% today and rates continue to drop for the next 12 months, it is possible that your actual earned income could be significantly lower. On the other hand, if rates rise, then your income at the end of the year could turn out to be quite a bit higher.

Money funds often provide both a 7-day and a 30-day compounded yield. Again, because these yields are compounded, they assume reinvestment of all dividends at today's rate. Depending on how the market moves in the next year, you may or may not actually receive this yield as income.

## 30-Day SEC Bond Fund Yield

When a bond fund advertises a yield, it is required to produce a standard-ized *30-day SEC yield*. The formula for its calculation was determined by the Securities and Exchange Commission (SEC). This standardization allows you to compare apples to apples among various bond funds. A bond fund's 30-day SEC yield is similar to a yield to maturity for the entire portfolio in that it takes into consideration bonds selling at discounts and premiums. It is calculated by dividing the net investment income (less expenses) per share over a 30-day period by the current maximum offering price. When a yield is advertised by a fund, it must be accompanied by recent total return data as well.

It is important to note that the 30-day SEC yield is similar to a yield-to-maturity figure for a regular bond in that it does not give an accurate description of the income you will actually receive. In addition, a bond fund never matures, which makes this standardized yield even harder to understand and use. As an income investor, a better yield might be the 12-month distribution yield.

## The 12-Month Distribution

The distribution yield takes the sum of the dividends actually paid over the last 12 months and divides them by the current price of the fund. This yield gives you an historical perspective of the actual income received by investors during the last year. Quite often, this yield is substantially differ-ent from the fund's 30-day SEC yield. The reason is that the 30-day yield annualizes the income results over only the last month. If rates are rising, this yield will be higher than the distribution yield, and if rates are falling, it will be lower than the distribution yield. For example, the Fidelity New Market Income fund recently had a 30-day SEC yield of 9.69% and at the same time a distribution yield of 8.82%. Since both yields are readily avail-able from the fund families, it's best to get both and ask questions if they are not consistent.

## Dividend Yield

Another yield often used by income investors is the *dividend yield*. This is really the same as the distribution yield and attempts to quantify how much income can be expected from a stock fund. The yield typically describes the dividend income distributed over the last 12 months (usually quarterly dividends) as a percentage of the fund's current price.

Sometimes you will see a dividend yield annualized based just on the basis of the most recent payment. This yield is very helpful if you are considering buying an equity/income-oriented fund for income since it allows you to compare it with other bond or money fund choices. For example, in 1995 Fidelity's Equity Income fund had a total dividend distribution of 96 cents. When you divide the 96 cents by the recent price of the fund, you get a dividend yield of about 2.3%. Of course, that's not the whole story for the fund, because it also had capital gains distributions and an increase in the price per share, which amounted to a total return of 31.81%. However, if you're trying to isolate just the expected dividend income yield, this calculation can be very handy.

## Taxable Equivalent Yield

Municipal bond fund yields are calculated exactly as other fund yields, but there is one added advantage. The interest earned on a municipal investment is exempt from taxes on the federal level—and on the state level for those investors buying bonds of their home state. In comparing a tax-

**F I G U R E   3-1**

Fund Yields by Category

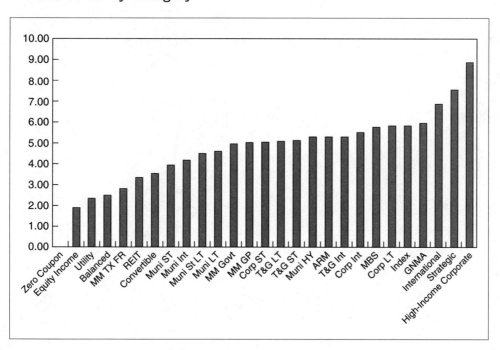

exempt yield with taxable yield, a *taxable equivalent yield* (TEY) is often used. The TEY tells an investor what interest rate they must get on a taxable fund to equal the value of the tax-exempt fund yield, based on her or his current tax bracket.

Let's say, for example, that an investor is looking at two funds. The first is a municipal fund that provides a tax-free rate of 5.0%. The second is a corporate bond that has a yield of 8.0%. The investor is in the 39.6% federal tax bracket. Which fund is better in terms of the income?

To answer this, a TEY is calculated as follows:

$$\text{TEY} = \frac{\text{Municipal yield}}{100\% - \text{tax bracket}} = \frac{5\%}{100 - 39.6} = 8.27\%$$

In this example the TEY is 8.27%. This means it would take a yield of 8.27% to equal the value of a tax-free yield of 5.0% for an investor in the 39.6% federal bracket. In this example the tax-free yield is the better yield.

In Figure 3-1 you can see the average yield for each of the major income fund categories. This provides you with a good guide as to how much yield each fund category should offer.

# CHAPTER 4

# Assessing the Fund and the Fund Manager

If you are having surgery, you want a well-educated and knowledgeable surgeon that you can trust. You also want to make sure this is not his or her first procedure and that his others have gone well. Makes sense doesn't it? It's no different when you're investing. In many cases you are handing over your life savings to a manager you'll probably never speak to or meet, and who works in a city you'll probably never visit. Sending a check in the mail or watching your company turn over your retirement plan to a fund manager can be a very anxious experience, and it's one you should not take lightly.

In the review that follows, I outline several things you should look for in evaluating a fund company and a fund manager. These items are not the end all nor do they guarantee that you'll end up with the highest quality manager. However, they are important factors to consider and should guide you in the right direction.

Evaluating a fund company and the fund manager is something every investor should do prior to sending any money their way. You will want to be comfortable not only with the manager but with the company as a whole. Remember, your life savings will hopefully be with this company a very long time. Therefore, you want to make sure they have the expertise and ability to do a good job.

## REVIEWING THE FUND COMPANY

Determining how good a fund company is is not a simple task. Most fund families are private companies, so financial information can be scarce. In addition, determining a company's reputation is often a subjective matter that requires some interpretation on your part. There are three factors to consider.

## Assets Under Management

A good start on the task is to look at how much money the fund company has under management. While more money doesn't necessarily mean quality, it does show that others have confidence in the firm. At the top of the heap might be a firm such as Fidelity Investments, which has close to $500 billion under management. At the bottom of the fund universe are those one-fund families who have less than $50 million under management. **While not a perfect indicator, sticking with firms that have at least $500 million under management is preferable.**

## Reputation

Reputation is a hard thing to quantify, but there are a few things that should help your review. The first is how a company's funds do against its peers. A fund family that consistently has funds near the top of their respective ranks must be doing something right. If a fund family consistently has all their funds near the bottom of the pile, they are not doing their duty for the shareholders. Keeping bad managers and failing policies in place is a sign of incompetent management.

## Longevity

Fund families that have managed to survive over the last several decades should be given some consideration. Since 1960, there have been several serious bear markets and financial market shakeouts (1987) that have caused many a firm to close its doors. If a fund company has been able to keep its clients and assets under management since the 1960s, it's doing something right. Firms such as Vanguard, T. Rowe Price, Fidelity, Scudder (Kemper), Mass Financial Services, and others fall into this category.

## REVIEWING THE MANAGER

Like the fund company, the ability of the fund manager is extremely important when managing money. Traditionally, mutual funds were managed by one person. This person was the trader, analyst, portfolio manager, and policy maker. Today, many of these jobs are split up. In recent years, even the fund manager's job itself has been split into what is called "team management," where there may be several managers, each responsible for a specific part of the portfolio. Most funds, however, are still managed by one person. The name of the manager is readily available from a number of sources, including the fund itself. To do a complete job, you'll need some additional information.

### Education

While it is certainly true that many of the top managers did not go to the best known schools, it's still a good guideline to see high-quality universities in the biography. At a minimum, a manager should have gone to a graduate business program. It is also a plus to see that the manager is a certified financial analyst (CFA) or a certified public accountant (CPA). These designations tell you the person has gone an extra step beyond traditional graduate work.

### Experience

Diplomas on the wall don't necessarily make for a good manager. Having been out in the real world of investing can often be more important than having gone to a great school. A manager should have seen some active duty before running the fund you are considering. Does anybody want their fund to be the manager's first job? It is estimated that about 85% of all fund managers were not managing money before 1990. This means most have never seen a bear market or a prolonged recession.

As a rule, a minimum of five years' experience is necessary (even doctors and lawyers need three to five years before they are able to practice their profession). It doesn't need to be all at the fund in question as long as it has been in the same investment discipline. For example, if you were buying a junk fund, you wouldn't want to see that the manager's only experience is managing a Treasury index fund. There's a big difference between the level and sophistication of analysis between the two. On the other hand, if the manager of a national tax-free fund has done 10 years as a manager of a state tax-free fund, then you should be confident in the manager's experience level.

### Tenure

Like education and experience, tenure is a key component in evaluating the fund manager. The longer the manager has been at the helm, the more experience and market environments he or she has seen. While longer tenure does not necessarily guarantee that the manager has been doing well, fund families usually don't keep poor managers on the staff very long. Hopefully, they have learned their lessons well and have been able to produce consistent returns. If you are investing in well-known, large funds, it's smart to choose a manager who has been on board for at least five years. An exception to the rule may be where a fund manager has just joined the firm after managing another fund family's portfolio for many years. Often the tenure data says the manager has been around for only one year. In this case, check the manager's previous experience.

## Strategy

We've probably all known people we thought were brilliant but were doing nothing with their life. It's sad but true that some of the brightest people don't have a clue when it comes to putting their intelligence to work. It's no different with fund managers. They might look great on paper, but when you hear them speak, you're convinced that you'd never let them touch a dime of your money.

One factor that helps you overcome this uncertainty is to know that there is a specific plan in place that the manager will follow. For example, the prospectus should clearly state the fund's objectives and how it intends to meet those goals. If the prospectus simply says the fund will invest in any stock for growth or any bond that produces income, be wary. You want to read about the exact types of investments, such as high-quality or low-quality bonds, or undervalued or growth securities. Another way to evaluate a manager is to read or hear manager interviews in various financial publications, TV, radio or from the fund family itself. These will bring yet another, more personal insight into how the manager thinks.

## Performance

There is no substitute for performance. A manager who has been able to consistently provide good returns without excessive risk has done his or her job. Consistency is a key measure when assessing performance. Some managers can get lucky by picking the right stock or bond at the right time. For a short period of time they may look like winners and reach the top of their respective ranks. The really great managers are regularly at the top of their ranks. What you don't want to see is a fund that is regularly at the bottom. If this is occurring, there are two big problems. The first is that the manager is just not good at what he or she does. The second is that the manager's boss, the fund company, is not doing their job. A bad manager should be replaced. It's the same predicament that a baseball team experiences each year. If a pitcher continually loses games, he's gone. It should be the same way for the investing industry. Unfortunately, sometimes it's not, especially when the manager is also the head of the fund company. As mentioned previously, this can occur with the small, one-fund fund family.

## ONE FOR THE RECORDS

If you are still not confident in the quality of the fund manager or the fund, you can check with the legal side of the fund business to see if any complaints have been filed against the fund. There are two places you can inquire. On the federal level, all mutual funds are required to comply with the Investment Act of 1940. To do this, they must be registered financial advisors or RIAs. All RIAs must file with the Securities and Exchange Commission. The filing explains the structure of the company and names the principals involved. Fund companies are required to provide investors with this filing if requested. All of this information is in the public domain and may be requested.

If you can't get the information from the fund, contact the National Association of Securities Dealers (NASD) in Washington, D.C. at 1-202-728-8015. They will be able to give you company information. You can also call the SEC at 1-202-942-8088. Their public reference branch can send you the fund's ADV form, which explains all about the structure of the fund and its officers. You'll need to write to 450 5th St. NW, Washington, D.C. 20549, Att: Public Reference Branch, and ask for the documents. As of mid-1998, they charged 24 cents per page for the information. At the state level, you should contact your state's Department of Investments and Securities. They will direct you to the correct person to request information on the fund company.

# CHAPTER 5

# Fees and Loads

There is no such thing as a free lunch in the financial world. Every mutual fund, load as well as no-load, charges its shareholders fees to cover fund management and expenses each year. Unfortunately, it is often hard to understand how these fees are broken up. There are 12b-1 fees, management fees, operating fees, and loads. Each impacts your fund's performance.

Mutual fund expenses are generally lumped into two categories, expenses you pay once and those you pay on an ongoing basis. The one-time fees are called *load* charges. Essentially, this is a sales commission for the brokerage firm and will directly reduce the amount you invest. The ongoing ones are those charged to shareholders for the annual management of the fund. Rather than getting a bill for these costs, the fund deducts them from the assets under management as they calculate the price of the fund. This is why the price of a mutual fund is called the *net asset value,* or NAV. It is net of these expenses. The ongoing costs are summed into one number called the *expense ratio.*

## THE EXPENSE RATIO

The total expense ratio is stated in percentage terms and represents how the total expenses of a fund relate to the total assets of the fund. These fees are paid out of the fund's assets. They do not include the load charges or other direct fees. In general, a fund's expense ratio ranges from less than ½% to as much as 2% per year. The range in the expense ratio often reflects the complexity of the fund's holdings. For example, money funds, which are usually less complicated, will normally have expense ratios of ½% or less. International stock funds, which are very complex and for which research and management can be very expensive, may have expense ratios of more than 2%.

The expense ratio comprises all the ongoing fees of the fund, including the management fees, 12b-1 fee, and other expenses. All of a fund's expenses fall under the category of annual fund operating expenses.

As a shareholder, you never really see these expenses being subtracted because they are calculated into the fund's net asset value. It works this way: After subtracting the fund's expenses from the fund's assets, a "net" number is produced. In turn, the total number of shares is divided into this net number. The NAV that results from this calculation reflects assets from which the liabilities (i.e., expenses) have been subtracted.

## 12b-1 FEES

Some fund companies charge shareholders a 12b-1 fee to cover the fund's distribution and marketing costs, including advertising and broker-dealer

### FIGURE 5-1

Income Fund Expense Ratios by Category

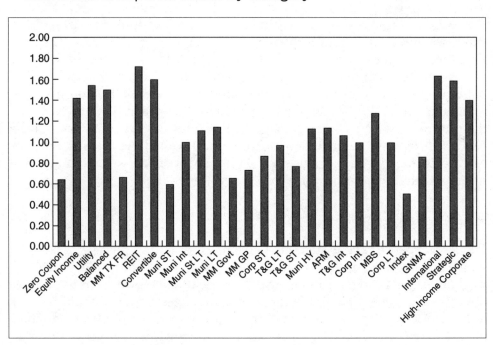

compensation. The fee is named for the SEC ruling that permitted fund management to dip into their assets to pay for distribution costs. Shareholders of both load and no-load funds may be subject to this fee. For example, if a fund wants another company such as a discount broker to sell its fund, it may pay the broker the 12b-1 fee for this service. The shareholders of the fund are charged the expense. Again, this is an ongoing cost.

## OTHER FEES

*Exchange fees,* typically between $5 and $25, are assessed when shares of one fund are exchanged to another fund within the family. Most funds today do not charge for exchanges, but it is still wise to ask before you invest. *Account maintenance fees* also may be assessed on all accounts but are generally charged against accounts that fall below a specified amount. This charge, typically between $10 and $25, is meant to fairly apportion expenses among shareholders, since fund accounts, regardless of size, cost approximately the same to manage. Retirement accounts, IRAs, for example, often have such charges. These are considered a direct cost because they reduce your investment by the amount of the fee.

The place to find the expense details on a particular fund is in the prospectus. At the front of each prospectus is a table of all expenses along with an explanation of the data. If you have questions about expenses that are not answered by the prospectus, you should call the fund's service reps and have them explain, line-by-line, the fund's expenses and what you are expected to pay.

## REVIEWING FEES

There is a running debate in the fund industry about expenses charged to clients. One faction suggests that high expenses make a fund unattractive because the fees significantly impact the performance of the fund. Indeed, fees do reduce returns because they reduce the assets of the fund. This group believes that the lower the expense ratio, the better. The biggest proponent of this philosophy is John Bogle, founder of Vanguard. The Vanguard funds are known for some of the lowest fees in the industry. On the other side of the issue are those who suggest paying higher fees for superior performance is not a bad thing. If you could get 25% each year, you might not mind a high level of expense. This debate will most likely go on for a very long time.

When it comes to income funds, fees can make a great deal of difference in yields. For example, money fund yields are already low. High fees would make a money fund yield very unattractive. For example, if the fund had a yield of 5% and an expense ratio of ½%, the yield to the shareholder would be just 4.5%. In the money fund world, this is significant. This is why more than half of all money funds waive all or part of their expense ratios. With junk bond funds, the expenses are usually higher because the securities are more complicated to manage and require greater research.

*As a general guideline, if a fund has a high expense ratio and high returns, it shouldn't be a problem. However, if the fund charges high expenses to its shareholders but continually offers low yields or returns, the fund should be avoided.*

## LOAD CHARGES

A sales charge, or sales *load*, is a one-time fee assessed by the fund. The fee is normally taken out of the amount you are planning to invest. This is called a *front-end load*. Rather than charge you on your initial investment, some funds charge a redemption fee that is a commission on the amount you sell. This is called a *back-end load*. The National Association of Securities Dealers (NASD) limits the maximum sales load to 8.5%. Most load funds charge between 3% and 4.5%. Fund families or funds that are offered without sales commissions are called *no-load* funds.

The sales load percentage is computed by subtracting the NAV of the fund from the public offering price and dividing the result by the public offering price. The NAV and the public offering prices are often listed in the mutual fund section of most major newspapers, although in recent years only the NAV is shown in many papers. The NAV will be on the left (the lower number) and the offering price (ask price) will be on the right (the higher number). For no-load funds, those with no sales charge, the NAV and the offering price are the same.

Let's look at an example of the purchase of a front-end load fund. Fund ABC is listed in the paper with an NAV of $9.97 and an offering price of $10.50. To determine the sales charge, you first subtract $9.97 from $10.50. You then divide the result ($.53) by the offering price of $10.50. The result is 5%. This means that if you were to invest $10,000, it would cost you 5%, or $500. Your investment, net of the sales charge, would be $9500. If you wanted to sell the fund, the order would be transacted based on the NAV, not the offering price.

The amount of the load percentage may vary depending on the amount you plan to invest in the fund. This is called a *sales break-point* plan.

For example, if you buy $10,000 of a fund, you might have to pay the full load charge of, say, 5.0%. However, if you plan to invest $1 million, the fund might reduce the load fee to, say, 1%. If you plan to invest a significant amount of money, make sure you inquire about these break-point options.

## LOAD OR NO-LOAD?

Like the expense debate, the load versus no-load debate is ongoing. Some experts suggest that a sales commission is worth paying if the fund consistently generates superior returns. This argument is valid if you are trying to invest in a fund that has a superior fund manager. There is also some justification for a load charge for personalized service you may receive from a full-service broker.

> *General guideline: When it comes to income funds, paying 4.5% load is essentially giving away your first year's income on most funds. There are just as many good income funds that are no-load as there are load. As for money markets, you should never pay a load.*

# Understanding Fund Returns and Risk

The return on your investment with a mutual fund is determined the same way it is with any other investment, by calculating the percentage change in value from one point in time to the next. This is normally called the *total return* because it includes all gains or losses made by the fund during the time period. An appreciation or decline in price, a distribution of regular dividends, annual capital gains, and the compounding process are all ways that gains and losses can occur. A total return can take several forms, including cumulative total return and average annual total return.

On the other side of the investment scale is risk. No investment should be examined without a review of the amount of risk associated with the expected return or yield. Three methods for measuring fund risk are widely used. They include standard deviation, beta, and duration which will be discussed in detail later in this chapter.

## TOTAL RETURN BASICS

### Return from Price Change

The simplest way a fund increases in value is through the change in NAV (price) between the time of purchase and a specific date. For example, if the fund is bought at a price of $10 in January and increases in value to $11 by February, the fund has gained 10%. The change in value of the securities in the fund dictate the movement in the fund's price. This part of the total return is often called the *return on principal* because it deals strictly with price. For most income funds, this is only part of the total return.

## Return from Dividends

Most income funds produce regular dividends. These are usually distributed on a monthly, quarterly, or annual basis. The dividends are earned by the bonds and stocks held in the portfolio. They accumulate independent of the change in the fund's NAV. An investor has the option to either have the dividends distributed directly or have them reinvested into additional shares of the fund. If they are reinvested, they add new shares to the original shares purchased and must be added to the total return equation.

## Return from Capital Gains

Like dividends, capital gains are paid to the shareholder as a separate payment, independent of dividends and NAV changes. Capital gains are derived from the fund manager's trading securities at a profit that year and are normally paid in the late fall. When capital gains are reinvested, they buy new shares of the fund and add to the overall value of the account. The fund's NAV will normally decline by the amount of the capital gain distribution on the day the fund officially distributes the gain, but the investor earns more shares.

For example, if an investor owned 1 share of Fund ABC and it was selling for $10 per share, the value of the account would be $10 (1 share × $10 NAV). If on November 25, an annual capital gain of $1 per share was paid by the fund and the investor elected to have it reinvested, the fund's NAV would decline to $9 and the investor's total value seems to decline to $9 (1 share × $9). However, they would have gained an additional 0.1111 shares ($1 cap gain/$9 NAV = 0.1111 new shares). The investor now has a total of 1.1111 shares at an NAV value of $9. Again, when shares (1.1111) are multiplied by NAV ($9) the total value is the same, $10. The important aspect of the reinvested capital gain is that now, as the fund increases in price, the investor's fund value grows more rapidly because he or she now has more shares.

For tax purposes, capital gains may be long-term or short-term, depending on how long the fund held the securities that were traded. The fund's capital gains distributions have nothing to do with the capital gain or loss as a result of the shareholder buying or selling shares of the fund.

## Return from Compounding

As was mentioned in Chapter 2, compounding is the process by which an account grows by earning interest on interest. If an investor reinvests her distributions, both dividends and capital gains, she will accumulate more shares. These new shares are then used to calculate the next round of dividends paid. This significantly adds to the growth of the account over time.

## Total Return

Having broken down the ways investors can increase the value of their accounts, we can now calculate the total return of the fund. This is done by adding all shares accumulated by all distributions and capital gains and then multiplying the total shares by the NAV. Here's the process for calculating a fund's total return.

**A.** Identify initial fund value by multiplying the initial NAV by the initial shares purchased.

**B.** Include all shares accumulated during the period being examined and multiply them by the current price.

Total return for the period examined is the percentage change between the initial value and the ending value. This is calculated as follows:

$$\text{Total return} = \frac{B - A}{A} - 1$$

For example, if you bought 10 shares of a fund for $10 ($A = 10 \times 10 = \$100$), then earned an additional 10 shares from reinvested dividends (10 original shares + 10 new shares = 20 shares) and the fund's price gained $2 to $12, your total current value would be $B$ (20 shares $\times$ $12 = $240). Now you plug those values into the formula:

$$\text{Total return} = \frac{\$240 - \$100}{\$100} - 1 = .40, \text{ or } 40\%$$

As you can see, a return of 20% resulted solely from the price movement from $10 to $12. The other 20% was realized through the reinvestment and compounding of shares over the period.

## Cumulative Total Return

The return just calculated is the cumulative total return because it encompasses the return for the entire observation period. The cumulative total return simply describes the actual total return over a period of time but does not annualize the data. Cumulative returns can be calculated for any period of time—one week, one month, one year, five years, or since the inception of the fund. The key factor is to simply calculate the percentage change from time period A to time period B.

### Annual and Annualized Return

The annual return for a fund describes the total return for a one-year period of time. Annual returns are normally defined for calendar years. The annualized total return, or *average annual return,* is a bit trickier, but it is key in evaluating a fund's long-term performance. It describes the average return over a period of time, but this is not a simple averaging or adding of the annual returns for the period. The annualized return also takes into consideration the effects of compounding over time.

The annualized return, often called the *compound annual growth rate,* accounts for the reinvestment of dividends and capital gains as well as the change in the price (NAV) of the fund over a specific period of time. It is a hypothetical rate of return which, if achieved annually, would have produced the same cumulative return if performance had been constant over the entire period. Most mutual funds must show average annual returns for one-, three-, five-, and ten-year periods.

## MEASURING FUND RISK

Any reasonable investment analysis should seek a balance between return and risk. In the last section, we discussed the various types of return that are reported for funds. However, at what "cost" those returns were gained is also of key importance.

As mentioned in Chapter 2, there are many types of risk associated with individual bonds and bond funds—credit risk, interest rate risk, and currency risk, to name a few. When dealing specifically with funds, there are several measures that are quite valuable in helping you gauge the fund's possible return volatility. The three main ones are standard deviation, beta, and duration.

### Standard Deviation

Knowing the standard deviation of a fund, its peers, and the market can be a very powerful tool in your investment arsenal. In its simplest definition, the *standard deviation* of a fund measures, in percentage terms, the monthly return volatility over a specific period of time. In the vernacular of the statistician, the standard deviation measures the variability in return about the mean return for a given period of time.

The mutual fund industry has adopted the standard deviation as the baseline measure of a fund's risk. So when you hear someone talking about the risk of one fund versus another, you can assume they are talking about standard deviation. The common time frame for mutual fund standard deviations is three years (36 months). Time frames that are shorter or longer can also be useful if you are trying to isolate a specific period of market activity.

*Funds that have higher deviations have historically experienced greater return volatility, whereas those that have lower deviations have had more stable return histories.* When matched with return, the standard deviation allows you to judge the relative risk and reward of a fund.

For example, let's say you are considering two funds, A and B. They both have the same three-year annualized return and are managed by reputable fund companies. Which is the better fund? To answer this, you can examine their standard deviations. Fund A has an annualized standard deviation of 5% over a three-year period. Fund B has a standard deviation of 10% for the same period. In this case, Fund A provided the same total return with half the volatility of Fund B. Naturally, the most desirable fund would have a very high return and a very low risk. Conversely, funds with very low returns and very high risk are the least attractive. It goes back to the basic principle that investors should be compensated for risks they must accept.

### Compare Against Peers

In the previous example, we only examined the return and the risk of the two funds. We didn't examine whether the two funds should in fact be compared. For example, it may be inappropriate to compare a money market fund with an equity income stock fund because the two funds have vastly different holdings, expected returns, and risk. Generally, funds should only be compared against their peers. This means money markets should be compared against money funds, municipal funds against municipal funds, and equity income funds against equity income funds. However, if a peer comparison doesn't provide enough insight, it is also a good idea to measure a fund against a well-known benchmark such as the S&P 500. In this way, you can get a better sense of a fund or even a peer group's volatility against a major market index.

### Not the "End All" Measure

Like any other measure, standard deviation alone can lead you astray. It should be used in combination with other measures. Here's why.

*One of the most important downsides in this measure of risk is that it is a function of historical returns and does not attempt to forecast future risks. In many ways, it's using a rearview mirror to drive forward.*

While the fund's historical results may look great, a change in manager or strategy can significantly alter the volatility of a fund's return over time. Another downside of using just standard deviation as a measure of risk is that it assumes every investor believes risk is volatility rather than some other concept. Some would suggest that a fund that never loses money has very little risk, even though its standard deviation may be very high. While all of these considerations are certainly valid, the concept of standard deviation is widely accepted as the most important measure of fund risk in the fund industry.

Figure 6-1 shows the annualized standard deviations for several mutual fund categories.

## Beta

Like standard deviation, beta is an historical data-based measure. *Unlike standard deviation, which measures volatility based on the fund's own return movement, beta measures the volatility of a stock fund's price relative to the general mar-*

**FIGURE 6-1**

Income Fund Standard Deviations by Category

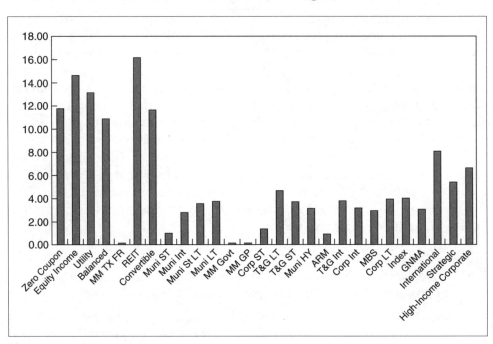

*ket.* It also relies on historical relationships between the fund and the market. In almost all uses of beta, the S&P 500 is used as a proxy for the market.

Beta represents the percentage of the market index the fund is expected to move for a given move in the index. For example, a fund with a beta of 1.0 would be expected to move up and down in lockstep with the S&P 500. A fund with a beta of 1.5 would be expected to move 50% more than the index in either direction. This type of fund would be considered more aggressive than the market because its movements are a multiple of the market's. Conversely, a fund with a beta of 0.50 would be expected to move 50% less than the market in either direction. This type of fund would be considered a more defensive fund in that it's return moves less for a given return change in the overall market.

Before drawing any conclusions about a fund from its beta statistic, it is important to determine if the fund correlates with the general market. For example, a gold fund's beta may be very small because it is not necessarily driven by factors that drive price changes in the overall market. On the other hand, we would expect an S&P 500 index fund to have a beta of 1.0 and move exactly with the market. To help you know whether or not a fund is appropriately correlated with the market, another statistic is used called *R-squared.*

The R-squared of the fund shows the degree of correlation between the fund and the general market. Funds with R-squareds of 1.0 correlate perfectly with the market, while funds with low R-squareds, say 0.50 or lower, are considered to be generally unrelated to the market. If a fund has an R-squared of less than 0.60, consideration of beta is less reliable.

It is best to use beta just with stock fund analysis (see Equity Funds for Income, Chapter 7) because bond funds do not typically have a correlation with a stock index. To compare a bond fund's return with that of the market, a measure called *duration* is used.

## Duration

Duration is probably one of the most powerful measures a bond fund investor can use. *Unlike standard deviation, duration does not look at the historical volatility of the fund, but attempts to quantify return movements based on expectations of future market activity.*

### The Mechanics
The duration of a bond or bond fund measures its sensitivity to interest rate changes. If the duration of a bond is 2.0, the bond would be expected

to move 2% in return for every 1% move in interest rates. If the duration is 10 and rates declined 1%, the fund's value would be expected to gain 10%.

Duration is an extremely helpful tool in understanding, quantitatively, just how much interest rate risk must be accepted when buying a particular bond fund. However, duration has limitations and does not work well with extremely large changes in rates.

Duration was developed because the maturity of a bond does not allow an investor to measure the expected price change of the bond or bond fund. We know that longer maturity bonds and bond funds have greater price volatility when rates change, but duration tells us how much. Maturity takes into consideration only the final payment, whereas duration takes into account all cash flows throughout the life of the bond. Duration is a weighted-average term-to-maturity in which cash flows are in terms of their present value.

There are two major properties important to duration:

1. Duration is inversely related to a bond's coupon rate. In other words, comparable bonds with lower coupon rates will have higher durations than those with higher coupon rates.

2. Except for zero coupon bonds, the duration of a bond is less than its maturity. Duration usually equals maturity with a zero coupon bond.

In applying these properties, an investor knows that buying premium bonds (high coupons) will help minimize the effects of rising rates. Conversely, a low coupon rate, as with a discount bond, will cause greater duration and greater price sensitivity.

### Application with Funds

Most mutual fund companies now offer duration along with average maturity to shareholders. When you are considering buying a bond fund, you can get a good idea of just how much interest rate risk (Chapter 2) might be associated with the fund. For example, let's say you believe rates are heading lower and you want to take advantage of this with a bond fund. If you could accept the risk, you would target a bond fund with long maturity and, more importantly, long duration. In the extreme case of a zero coupon bond fund, the maturity normally equals the duration. This means that a 20-year maturity zero coupon bond fund would be expected to increase in value by about 20% if rates declined 1%.

Conversely, if you want a defensive income portfolio, you want to have lower duration funds. Included among these are intermediate- and short-term funds. A money market fund's price is always held constant at $1 per share. Because of this, its duration is zero.

### Adjusting Duration—A Manager's Value

One of the values of a bond mutual fund is having active investment management. A good fund manager will not only buy the right bonds at the right time but should also work to protect fund investors in times of interest-rate uncertainty. One of the ways to accomplish this is by adjusting the duration of the fund to meet market conditions.

Usually, a fund manager runs the portfolio within tight parameters. For example, general fund quality, maturity, and bond types are highly defined by the prospectus. However, a manager can adjust certain aspects of the portfolio, including cash positions and individual bond characteristics. A typical bond fund will have 5% to 10% in cash with the remainder invested in bonds. The cash is used to meet redemptions, exchanges, and the purchase of new bonds for the portfolio.

If the manager believes that rates are heading higher, he or she can increase the cash position. Greater amounts of cash in the portfolio cause it to be more stable, as short-term cash securities are far less volatile than longer-term bonds. The increase in the cash position also reduces the duration of the fund. As the duration declines, the fund becomes less sensitive to interest rate changes. Some funds have been known to increase cash positions to as much as 20% in rapidly rising rate markets, but most don't exceed 10%.

Once rates have peaked, the manager will put the excess cash back to work by buying new, higher-yielding securities. This management strategy allows the fund to become more stable in down markets and helps protect shareholders' principal value. The downside of this strategy is that the higher cash positions usually provide less income, which results in lower fund yield.

Another duration strategy a manager can employ is buying "cushion" bonds. *Cushion bonds* are those that act as a cushion or stabilizing factor during market volatility. For example, if a manager believes rates are going to rise but does not want to sacrifice portfolio income, he or she can buy bonds that have lower duration characteristics. These might be bonds with higher coupon rates, or as is usually the case, bonds with slightly lower maturities. For example, if a manager is running a long-term municipal bond fund with an average maturity of 25 years, the duration would be very high and the fund would be quite interest-rate sensitive. To protect the fund in times of significantly rising rates, the manager can buy more

**FIGURE 6-2**

Income Fund Duration by Category

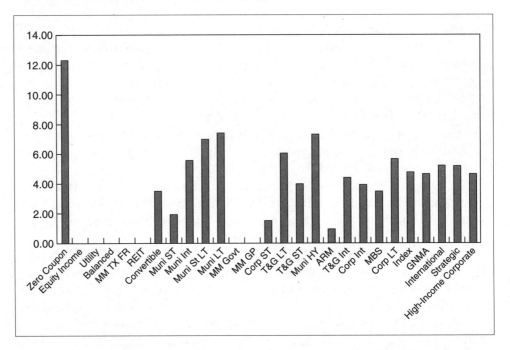

bonds with maturities of, say, 15 years. This would reduce the fund's average maturity and duration and cause it to be less rate sensitive. At the same time, the income levels would generally be kept intact.

## Using Fund Duration and Maturity as a Sentiment Indicator

Since most funds adjust their maturity and durations as market conditions change, tracking these adjustments can help you understand market sentiment. As rates increase, funds will normally shorten duration and maturity. Conversely, as rates decline, duration and maturities will lengthen. Taking this another step, if you can regularly track a fund or fund group's maturity and duration, you can develop a sense of how the institutional players feel about the market. For example, in late 1993, prior to the early 1994 Federal Reserve rate hikes, funds started to rapidly shorten maturities and durations. This provided a signal to many income fund investors that Wall Street was preparing for a rough market ahead. In this case the fund managers were correct. Having this kind of information can greatly help you in your decision-making process.

# CHAPTER 7

# Fund Types

## INCOME FUNDS—HOW THEY WORK

Like all mutual funds, income funds are "pools" of actively managed securities. What differentiates income funds from other funds is an orientation toward providing regular income distributions to shareholders. Mutual fund distributions are considered dividends rather than interest because they are distributed by a fund company. This makes a tax difference in states that treat dividends and interest separately. In general, distributions are made on a monthly basis, although some of the equity funds distribute only on a quarterly basis. Distributions can also be reinvested back into the fund. The ability to reinvest is one of the great benefits of owning a fund, since reinvestment vastly increases returns over time through the compounding process.

Another upside feature of funds is their availability, which sets them apart from an individual security. To purchase an individual stock or bond, you normally are required to have enough money to buy a minimum denomination. For example, municipal bonds require a minimum purchase of $5000 per issue. Most funds require only $2500 for the initial purchase and far less for subsequent purchases.

Shares are bought and sold through a fund company. They are either bought directly from the company or through a broker or investment advisor. Fund shares can be issued in fractional amounts so that an investor's entire purchase can be put to work in the fund. Usually a fund offers "exchange" privileges, which allow an investor to sell a fund and invest in another in a simultaneous transaction. Funds also offer several forms of redemption, or sale. Shares can be exchanged into another fund, sold and redeemed by check to the owner, or sent electronically to a shareholder's bank account.

The fund's price, or net asset value (NAV), is determined by the value of the securities in the portfolio minus the expenses charged by the fund. Every fund is *marked to market* each day at 4:00 PM EST. This means that the value of each security in the portfolio must be determined each day. At times, a security may not be able to be priced because it did not trade that day. In this case the fund estimates the price based on one of several complex pricing models that attempt to accurately reflect what the security is worth. This is often called *matrix pricing*. The fluctuation of the NAV each day will be a function of the security itself. Funds that buy more speculative securities for their portfolios tend to have greater day-to-day NAV movement, whereas funds that own high-quality, conservative securities tend to move less.

There are many different types of income funds. What differentiates each is the composition of the portfolio. The primary securities bought by true income funds are money market and short-term and long-term bonds. Some funds purchase very short-term securities that are very high quality. Others buy long-term, more speculative securities. Funds are also differentiated by issuer and include Treasury, corporate, municipal, mortgage, and others. There are also equity funds that have a strong orientation toward income. These include the balanced, equity income, growth and income, utility, and real estate funds. While high levels of income are not the primary focus of these funds, they do offer higher yields than most stock funds and often will hold significant allocations in bonds.

When it comes to diversification, funds can be broken down into two varieties, diversified and nondiversified. The Securities and Exchange Commission has strict guidelines that the funds must follow based on the Investment Company Act of 1940. A *diversified fund* is one that, with respect to 75% of its holdings, can't own more than 10% of the voting rights of any one company. A diversified fund also can't own more than 5% in any one security with respect to all assets under management. The regulation does not apply to government securities. The fund typically has more leeway with the other 25% of its investments but will normally keep the investments "diversified" with respect to all assets. A fund company will often impose additional diversification restrictions on its fund within its prospectus. For example, the Vanguard Municipal Fund keeps at least 75% of the municipal bonds held in the portfolio invested in the top three credit-rating categories, and no more than 20% of assets may be invested in bonds rated BAA.

The main advantage of a diversified fund is that if there is a problem with any one security, the impact on the entire portfolio is small. The vast majority of income funds are diversified funds.

Nondiversified funds have the ability to *concentrate* holdings. This means they can hold a large percentage of one company. In the extreme, there are some stock funds that own just a handful of securities, all in the same industry. The advantage of a nondiversified fund is that it provides an investor with a specific focus and possibly better returns. The downside of a nondiversified fund is that if something negative occurs with either the sector or the securities, it can have a significant impact on the fund's return.

In the next several sections, we will discuss the many different types of income funds. At the top of each section is a matrix that describes the composition, return, yield, risk, and other elements of the fund category. This provides you with a quick reference if you need to review the fund category. At the end of the book are the top funds for each category.

## EQUITY FUNDS FOR INCOME

### Balanced Funds

Balanced funds seek to maximize total return through a combination of capital growth and current income. Typically, about 60% of a balanced fund's assets are invested in equities, mostly with large-cap companies, which have market capitalizations of more than $5 billion. Some balanced funds buy small-cap or mid-cap stocks for their equity allocation,

### TABLE 7-1

Equity Funds

| Item | Balanced | REIT | Utility | Equity Income |
|---|---|---|---|---|
| Credit quality | Medium | High | High/medium | High/medium |
| Interest-rate risk | High | Medium | Medium | Medium |
| Maturity | Na | Na | Na | Na |
| Yield | 2.49 | 3.32 | 2.29 | 1.87 |
| 3-year total return | 11.79 | 9.79 | 15.10 | 15.15 |
| Standard deviation | 10.85 | 16.13 | 13.14 | 14.61 |
| Income level | Low | Low | Low | Low |
| Expense ratio | 1.51 | 1.72 | 1.54 | 1.42 |

but most stick to the big names. The remaining assets are normally invested in corporate, Treasury, or government agency bonds. While the manager usually keeps a constant mix between the asset classes, many fund managers adjust their holdings and allocations to reflect market conditions.

Many of the funds, such as asset giants Fidelity Puritan and Vanguard/Wellington, have been in existence for many decades. These funds have traditionally used a "classic" approach to the market, that is, the fund manages a balance between equity and debt. In many respects, the balanced funds were the first asset allocation funds. Before the capitalization, style, and sector segmentation that has enveloped the fund market in the last few years, investors simply put their money into stocks and/or bonds. The balanced funds provided a way to take advantage of the power of an institutional advisor in these two disciplines simultaneously. With the proliferation of thousands of funds in every imaginable sector, this basic, but attractive approach is often overlooked.

Currently, the average allocation for all balanced funds available to the investing public is about 56% stocks, 35% bonds, 6% cash, and 3% other securities. In addition, of the 56% in stocks, about 9% is in foreign equities. There are now over 300 funds classified as balanced funds available to the average investor.

The combination of stocks and bonds in these portfolios allows for greater stability in the fund's return owing to the conservative nature of the fixed-income portion of the portfolio. The equity portion of the portfolio boosts overall returns, and the bonds anchor the volatility. The bond percentage in the portfolio will typically have standard deviations that are about one-quarter of those of the stock portion of the fund. With as much as 40% in bonds, this provides excellent stability for the fund. Of course, the drawback of these funds is that upside appreciation is often limited by the very bond exposure that helps performance on the downside.

Incomewise, the portfolios normally provide an investor with quarterly dividends. The quarterly dividend can be reinvested, which, again, helps the overall compounding process. Usually, the dividend yield is less than 3%, which is less than a taxable money fund (currently about 5%). This yield, however, is still significant in that it is more than twice the current dividend yield of the S&P 500. As you can see from the table below, the average annual return over the last three years is very respectable, just over 17%, compared to the return for all domestic equity funds at 22.67%. The exciting fact is that this return was achieved with about half the volatility.

| Fund Category | 3-Year Return | Standard Deviation | Yield |
|---|---|---|---|
| Balanced funds | 17.16 | 8.9 | 2.25 |
| Top 30 balanced funds (by assets) | 17.73 | 9.0 | 3.00 |
| All domestic equity | 22.67 | 16.4 | 0.47 |
| Vanguard Index 500 | 30.13 | 15.2 | 1.25 |

The stability, return, and yield of these funds becomes attractive to investors who are looking for both exposure to the stock market and some income generation. When the stock market reaches record highs or is in a protracted consolidation, investors often look to the balanced funds as a way to reduce overall risk.

## Other Stock Income Funds

In addition to the balanced funds, there are several other types of funds that offer income with total return. In each case, the fund has greater volatility than regular bond funds, higher total returns, and generally lower income levels. As part of an income strategy, it is advisable to use these funds in conjunction with more stable bond and money market funds. However, their total return orientation provides an opportunity to increase the overall value of the account.

## Real Estate Funds

Real estate funds typically invest in real estate investment trusts, or REITs. REITs are similar to mutual funds in that they often pool together many real estate projects, especially commercial projects. These projects provide steady income streams that are then passed on to shareholders. Income levels, however, are generally low compared to money and bond funds. Currently, there are about 75 real estate funds available to the individual investor. Yields typically come in under 3%, but some of the top funds, such as Vanguard's Special REIT Index Fund (VGSIX) and the CGM Realty Fund (CGMRX), offer yields in excess of 4.5%. Total returns have averaged about 9% over the last five years. However, standard deviations on these funds average near 14%, which is only a bit less than the S&P 500 Index. This may not make it worth the risk compared to more defensive fund groups. In 1990, when the market was lower, these funds lost an average of 13% of their value. Conversely, in a good equity market they can have solid returns, as evidenced by the 29% average total return achieved in 1996.

## Utility Funds

Utility funds are traditionally regarded as the safe haven of the equity world. Investors have been able to count on high dividends, low volatility, and steady returns. Utility stock funds typically buy shares of electric utility and telephone companies. There are about 70 utility funds available to the individual investor. Most of these have load charges. Average yields offered are between 2% and 2.5%, which is nearly 150 basis points better than the S&P 500's yield. Top-yielding funds offer yields above 3.5%. The three-year average return for the sector is just under 20%. In 1997, the group posted an average return of just over 25%. In 1994, however, the funds lost an average of 8.9%. The average standard deviation for the group is about 12%, which is about 20% lower than that of the S&P 500.

## Equity Income Funds

Traditionally, equity income funds were very similar to balanced funds in that they held most of their portfolios in equity positions, but they also own some bonds and preferred stocks for added income and stabilization purposes. The difference between balanced funds and equity income funds is that with the latter, the major focus is on growth, with income as a distant objective. In recent years, the income orientation of equity funds has diminished. For example, the average bond holdings in the 160 equity income funds available to investors is only about 5%, whereas stocks make up about 83% of the holdings. This leaves the yield on these funds at levels nearly equal to the S&P 500, which was about 1.5% in mid-1998. However, the top-yielding funds in the category, such as Vanguard Equity Income, offer yields in excess of 3%. Standard deviations on these funds average about 11.5%. This is far higher than most bond funds but slightly lower than the S&P 500. The great advantage of these funds is in their total return. In 1997, the average fund in this category gained 26%. In 1994, when times were not so good, the average fund lost just under 2%. Like all of the equity funds mentioned in this section, the equity income funds should be used as a total return supplement in an income portfolio.

## MONEY MARKET FUNDS

Money funds are often the "Rodney Dangerfields" of the fund industry: They get no respect. Most investors think they are just substitutes for a bank checking account, are all alike, and are as safe as T-bills. All of these

**TABLE 7-2**

Money Funds

| Item | Government | General Purpose | Tax-Free |
|------|------------|-----------------|----------|
| Credit quality | High | High | High |
| Interest-rate risk | None | None | None |
| Maturity | Short | Short | Short |
| Yield | 4.98 | 5.04 | 2.79 |
| 3-year total return | 4.92 | 5.09 | 3.09 |
| Standard deviation | .14 | .14 | .19 |
| Income level | Low | Low | Low |
| Expense ratio | 0.65 | 0.73 | 0.66 |

impressions are wrong. Indeed, in the years ahead, money funds may become a portfolio balancing investment for many equity investors and a great source of safe yield for income investors.

## The Basics

There are now over 1300 money markets available to U.S. investors. Assets of these funds stand at over $1.1 trillion dollars and make up about 22% of all fund assets. At some time, almost all mutual fund investors have owned a money fund. It's hard to believe, but in 1982 money fund assets commanded a 74% share of all mutual fund assets. It wasn't until 1993 that stock fund assets surpassed those of money funds. According to Peter Crane, editor of *IBC's Money Fund Report,* an institutional money fund publication, "Over the last year, assets have risen over $200 billion (21.8%) with the continued popularity of money funds [with] both individuals and institutions." Crane sees continued growth in assets, approaching the 20% rate of the last three years.

While no fund, including a money fund, is guaranteed, a money fund's primary objective is to maintain a constant price of $1 per share. In this way, an investor's principal amount never loses value. At the same time, a money fund provides a monthly income distribution (daily accrual) which can be reinvested in additional shares or distributed. The income component is not fixed like a T-bill. It fluctuates each day depending on the levels of short-term interest rates. As rates increase due to inflation or a tightening in Federal reserve monetary policy, the yields on money funds will rise.

As with any portfolio, a money fund is always rotating securities in and out of the fund, mostly because the securities are maturing. As the fund buys new short-term investments, its yield will reflect general levels of short-term rates. This is why in declining rate markets, money fund yields will fall, and in rising rate markets, money fund rates will increase.

In the early 1980s inflation was soaring and interest rates were at record highs. This hurt both stock and bond fund prices and total returns. Money fund assets, however, were surging. The reason is simple. Money funds were offering yields in excess of 15%, and some got to as high as 20% for a short period of time. With a high rate of return and a constant price, it was an easy decision to buy a money fund.

## Why Money Funds Today?

Money funds are used for a wide variety of reasons. They may be a starting point for an investor's first fund purchase, a sophisticated cash position for a major corporation or bank, or anything in between. Typically, though, money funds are used as a conservative allocation in an investor's portfolio. They are also commonly used as a safe haven in times of market volatility. Since the share price is held at $1.0 per share, market activity does not impact these funds. Indeed, in times of inflation, when most bond and stock fund prices are declining, a money fund's yield will increase and the investor will make money rather than lose it. This was evident in 1994, when rising rates hurt both stock and bond markets, but money fund investors reaped the rewards of increasing yields without loss of principal.

In today's market, where equity prices and valuations are at all-time highs and the yield curve is flat, money funds offer an equity investor a great way to stabilize and moderate their portfolio's risk-and-return profile. If the market corrects, the money fund allocation will remain intact and can then be used to reinvest in the equity market at lower, more reasonable prices. If you are an income investor, there is also a strong case to be made for money funds.

Income investors have been faced with a *yield squeeze* for nearly three years. This means that yields have been declining and the yield curve has been flattening. This leaves income investors faced with a 30-year Treasury bond offering less than 5.3%. Excepting long-term municipal and high yield "junk" funds, most income fund yields are only marginally (if at all) higher than the average money fund yield. So on a risk/return basis, the money funds are extremely attractive.

## Money Fund Regulation—An Added Security Blanket

Like all mutual funds, money funds are regulated by the Securities and Exchange Commission under the Investment Company Act of 1940. However, money funds also have another layer of regulation called Rule 2a-7, or "The Rule." The Rule restricts what money funds own so that they maintain the highest quality and greatest amount of stability in price.

For example, a taxable money fund cannot own more than 5% of its total assets in the securities of any one issuer—other than the U.S. government. This restriction forces money funds to have a well-diversified portfolio. State tax-exempt funds have a bit more leeway with the diversification rule, which pertains to only 75% of a fund's assets. With respect to quality, a taxable money fund cannot invest more than 5% of its total assets in securities that carry "second tier" quality ratings. *Second tier* means any paper not holding the highest rating by the major rating agencies. The regulation forces the fund to hold only the highest quality securities. Another restriction holds the average maturity of a money fund to 90 days. While some of the holdings can have longer maturities (a maximum of 13 months), the fund itself cannot exceed 90 days. This ensures that the fund does not extend maturities to the extent that the price per share could be impacted by changes in interest rates. Under current SEC regulations, a fund cannot even call itself a money market fund unless it meets these and other strict regulations.

Although there is clearly a great deal of regulation, this still does not guarantee that a fund will stay out of trouble. In fact, in 1994 an institutional fund "broke the buck;" its NAV dropped below $1. Subsequently, the fund was liquidated at 94 cents on the dollar. In addition, at least 100 money funds had to be bailed out of trouble by their parent companies in that same year. Many of the problems arose from aggressive investment polices and the use of specialized money fund derivatives. Since then, the SEC has again tightened the regulations and now prevents the use of these more speculative securities.

As you can see, there are a number of SEC regulations that confine a money fund to very specific types of investments. Because of this, the yields on money funds tend to be very similar. Since these funds own only high-quality, short-term securities, the yields on the funds are usually the lowest for all income funds. This causes a lot of competition among funds. Typically, the highest yielding funds cut most, if not all of their expenses to achieve the highest yields. According to IBC's Crane, currently, 58% of all money funds waive their fees.

## Taxable and Tax-Free

There are two basic varieties of money funds, taxable and tax-free. Taxable money funds invest in securities that have taxable income, and tax-free funds invest in municipal securities whose income is tax-exempt at the federal and often at the state level. Within the taxable and tax-free categories, there are subgroups based on portfolio composition.

### Taxable Money Funds

Taxable money funds invest in a wide variety of securities, including Treasury securities, government agencies, repurchase agreements, or "repos," domestic and foreign certificates of deposit, commercial paper, bankers acceptances, foreign bank obligations, and many others. All of these securities pay interest that is taxable. Take the case of Treasury securities and some qualified government agencies, for example. The income is taxable at the federal level, but it is exempt at the state level. Typically, the issuers of the securities are public corporations such as banks or major industrial firms. Each issue must be of the highest quality for the funds to include them in their portfolios.

Taxable money funds have been split into two general categories, general purpose funds and government funds. *General purpose funds* are by far the most numerous of all money funds. They can purchase any security that qualifies as an approved money market security by the SEC. These funds normally offer the highest yields of all the money funds. *Government money market funds* invest in Treasury securities such as T-bills, agency securities, or both. Funds that invest solely in Treasuries and therefore have their income exempt from state taxes are called *100% Treasury money market funds.* These are considered the safest of all money funds since the securities are backed by the full faith and credit of the U.S. government. As you might expect, these funds have the lowest yields.

### Tax-Free Money Funds

As their name implies, tax-free or municipal money market funds' income is exempt from federal taxation. In addition, the income is exempt at the state level to the extent that the fund owns securities in the shareholders' state.

These funds buy issues of municipal governments and entities such as a state, city, town, public works district, or public service company. The most common type of security is a general obligation of a state. These securities are backed by the full faith and credit of the issuer (usually a state), and interest is derived from taxes of residents of the state. Funds can also purchase revenue bonds. A revenue bonds' interest is derived from a public project that generates income—a toll road or municipal airport, for example. Tax-exempt funds also buy tax-free commercial paper issued by other tax-free agencies such as schools or development authorities. Each municipal issue carries a credit rating that describes the issuer's ability to pay. Unlike Treasury securities, the issues don't automatically get the highest credit ratings, but they still must be of the highest quality to qualify for fund purchase under Rule 2a-7.

### National Funds

The most popular and common type of tax-free money fund is the national money fund. These portfolios hold tax-free securities from many different issuers from around the country. They offer great geographical diversification. The income from these funds is exempt at the federal level and at the state level to the extent the fund owns securities from the shareholder's state.

### State Tax-Free

Certain types of money funds called *state tax-free funds* purchase securities of just one state. In this way the income is exempt from federal taxes as well as all state taxes. These funds are most popular in states with high tax brackets and lots of issuing agencies, such as New York, California, Massachusetts, New Jersey, Ohio, Michigan, Illinois, and Connecticut. There are no capital gains on the sale or exchange of a money fund because the fund is always bought and sold at $1.0 per share. However, there can be taxes due on money fund income, as mentioned for taxable funds, depending on the fund's holdings.

## Money Fund Yields—Which Fund Is Best?

The standard yield by which most money funds are judged is the SEC 7-Day standardized yield. This yield is calculated by adding the seven daily dividend factors of the fund together and then dividing the amount by seven. The number is then annualized and turned into a percentage. This yield is found both in a simple yield as well as a compound yield. Yields are normally found weekly in major financial newspapers.

Tax-free yields are calculated the same way as taxable yields, but an investor would normally want to calculate for himself a taxable equivalent yield (TEY). The TEY tells an investor how the income of a tax-free fund compares to a taxable fund's yield based on the investor's tax bracket. The calculation is as follows:

$$\frac{\text{Tax-free yield}}{1 - \text{tax bracket}} = \text{TEY}$$

For example, if the tax-free yield was 5% and an investor was in the 39.6% federal tax bracket, she would have to get a taxable yield of at least 8.27% to equal the tax-free yield. This simple calculation allows an investor to determine whether a taxable or tax-free fund offers greater after-tax yield.

## TREASURY AND GOVERNMENT BOND FUNDS

Treasury and government securities bond funds are those that invest in securities that are issued or guaranteed by the U.S. government (direct obligations) or by an agency of the U.S. government. The most common types of government securities are Treasury bills, notes, and bonds. The Department of the Treasury issues these securities, and their interest and principal is guaranteed by the "full faith and credit" of the U.S. government. Treasury securities are taxable at the federal level, but exempt from income tax at the state level.

Treasury bills have maturities of one-year or less, while Treasury notes have maturities of two to five years. Longer maturity securities are called bonds, such as the bellwether 30-year Treasury bond. Treasury securities are considered the most liquid debt instruments in the world. They carry AAA rating and are viewed as having no credit risk. They are, how-

**TABLE 7-3**

Treasury and Government Bond Funds

| Item | Long-Term | Intermediate-Term | Short-Term |
| --- | --- | --- | --- |
| Credit quality | High | High | High |
| Interest-rate risk | High | Moderate | Low |
| Maturity | Long | Intermediate | Short |
| Yield | 5.10 | 5.31 | 5.10 |
| 3-year total return | 7.52 | 7.07 | 7.05 |
| Standard deviation | 4.64 | 3.80 | 3.70 |
| Income level | Moderate | Moderate | Low |
| Expense ratio | 0.97 | 1.06 | 0.77 |

ever, subject to interest-rate risk. As with any bond, shorter maturity issues will have less return volatility for a given change in rates than a longer maturity bond.

In addition to Treasury securities, there are a number of other government securities called *agency securities* that U.S. government entities issue. One of the most visible agencies is the Government National Mortgage Association (GNMA), or "Ginnie Mae." The purpose of this agency is to finance residential housing. Its issues are essentially pools of mortgages that are backed by the agency and whose interest and principal payments are backed by the U.S. government. Many funds focus solely on GNMA securities because they are very liquid and there is an active trading market in the issues. GNMA securities are taxable at both the federal and state levels.

There are a number of other "government-sponsored" securities. The U.S. government does not insure or guarantee government-sponsored securities as it does with *government-backed* securities. However, they are still seen as extremely high quality and thus carry AAA ratings. The best known of these are the Federal National Mortgage Association (FNMA), or "Fannie Mae" bonds. They are subject to federal and state taxes. Other agencies include the Federal Home Loan Mortgage Corporation, or "Freddie Mac," and the Student Loan Marketing Association, or "Sallie Mae." Freddie Mac securities are taxed at the federal and state levels, but Sallie Mae securities are only taxed at the federal level.

From a yield perspective, Treasury bonds usually have the lowest yields for a given maturity because of the high degree of safety. Agency securities are also considered very high quality, but yields will normally be a bit higher than Treasuries for comparable maturities.

The difference between Treasury and government security bond funds is in what they own. Typically, the majority of a Treasury fund's holdings will be in Treasury notes and bonds. One of the advertised features of most Treasury funds is that the monthly dividend is exempt from state taxes. For investors in high tax bracket states, this is a very attractive factor.

A government securities fund will normally hold both Treasury issues and agency issues. Government security funds typically have slightly higher yields than Treasury funds. The dividends from these funds may have some exemption from state taxes, to the extent that they own qualified securities.

Both Treasury and government security funds are available in a variety of maturities, including short-, intermediate-, and long-term. They are most often used in conservative portfolios that have safety and income as their main objectives.

## MORGAGE BOND FUNDS

There are now over 200 mortgage bond funds available to the individual investor. They generally come in three varieties: adjustable rate mortgages (ARMs), Ginnie Maes (GNMAs), and government/mortgage securities. While each type carries different levels of risk and contains a different array of bond types, they all have one thing in common: They buy mortgage bonds.

Mortgage bonds are pools of loans, typically residential home loans, packaged by various government agencies. As with all bonds, interest rates have a definite impact on them. The differentiating element in mortgage bonds is their prepayment risk.

### Prepayment Risk

Prepayment risk is the risk that the loans in the packaged pools will be repaid earlier than expected. This is a risk because a purchaser of the loan pool expects the pool, like a bond, to pay the stated interest rate until final maturity. However, if the loan is paid off early, the income flow stops and principal may be returned. One of the biggest enemies of mortgage bonds is rapidly declining interest rates. Normally, you'd think falling rates are good for all bonds, but for the mortgage market, this doesn't necessarily hold true.

Early payment can occur for a variety of reasons, including selling a home to buy a new one. In this case, the original loan is paid off and

**TABLE 7-4**

Mortgage

| Item | Government Mortgage | GNMA | ARM |
|------|---------------------|------|-----|
| Credit quality | High | High | High |
| Interest-rate risk | Moderate | Moderate | Low |
| Maturity | Medium | Medium | Short |
| Yield | 5.81 | 5.98 | 5.30 |
| 3-year total return | 6.94 | 7.59 | 5.45 |
| Standard deviation | 2.93 | 3.00 | 1.01 |
| Income level | Moderate | Moderate | Low |
| Expense ratio | 1.28 | 0.86 | 1.14 |

replaced with a new one. Another reason for prepayment is loan refinancing. If you have an outstanding loan at a high interest rate and rates start to decline, you often can refinance the loan at a lower rate. This activity is very common in the residential home mortgage market.

The rate at which loans in a pool repay is called the *prepayment experience.* The prepayment experience will vary from pool to pool and from market condition to market condition. Understanding this special risk is important for fund managers because they must make a number of assumptions about future prepayments when setting strategies for their funds.

Each of the three types of mortgage funds mentioned has a different level of risk based on the mortgage pool composition.

## ARM Funds

Adjustable rate mortgage funds are generally considered to be the least volatile of the funds, although several ARM funds have had huge declines in recent years due to investment in highly leveraged short-term securities called *principal-only loans* (POs). (POs act like zero coupon bonds.) If these funds are set aside, this fund category usually has a lower standard deviation of returns when compared to the other mortgage categories.

The reason for the lower volatility is that these pools are made up of mortgage securities (often GNMAs and FNMAs) that adjust or rest on a frequent basis. They act similarly to bonds with annual call dates (equal to a one-year maturity). The market prices them as short-term securities, which causes them to have very short durations.

## GNMA Funds

As the name implies, GNMA funds are those that primarily purchase mortgages from the Government National Mortgage Association. GNMA is a wholly government-owned corporation within the Department of Housing and Urban Development, and it carries the full faith and credit of the U.S. government. Because of the underlying high credit quality and the abundance of these securities, they have become the only specific mortgage security to have funds created for it. GNMA funds typically have longer maturities than ARM funds and, subsequently, higher levels of return volatility. Investors are rewarded for the increased risk with higher income rates and greater total return potential.

Most of the funds have at least 65% of their holdings in GNMA securities. Because GNMAs are not Treasury securities, they tend to offer a bit more yield, while still offering the "government-backed" guarantee. However, GNMAs, like other mortgage securities, have prepayment risk. When people refinance a mortgage, they are terminating loans in a mortgage pool such as GNMA. This causes a return of capital to the GNMA owner, which in this case would be the mutual fund. The investment world does not consider return of capital to be a good thing. These returns negatively impact a mortgage security's price. It is for this reason that GNMA funds often underperform other bond funds as rates decline. Fund managers attempt to reduce the downside impact by purchasing GNMAs that are less susceptible to prepayment risk, but it remains an ongoing challenge for managers to do this.

### Yield Advantage

Despite the challenge of prepayment risk, GNMA funds have become very popular in recent years as investors search for high-quality, higher-yielding funds. Currently, the average 12-month distribution yield on a GNMA fund is just under 6.2%. Compared to the average Treasury bond fund yield of about 5.25%, it's a good deal.

## Return and Risk Review

In the last three years, the average GNMA fund has produced an annual total return of 8.5%. The group's best return in the last 10 years was in 1995, when the average fund produced a 16.5% return. Because these funds tend to be very conservative, they typically are not at the top of the bond fund charts for return. With respect to risk, the funds are usually very stable. The average standard deviation, or annual fluctuation in return, for the group is 3.5% (S&P 500 is about 15%). This makes them very attractive candidates for income portfolios that require a high level of quality in the underlying portfolio composition. Rather than having to stick with a Treasury bond fund, investors have a fund choice that equals the quality but allows for more income.

## CORPORATE BOND FUNDS

Corporate bond funds are those that buy bonds issued by corporations. There are two major types of corporate issues, secured and unsecured bonds. In each case, the income paid to bond holders and bond fund shareholders is taxable as ordinary income at both the state and federal levels.

*Secured bonds* are backed by a specific pledge of assets by the issuer. If a secured bond were to default, the bondholder would have a claim on

**TABLE 7-5**

High-Quality Corporate

| Item | Long-Term | Intermediate-Term | Short-Term |
|---|---|---|---|
| Credit quality | High | High | High |
| Interest-rate risk | High | Moderate | Low |
| Maturity | Long | Intermediate | Short |
| Yield | 5.83 | 5.55 | 5.08 |
| 3-year total return | 7.28 | 6.97 | 5.68 |
| Standard deviation | 3.85 | 3.14 | 1.31 |
| Income level | Moderate+ | Moderate | Low |
| Expense ratio | 0.99 | 1.00 | 0.87 |

those specific assets of the company. Within the secured bond category, the most common bonds are *mortgage bonds,* those secured by mortgages on property, and *equipment trust certificates,* those secured by equipment.

*Unsecured bonds* are issued by a corporation but are not backed by a specific asset, just by the "good faith" of the company. These are commonly known as *debentures.* If the company defaults, the secured bondholders would be paid first, then the unsecured debenture bondholders. This added risk associated with debentures is why they typically have higher yields than secured bonds. The next lowest level on the credit line are corporate issues called *subordinate debentures.* In case of default, these bonds are paid off after the debentures and after the secured bonds. As you might have guessed, yields on these bonds are on the higher end of the corporate bond yield scale.

Each type of bond described above can have different ratings. The rating will depend on the ability of the issuer to pay interest and principal on a timely basis. Most corporate bond funds are high-quality funds. This means the majority of their portfolio consists of bonds with ratings of 'BBB' and above, with most having average quality in the 'AA' zone. There are also many "general" corporate funds that can buy both high-quality and some lower-quality issues. Corporate funds that primarily buy low-grade bonds are called *high-income* or *junk funds.* These are discussed in the next section.

In addition to quality differences, corporate bond funds can also vary in target maturities. For example, short-term corporate funds normally have maturities of three years and under, intermediates three to seven years, and long-term funds have maturities in excess of seven years. *As the maturity increases, so do the yield, the expected return, and the fund's return volatility.* Yields and total returns on corporate bond funds are usually higher than those of Treasury funds of comparable maturity but lower than those of high-income funds.

An investor with a short time horizon, say one to three years, is best suited by short- or intermediate-term funds. Investors with time horizons of five years or more should focus on long-term funds. Since the income on corporate funds is taxable, they are best suited for investors in low tax brackets or for conservative qualified accounts such as IRAs or 401(k)s.

### Comparative Risk and Return

On average, higher-quality corporate bond funds produce income levels above those of the Treasury funds but below those of the high-income funds. For example, in 1998 the average 12-month distribution yield (midyear) on the corporate high-quality fund category was 5.58%, compared to the Treasury category at 5.04% and the high-income group at 9.03%.

Long-term total returns for the corporate funds should be on par with those of the Treasury and municipal categories at all maturity levels. Over a five-year period ending August 1998, the high-quality corporate fund's average annual total return was 5.7%, compared to the Treasury group's 6% total return and the municipal average of 5.48%. In times when the market is concerned about recession, the high-quality corporate funds will normally see an increase in demand. This often causes the group to considerably outperform lower-quality funds.

Regarding risk, the corporate funds' long-term standard deviations have been slightly lower than those of the Treasury and municipal funds. For example, for the five-year period ending mid-1998, the standard deviation for the corporate high-quality group was 3.5%, compared to the municipal funds' 4.5% standard deviation and the Treasury funds' 5.2% standard deviation.

### HIGH-INCOME CORPORATE FUNDS—"JUNK"

It wasn't so long ago that the words "junk bond" meant just that—junk! Bonds that were rated below BBB were viewed as the most speculative of all bonds, and they did not have a good chance of making interest and principal payments. The tarnished reputation of the high-income bond and bond fund market has seen a dramatic evolution in the last few years. Junk bond funds have turned to gold for the bond mutual fund industry and for those investors who have invested in the funds since late 1990. But before

**TABLE 7–6**

High-Income Corporate

| Item | High-Income |
|---|---|
| Credit quality | Low |
| Interest-rate risk | High |
| Maturity | Int/Long |
| Yield | 8.89 |
| 3-year total return | 8.84 |
| Standard deviation | 6.57 |
| Income level | High |
| Expense ratio | 1.40 |
| Event risk | High |

you invest in these funds, it's important to look at the risk side of the junk fund story.

One of the main reasons these bond funds have done well in recent years is not so much a bond story as it is a stock story. Junk bond funds have traditionally had a high correlation to the stock market. Because junk bond values are closely tied to company earnings, they act very much like the company's stock price.

On a comparative return and yield basis, the junk funds have fared very well against both their high-quality corporate cousins and their municipal neighbors. In strong bond years, such as 1993 and 1995, they matched or exceeded the total returns of the other two sectors. In poor bond market years, such as 1994, they held their own. *While the total returns of junk funds are clearly exceptional, the yield component has been the greatest advantage for most income investors.* The junk funds have consistently held yield premiums against all other income markets. In mid-1998, yields on junk bond funds averaged about 8.25%, which was about 300 basis points higher than long-term corporate and Treasury bond funds.

## Comparative Risk

Judging fund risk can be a tricky endeavor, especially in cases with multiple definitions of risk. In reviewing risk of the junk fund sector, one can look at two items, standard deviation and duration. Using standard deviation (monthly return volatility), the junk funds appear to have about the same risk as the high-quality corporate funds and the municipal funds. On a duration basis (a fund's sensitivity to changes in rates), the junk funds appear to have even better results. One explanation for the lower duration numbers (lower rate sensitivity) is the fact that the junk funds purchase high-income bonds that will mathematically have lower durations.

| Items | Junk Funds | High-Quality Taxable Funds | Municipal Funds |
|---|---|---|---|
| 3-year standard deviation | 4.81 | 4.57 | 5.78 |
| 5-year standard deviation | 4.66 | 4.72 | 5.78 |
| Average maturity | 7.5 | 9.3 | 18.6 |
| Average duration | 4.5 | 4.9 | 7.5 |

There are, however, other elements to this market which are less obvious, but which could be far more important in evaluating a junk bond fund.

## Hidden Risks and the Summer of '90

A risk that is less quantifiable but extremely applicable to the junk market is *liquidity risk*. Liquidity risk is the risk that a lack of buying demand will affect prices. Liquidity in the junk market is notorious for disappearing at the first sign of adversity. Even though the high interest payments cushion junk bonds (typically lower duration) from decline, liquidity risks are often masked. It is this element of the junk bond market that requires some caution, and it is why this part of the bond market is called junk.

In the summer and fall of 1990, the junk bond market experienced a near collapse. Bonds were defaulting at an alarming pace as the economy went into recession. In addition, the famous insider trading case involving Mike Milken was in full swing. These events caused the demand for high-income bonds to nearly disappear. Subsequently, assets were drawn out of the funds and liquidity was as thin as it ever gets. It was in this environment that junk bonds and the junk funds showed their ugly underside.

In the brief 3-month period from August to October 1990, junk funds experienced huge declines. Some funds lost as much as 25% in those 90 days. No fund really escaped, even those of the biggest and most prestigious fund companies. By the end of the year, the average total return loss was more than 9%. While a 9% loss in the sector's worst year doesn't seem so bad, the important thing to remember is that returns on these funds can decline very quickly. This consideration should give pause to any potential new investor who believes there is a free ride in high-income funds.

Since that 1990 episode, the high-income market has shown a tremendous recovery. In 1991, the year after the near collapse of the sector, the average fund gained more than 35%. In the last five years, the average total return for the group has been just under 10%. Many of the top funds have produced total returns above 14% for the same period. The superior return and yield of the funds have made them extremely popular for investors looking for additional income for their portfolios.

On a risk basis, the standard deviation for the group is just over 4%. This is 25% that of the S&P 500 and in line with most other long-term bond fund sectors. However, these funds are still susceptible to lots of volatility if the economy moves into a recession or even a slowdown in economic activity. Basically, the standard deviation and duration figures do not cover all of the risks involved with a junk bond fund. Because of this added inherent risk, they should be used in conjunction with other funds that are more stable, such as money funds and short-term bond funds.

## MUNICIPAL BOND FUNDS

Tax-exempt securities have been an important feature of the debt markets in the United States for over 100 years. The great value of these funds is that their income isn't taxed by the federal government, and states exempt tax on income derived from bonds they issue. Today, there are tens of thousands of issuers of tax-exempt bonds. In 1978, the federal tax laws pertain-

**TABLE 7-7**

Municipal

| | Long-Term | Intermediate-Term | Short-Term | Long-Term State | High Yield |
|---|---|---|---|---|---|
| Credit quality | Medium/High | Medium/High | Medium/High | Medium/High | Low |
| Interest-rate risk | High | Moderate | Low | High | High Yield |
| Maturity | Long | Medium | Short | Long | Long |
| Yield | 4.59 | 4.17 | 3.93 | 4.49 | 5.28 |
| 3-year total return | 7.25 | 6.04 | 4.33 | 7.13 | 7.70 |
| Standard deviation | 3.69 | 2.72 | 0.90 | 3.52 | 3.14 |
| Income level | High | Moderate | Low | High | High Yield |
| Expense ratio | 1.15 | 1.00 | 0.59 | 1.11 | 1.13 |

ing to bond funds changed to allow a "passthrough" of tax-free income from municipal securities via municipal bond funds. This marked the beginning of the rapid growth in tax-free funds.

There is a wide variety of municipal bond funds now available to the individual investor. They range from the very short-term tax-free money market funds discussed at the start of this chapter to aggressive high-yield funds. However, they all have one thing in common: They purchase municipal securities.

As the name implies, municipal bonds are issued by municipal entities such as states, cities, towns, public works projects, highway authorities, school districts, and the like. The interest income paid by these issuers to the bondholders is exempt from federal taxation. The income is also normally exempt from state taxation for bondholders in the issuer's state. Such bonds are called *double tax-free.*

There are two main types of municipal bonds: general obligation, or "GOs," and revenue bonds. *General obligations bonds* allow interest and principal to be paid from the taxation power of the issuer. This type of backing is commonly referred to as "full-faith and credit." State-issued bonds are usually general obligations and are backed by the issuing state. The GO is considered the safest type of municipal bond. Even though they are considered safe from a credit risk perspective, they are given different credit ratings depending on the stability of the underlying issuer.

The revenue generated by a public project pays a revenue bond's interest and principal. An example might be a toll road, where the money earned from commuters would pay interest and principal. In general, this type of bond is considered to have more risk than a GO because the revenue of the project could be impacted by other events out of the issuer's control. For example, the toll authority can't force a person to use the toll road, whereas the state's department of revenue can force the payment of taxes. Given the difference in income-generating capability, revenue bonds typically have higher interest rates compared to comparable GO bonds.

Bond funds that specialize in municipal issues typically own both GOs and revenue bonds. The elements of quality, maturity, and issuer differentiate the various types of funds. Funds that hold bonds in many different states are called *national funds,* while those that own bonds of just one state are called *state tax-free funds.* The dividend earned on the national funds will be exempt from federal taxation. The dividend earned from the state tax-free funds will be exempt from taxes at both the federal and state levels.

Among the great advantages of municipal bond funds are the management and diversification they offer. Since most municipal bonds are issued in a minimum denomination of $5000, it is often very difficult, if not impossible, for an individual investor to construct a well-diversified portfolio without having at least $100,000. Most funds, however, allow a minimum initial investment of only $2500. In addition, nearly all municipal bonds are traded among institutional investors in large amounts, often in excess of $1 million per trade. If an individual investor tried to sell one $5000 bond from an obscure issuer, the amount offered on the bond might be far less than the investor had expected. The economies of scale allow fund managers to get better prices than a small investor could expect as well as better and less costly trade execution.

## Tax-Free Money Funds

The money market funds (described earlier) hold securities that have maturities of less than 90 days and are of the highest quality. Funds will usually buy tax anticipation notes (TANs), bond anticipation notes (BANs), revenue anticipation notes (RANs), tax-free commercial paper, and variable rate demand notes. Tax-free money funds are available in both national and state tax-free varieties. Evaluating the value of the dividend requires a comparison of the taxable and tax-free fund yield. The tax-free yield should be converted into a taxable equivalent yield (see Chapter 3). Tax-free money fund yields will normally be the lowest and safest of all the municipal funds. Since a money fund's NAV is held at $1.0 per share, the principal value will always remain steady. The best measure of performance for these funds (taxable money funds as well) is a comparison of yields.

## Short and Intermediate Municipal Funds

Unlike the money funds, the short- and intermediate-term municipal funds have a variable NAV. Like any fund, the NAV's movement day-to-day is a function of the market and the securities the fund owns. The short- and intermediate-term funds have average maturities greater than that of a money market (usually 1 year or more) but less than that of a long-term fund (about 10 years maximum maturity). These funds offer an investor a compromise between the low yield and low risk of a money market and the higher yield and greater return fluctuation of a long-term fund.

In a normal market, the yields on intermediate funds will be about 50% to 70% of the long-term funds and about 30% more than the money markets. In most cases, the short- and intermediate-term funds are of very high quality. Most investors are buying these shorter maturities for safety, so there has been little demand for low-quality portfolios. However, due to the demand of individuals in states with high tax brackets, there are numerous funds in this maturity range that are state tax-free. Again, this allows an investor in a particular state to buy a fund that owns bonds issued by that state only. This makes the dividends exempt from both state and federal income taxes.

## Long-Term Funds

Municipal bond funds with average maturities in excess of about 10 years are considered long-term funds. Most such funds have maturities between 15 and 25 years. As was mentioned in Chapter 2, the longer the maturity (and duration), the greater the volatility in a fund's price and return. For this added volatility, an investor is rewarded with higher yields. These yields can sometimes be twice that of a money market fund and about 30% more than an intermediate-term fund. The long-term funds have become the most popular type of municipal fund because of the higher yields available. Within the long-term sector, there are five common types of funds: national high-quality, national high-yield, state high-quality, state high-yield, and insured.

### National High-Quality

As the name implies, the national high-quality funds buy municipal bonds from many different issuers across many different states. These are the most popular types of municipal funds. Dividends are exempt from federal and state tax to the extent that the bonds are issued from an investor's home state. For example, if you owned ABC Municipal fund and 10% of the portfolio was bonds issued from your home state, the income attributable to that 10% would be exempt on the state level. To help you with your tax preparation, most fund families provide a complete breakdown of the fund's holdings by state at the end of each year. The quality level on these funds will typically be A or higher. Many consider these types of funds more secure because of the geographical diversification they offer. This helps protect them during times when a particular state may be downgraded and all the bonds issued from the state are impacted.

### National High-Yield

High-yield municipal bond funds are very similar to high-quality municipal funds. The main difference is that they generally purchase bonds with credit ratings of BBB and below, although the funds can purchase high-quality bonds. The lower-quality bonds provide a higher interest rate and higher dividends to shareholders. Yields on these funds can be as much as 75 basis points (1% = 100 basis points) higher than the high-quality funds with the same maturity. Typically, maturities on these funds are longer than 15 years.

The lower credit quality of the bonds owned in high-yield fund port-folios can subject the fund to greater uncertainty about payment of interest and principal. This can be accompanied by greater return volatility over the long term, especially during periods of economic recession when these types of bonds are more vulnerable to default. However, during the last 10 years, volatility in this fund category has not been significantly higher than that of the high-quality funds.

In times of strong economic growth and lower interest rates, these funds are favored for their higher yields. As increased buying occurs, the price of the bonds increases and yields decline. In fact, yields will often decline at a faster rate than yields on high-quality bonds because of the increase in demand. This decline causes a narrowing of the yield "spread," or difference, between high-quality and lower-quality yields. As this occurs, fund managers often move more of their portfolios into higher-quality issues, because the additional yield gained by buying lower-quality bonds is not worth the incremental risk. This helps increase the credit qual-ity of the funds and makes them act much more like higher-quality funds.

## State High-Quality and High-Yield

State high-quality and high-yield municipal funds or *double tax-free funds* are those that purchase bonds of a specific state. The difference between the two is the credit quality. The state high-yield funds have characteristics similar to those mentioned in the last section. Most state tax-free funds are currently high-quality funds.

The dividends of both types of funds are exempt from state and fed-eral tax. The obvious advantage of these funds is that on an after-tax basis, they provide greater income to an investor in that state than a national tax-free fund would.

The use of a taxable equivalent yield is key in comparing the differ-ences in yield. However, when using the TEY formula, you should use the state's total effective state and federal tax bracket rather than just the fed-eral bracket. For example, ABC California fund offers a yield of 5% while ABC National fund offers a yield of 5.25%. At first glance, it would seem that the ABC National fund is a better deal, based on yield. However, the

National fund investor will pay taxes at the state level on the dividends. Let's look at its TEY for an investor in the top tax bracket of 39.6%.

$$TEY = 5.25\%/(1 - .369) = 8.69\%$$

Now let's look at the 5% ABC California fund for the same investor, who happens to be a resident of California. An investor in the top federal and state tax bracket in California will have a total effective bracket of 46.24% (married filing jointly). Now let's recalculate the TEY using the total tax bracket. The ABC California fund 5% double tax-free yield would be:

$$TEY = 5\%/(1 - .4624) = 9.30\%$$

As you can see, despite the ¼% lower yield, the taxable equivalent yield was higher in the California fund (9.30%) because of the added tax-exempt value with the higher overall tax bracket. In this case, the state fund was a better deal on an income basis. So, what about total return and other risks?

The total return on state funds tends to be very close to that of national funds, and they track each other very closely. During some periods, especially when there are significant credit problems with the state in question, the state funds can exhibit much greater return volatility. This was most evident in 1994, when Orange County in California defaulted on over $1.5 billion in bonds. Even though many funds didn't even own Orange County bonds, most of the state's issuers had significant short-term price declines. National funds dipped only slightly through the crisis. This highlights the added risk when geographical diversification is removed, as is the case with state bond funds.

### Insured Municipal Funds

Insured bond funds are a special type of municipal fund that purchases insured bonds. The fund itself is not insured, only the bonds it owns. From a credit quality perspective, an insured bond fund is considered a AAA quality fund. Because the fund is of higher quality, yields can be as much as ½% less than a comparable high-quality municipal fund that is not insured.

Issuers of municipal bonds can purchase insurance from one of several commercial insurance firms that specialize in the bond business. The bonds are normally insured for the payment of interest and principal. In this way, if the issuer is unable to make timely payments, the insurance company will step in and make the payment. The issuer pays a premium to the insurance company for this option. Once a bond has been insured, it is assigned a AAA rating. The AAA rating allows the issuer to sell the bond at a lower interest payment, a significant cost savings.

While the insurance covers the interest and principal payment, it does not cover volatility in the price of the bond. Many investors incorrectly believe that an insured bond will not be subject to interest rate risk because it has a AAA rating. Indeed, evidence suggests that insured bonds have similar price and return volatility to an uninsured issue. In addition, many investors believe that once a bond is insured, it will always have a AAA rating. This is also incorrect. If an issuer defaults and the insurer can't make the payment, the bond's rating will drop. In addition, if the rating on the insurance company falls, the bonds that it insures may also be subject to rating decline.

There is much controversy over the perceived added safety of an insured fund. Many investors feel that an uninsured fund is actively managed and constantly monitored and, therefore, that management will be able to detect problems with individual issuers. This confidence, in effect, acts as assurance against default; therefore, the insurance is not necessary. It's a good case to be made. There are also those who feel that the insurance is only as good as the insurer, and if there were a large number of big defaults, the insurance companies would not be able to make timely payments.

## INTERNATIONAL BOND FUNDS

In recent years, many investors have attempted to diversify their portfolios by purchasing international funds to offset the risks of investing solely in the U.S. market. In addition, international investing has been a popular

**TABLE 7-8**

International Bond Funds

| Item | International |
| --- | --- |
| Credit quality | Moderate |
| Interest-rate risk | High |
| Maturity | Long |
| Yield | 6.91 |
| 3-year total return | 5.30 |
| Standard deviation | 8.10 |
| Income level | High |
| Expense ratio | 1.63 |
| Currency risk | High |

way to leverage higher yields and returns offered in foreign markets. However, international bond investing typically requires the acceptance of additional risks, including currency risk.

When buying foreign bond funds, it's important to know that they are not all alike. For example, funds that call themselves *global bond funds* generally invest in bonds of other countries, corporations within those countries, and some U.S. bonds. Funds that call themselves *international* are generally composed only of foreign bonds, with possibly with very small concentrations in the U.S. market. Today, however, there are even smaller subsets, including *emerging debt funds*. These funds specialize in more speculative high-yielding markets, such as Brazil, Argentina, Mexico, Hungary, and others. There are also funds that specialize in a certain part of the world, such as the European bond funds. They tend to be more stable and offer lower yields. As you might guess, all of the funds can act very differently, but they do have a common denominator—currency risk.

## The Currency Question

International bond funds can and do act very differently from U.S. bond funds. The main reason is the impact of changes in currency value. This is called *currency risk.* In addition, these bonds can be impacted by *sovereign risk.* This is the risk that political instability has on the liquidity and value of a country's debt. However, currency risk is probably the greatest risk with most international bond funds.

As the dollar strengthens against a country's currency, the value of that country's bonds in U.S. dollars weakens. Thus, a stronger dollar overseas can hurt an international bond fund's NAV, even if the bonds themselves are rising in value in the home country. The worst case scenario for international bond funds is when rates are rising in that country *and* the U.S. dollar is gaining ground. This "double whammy" can result in double-digit losses in a matter of days. This was seen in 1994 when Mexico devalued its currency. Rates in Mexico were rising and the dollar was rising. This resulted in losses of more than 20% for those bond funds that concentrated in Mexican debt securities.

### Hedging
Some fund managers attempt to soften the currency blow by *hedging* their portfolios with currency futures. A fund manager hedges by buying currency futures that gain value as the dollar rises. In this way, the losses in the portfolio securities can be offset by the gains in the futures contract. How-

ever, not all countries have liquid and reliable currency trading. Indeed, attempting to hedge an international bond portfolio that consists of emerging debt market bonds is almost impossible. Even those funds that claim to hedge often don't do a very good job, and don't completely hedge away the currency factors.

This added element of risk has caused these funds to have risk (standard deviation) profiles far in excess of U.S. bond funds. So what do you get for this added element of risk?

The answer currently is not very clear. The average yield on the long-term international funds as of mid-1998 was about 6.25%, while top funds offered yields in excess of 8%. The average yields have not been as high as the U.S. junk bond funds or even the long-term municipal bond funds (using a 39.6% tax bracket equivalent yield). Average total returns on the international funds over the last three years have been just under 8%. This is about the same return when compared with the U.S. corporate bond sector, yet lower than the high-income bond funds.

On a risk basis, the standard deviations for the international funds, at about 6.25%, have far exceeded those of most U.S. funds. One reason for this is the influence that the emerging debt funds have on the average. For example, Scudder's Emerging Markets Income Fund had a standard deviation of over 14% and a yield close to 8.5%, while their International Fund had a standard deviation of just 4.6% and a yield of 5.5%. As you can see, differentiating the funds is quite important.

In general, emerging debt funds should only be used in the most aggressive income fund portfolios. They should be viewed as the "junk" of the international markets. They offer higher yields and returns, but with far greater potential volatility. European bond funds also have the potential for solid total return, but yields have been equal to or less than those of U.S. securities. There are certainly times when these funds might be worthwhile, such as periods of declining dollar value versus the target currency. For example, buying European funds in early 1995 paid off when the dollar weakened against the German mark. However, you must be able to pick the fund that will actually reflect this relationship. What about the diversification advantages?

## Does the Diversification Story Hold?

One of the strongest cases in recent years for holding any international securities, stocks or bonds, has been diversification. The idea is that if you own funds that don't all move the same way at the same time, you can balance out the ebbs and flows of the markets. While this idea is certainly appealing in its concept, the reality of the markets these days is not so black and white.

Most of the world financial markets, the bond markets included, have become much more correlated, that is, they move together more closely. What happens in the U.S. now impacts to a much higher degree the fortunes of many other economies, including those in Europe and Asia. Conversely, the ups and downs in those markets impact the U.S.

If you are not familiar with the intricacies of the international markets and currency volatility, the best course is to stick with what you know in the U.S. bond markets. There is plenty of choice and diversity among fund categories to maximize both your income and total returns.

## SPECIALTY BOND FUNDS

### Bond Index Funds

Index fund investing has been extremely popular in the last several years, but most of the money has found its way into stock index funds. Less well known, but equally appealing, are *bond index funds.*

The concept of bond index funds is exactly the same as their stock fund counterparts. Rather than attempt to "pick" bonds in particular sectors, an index bond fund simply tracks the composition and performance of a major market index. By tracking an index, the fund is always *market neutral.* All this means is that the fund is not making bets that rates are rising or falling. Rather, it is always invested in a broad array of bonds. This is considered a "passive" approach to the market. In addition, the indexing

**TABLE 7-9**

Specialty Funds

|  | Zero Coupon | Convertible | Index | Strategic |
|---|---|---|---|---|
| Credit quality | High | Moderate | High/Moderate | Moderate/Low |
| Interest-rate risk | Highest | Moderate | High/Moderate | High |
| Maturity | Long | Medium | Medium | Medium |
| Yield | 0 (no dist.) | 3.51 | 5.87 | 7.57 |
| 3-year total return | 12.81 | 9.57 | 7.81 | 6.55 |
| Standard deviation | 11.73 | 11.64 | 3.91 | 5.37 |
| Income level | Low | Low | Moderate | High/Moderate |
| Expense ratio | 0.64 | 1.60 | 0.50 | 1.59 |

concept is usually less costly and should result in expense ratios that are less than "actively" managed funds.

For the average investor, index funds are very attractive because they don't have to pick a specific sector of the market, such as high- or low-quality bonds. Another benefit is that there are funds that index different maturities. This allows an investor to buy a short-, intermediate-, or long-term bond index fund in proportions that are consistent with their objectives for return, yield, and risk.

What is a bit more tricky with bond index funds is that the market indexes that the funds track are less well known to the average investing public. Generally, index bond funds track the Lehman Brothers Bond Index. Lehman Brothers is a large Wall Street financial firm which, among other things, specializes in producing many different types of composite bond market indexes. These indexes are well known and understood in the institutional bond world. For example, the Lehman Brothers Aggregate Bond Index includes fixed-rate bonds rated investment grade or higher by Moody's Investors Service, Standard and Poor's, or Fitch Investor's Service. All issues must have at least one year left to maturity and have an outstanding par value of at least $100 million for Government issues and $50 million for all others. The Aggregate Index is composed of the Government/Corporate, the Mortgage-Backed Securities, and the Asset-Backed Securities indices. Government and corporate bonds make up about 70% of the index.

One of the best-known fund families that offers bond index funds is the Vanguard Group. Vanguard manages the second largest stock fund in the world, the Vanguard Index 500 Fund, which is a stock index fund. They also offer four other bond index funds that range from their short-term Vanguard Bond Index Short-Term (VBISX) to their long maturity Vanguard Bond Index Long-Term (VBLTX). In total, these funds have in excess of $7.5 billion under management. The expense ratio on these funds is very low, at around 20 basis points, versus an average expense ratio of about 1.1% for all bond funds.

Generally, these funds are best suited for those investors who are less confident in selecting specific bond fund sectors but feel comfortable selecting the maturity. So far, the bond index funds are only available in taxable varieties (no municipal bond index funds yet), so they are very good for more conservative qualified accounts such as IRAs or 401(k)s.

## Convertible Bond Funds

Convertible bond funds are probably the least understood of all bond funds. They combine aspects of both the equity and bond market but usually find themselves orphaned from both. Equity investors think of them as strictly bond funds, whereas bond fund investors often view them as hybrid equity funds. Most investors don't even know they exist.

A convertible bond is issued similar to any other bond. It has a set maturity date and a set semiannual interest rate. The special feature of a convertible bond is that it allows the owner to convert the bond into the common stock of the issuing company. The ability to convert from the debt issue to the equity issue is called a *conversion feature* and is established at the initial offering of the bond. The bondholder normally can convert to stock at any time, although some bonds specify when a conversion may take place.

When the convertible bond is issued, a *conversion ratio* is established. The conversion ratio tells the investor how many shares he or she will receive when a conversion takes place. For example, a bond may have a conversion ratio of 50. This means that for each convertible bond owned, the investor will get 50 shares of the common stock. If the bond is issued at a normal par, or face value, of $1000, each of the 50 shares would be worth $20 ($1000/50 = $20).

The next step is where things start to get interesting. In our example, the conversion ratio is 50 and the stock value, based on the $1000 face value of the bond, is $20. If the company's stock is worth more than $20 per share, the bond could be converted to stock immediately for a profit. Here's how it would work: Let's say you are the owner of the convertible bond that is worth $20 per share of common stock upon conversion. If the value of the stock is $30, you could convert your 50 shares ($1000 value = 50 shares × $20) and receive $30 each. You would receive a gain of $10 per share, or $500. Not too bad!

### A Bond in Stock's Clothing

Unfortunately, the real world doesn't work quite that way. At the time of issue, convertible bonds normally have a conversion ratio that makes them unattractive to convert right away. The incentive for the bondholder is that the company's stock will rise enough to make it profitable to convert some time in the future. In the meantime, the convertible bondholder will get the semiannual coupon payment and hope the value of the company's stock continues to climb. This added value will also help the price of the convertible bond to appreciate.

Since higher stock prices increase the value of a convertible bond, convertible bonds typically appreciate more than normal bonds in rising equity market conditions. In this respect, they act very much like conservative dividend-paying stocks. However, when stock prices are dropping, the convertible bond's higher interest rate generally cushions price declines. In addition, if rates are declining, the bond's price will often get a boost, despite what's happening in the stock market.

### Why Funds Make It Easy

Even though we've just had our crash course on the mechanics of convertibles, it still may be a bit confusing. Luckily, you don't really need to know all the technical aspects of convertible bonds because you can simply buy convertible bond funds. When you own a convertible bond fund, you let the manager worry about the conversion factors, which bonds to buy, and which to convert. All you have to know are a few simple principles:

1. Convertible fund prices normally rise faster than other bond fund prices when the stock market rises.
2. Convertible bond fund prices normally fall less than stock fund prices when the equity market falls.
3. Convertible bond fund income levels are almost always higher than the highest stock fund dividend rates, but they are usually lower than comparable corporate bond fund rates.
4. The best time to own a convertible bond fund is when rates are steady or heading lower *and* stock prices are rising.

### A Place in Your Portfolio

Does this last scenario sound familiar? The stock market has been on a roll for several years. At the same time, interest rates have been falling. It is in this type of market that convertible bond funds will shine. On the upside, they give you bondlike stability with stocklike appreciation. The downside is that they pay less income and may exhibit greater price volatility than most corporate bond funds. However, if you want to add some spice to an income portfolio or some stability to an equity portfolio, they are a good choice.

## Strategic or Multisector Bond Funds

Strategic, or *"multisector," bond funds* are relative newcomers to the fund industry. The first showed up in the early 1990s. Managers of these funds attempt to buy any sectors of the bond market to gain income or total return. However, they primarily invest in three bond areas: high-income, foreign, and U.S. bonds. While the rewards of these types of funds can be excellent, the risks are more difficult to assess than those of other bond funds.

Since these funds can hold speculative-grade bonds, they have in recent years been heavily weighted in high-income bonds and are often classified that way. However, it's important to understand that these funds differ from regular junk bond funds in that they have the ability to shift into any sector of the bond market that happens to be "hot" at the time.

Currently, there are just over 100 funds in the strategic income fund category. The funds typically have income levels higher than those of U.S. corporate funds but somewhat less than high-income funds. For example, the current 12-month average yield for the multisector funds is just above 7%, while the junk funds offer an average yield of 8.26% and the high-quality long-term corporates are just above 5.7%. On a risk basis, these funds are similar to most bond funds (excluding convertibles and zeros), with an average standard deviation of about 4%. However, they have been much higher in the past.

### Rewards

The clear reward of these funds is the potential increase in income and total return. This is accomplished by assembling a truly globally diversified portfolio. Managers of the funds attempt to balance allocations between bond sectors so they can offer the best of all bond sectors without having to incur all of the risk associated with any one. The 3-year annualized return of this group stands at just under 11%, versus a 3-year return of 7.7% for high-quality corporates.

### Risks

Unlike a fund that invests in just one type of bond, such as a municipal or corporate fund, a strategic income fund holds bonds from a variety of sectors. This makes assessing and measuring risk difficult. When a fund holds high-income junk bonds, foreign bonds, and U.S. corporate issues, the investor is exposed to many types of risk, including credit quality, interest rate, event, political, and currency risk all at once. Another challenge for the investor in understanding these funds is the fact that the fund manager may change the allocation to any one sector at any time. In many respects, this often leaves investors blind in terms of knowing what they own.

## Zero Coupon Bond Funds

*Zero coupon bonds* are bonds that are issued without a coupon payment, hence the name "zero coupon." Instead of paying bondholders a semiannual income payment, the issuer sells the bonds at a deep discount to their face value. The discount value equates with current levels of interest. For example, a 30-year zero may be issued at a price of $200. At maturity (in 30 years), the holder will be paid the full face value of $1000, a gain of $800 over the life of the bond. The great advantage of these bonds for "buy and hold" investors is that they know exactly how much they will have at maturity. This is why zero coupon bonds have become so popular for funding a college education.

While zeros don't make a single interest payment during their life, an investor is still responsible for taxes on the bond each year. The taxes paid are called *imputed taxes*. They are based on the income amount that would have been paid on the same maturity bond were it a regular semiannual coupon bond. The only exception to this is if the zero is a *municipal zero coupon bond* (original issue discount bonds). In this case, no imputed tax needs to be paid.

Currently, there are only about a dozen zero coupon bond funds available to the individual investor. These tend to have fairly small amounts of assets under management because of their more aggressive nature. However, in declining rate markets, these funds tend to be very popular among investors with a focus on high levels of total return. In recent years, as rates declined, these funds have scored some of the highest total returns of any bond funds. However, like zero coupon bonds, they don't produce any distributed income.

Nearly all the zero coupon bond funds buy zero coupon Treasury securities. They tend to be the most liquid and easily priced. This gives them extremely high credit quality but also very high interest rate risk. An investment in zero funds is not a move to be taken lightly. If rates start to rise, the NAV on these funds drops very rapidly. They should be used sparingly for total return enhancement and never for income generation. In addition, only those who fully understand their volatile nature should use the zero coupon funds.

## Risk and Return

Even though many investors purchase zero coupon bonds for buy and hold purposes, there are many who use them to take advantage of short-term interest rate swings. The reason for this is simple. For a given change in interest rates, zero coupon bonds will move far more than a regular bond. In fact, they typically move as much as four times more. This presents great risk for uninformed investors and great reward for the savvy investor.

One way to examine just how much a zero will move is by looking at the bond's duration (interest rate sensitivity). A zero's return would be expected to move as much as its maturity. This is because a zero coupon bond's duration normally equals its maturity. This means that a 1.0% decline in rates on a 30-year zero coupon bond would return about 30%. Conversely, an increase in rates of 1.0% would cause the zero's return to drop by 30%. From an investor's perspective, the best time to buy a zero is when rates are dropping and the worst time to own them is when rates are increasing.

# CHAPTER 8

# Selecting Income Funds

## IT'S AN ART, NOT A SCIENCE

In the previous chapter we reviewed the various types of funds available to you for investing. Just knowing about different fund categories doesn't help you reach your goals if you don't know which fund to purchase. This chapter offers several different approaches to fund selection. It's important to know that there are probably as many different approaches to fund selection as there are funds. They range from the very basic quantitative to the bizarre. The ultimate goal is to find a fund or funds, whatever shape or form, that will achieve your specific investment goals for the long term.

There are no methods that consistently deliver the "top fund." This is because all methods attempt to forecast the future—something nobody can do. And with over 8500 funds now available, just getting close is really a more tenable objective. Indeed, simply defining a top fund can be complex. For example, is the top fund the one that has the best yield? Or is it the one with the best return? How about the best manager, or the fund that out-performs when the market is falling? Clearly, the top fund will be specific to the the set of investment goals you're trying to achieve.

It is very important to understand that in many ways, *fund selection is an art, not a science. It requires the use of both qualitative and quantitative data, and, as important, it requires common sense.*

The art of the process comes into play with the interpretation of qual-itative and quantitative data. The art is knowing just how important vari-ous factors are for a specific fund in a specific category. It also requires experience with the subtleties of the fund industry. For example, does the

ABC fund always maintain their fund approach, or do they continuously shift based on what's happening in the market? These types of questions are very difficult to quantify or simply put in a matrix or a database to then be sorted.

But are there approaches that make more sense than others? Yes. *The best approach is the one that first takes into consideration the objective of the investment.* For example, if aggressive income at any cost is the sole objective, then focusing on yield would probably be the primary methodology. On the other hand, an investor with high income and stability of principal as an objective would certainly want a balance between yield and fund risk. Once the objective is clearly understood, an appropriate selection process can be undertaken.

*In general, you should always take into account both return (total return and/or yield) and risk. There should always be balance between the two.* You should also never limit yourself to just one selection approach. It doesn't hurt—and usually takes little extra time—to review a fund from several different angles. Again, the selection process is not a defined science. When reviewing a fund for selection, it is important to ask yourself if it makes sense and if it is a fund you can stick with for more than just a few months. You should expect to hold this fund for several years, not several weeks, so having a high level of confidence in the fund is important.

## THE FUND FRONTIER

In Chapter 2 we discussed the *yield curve*. The yield curve is a chart that shows the relationship of yield and maturity. In many ways it is a graphical representation of risk and reward. As a first step in the fund selection process, we can take the yield curve concept and apply it to income funds by plotting their yields or returns against their risk. This will show us which funds provide the best or worst return or yield for a given level of risk. This is called the *efficient frontier,* or in the fund world, the *fund frontier.*

The efficient frontier describes a chart that shows the return on the vertical axis and risk on the horizontal axis. A three-year annual return is normally used for the return measure and a three-year standard deviation is normally used as the risk measure. However, other risk or return measures can be substituted, such as yield in place of return and duration in place of standard deviation. In addition, different time frames can and should be used to focus in on various market environments. For example, some suggest that a three-year time span is too short to really determine if a fund can produce consistent returns for the long haul, especially in exceptional market environments like the late 1990s.

This selection process is based on historical data; it relies on past performance to forecast future results. If the funds have exhibited consistent behavior over the years, this process can be quite valuable. However, if the funds in the category being examined are volatile, this approach is less reliable.

The fund frontier can include all fund categories, all income fund categories, or all the funds within a specific category. To help us select funds, we'll look at the income fund category chart. This chart will help us narrow our fund selections.

The chart is usually broken down into four quadrants.

QUAD 1—The upper left, quadrant 1, is where you find funds that have low risk and high returns. As you might expect, these funds are generally considered the most attractive. Typically, there are very few funds in this quadrant.

QUAD 2—The lower left, quadrant 2, is where you find funds that have low return and low risk. Most likely you will see money funds and short-term, high-quality bond funds in this sector. Based on the objective, these funds can be attractive.

QUAD 3—The upper right, quadrant 3, is where you find funds that have high risk and high return. Included among these funds might be the zero coupon funds and income-oriented equity funds.

QUAD 4—The lower right, quadrant 4, is where you find funds that have high risk and low return. Clearly, these funds should be the least desirable based on this examination. Who really wants a fund that has poor performance and subjects the investor to a high level of risk?

The selection process using this method is simple. Once the chart is drawn, your best fund selection should be found in or close to quadrant 1. As mentioned earlier, if the funds in this category exhibit wide variations in return or risk over time, the reliability of this process is diminished. This is why the selection process should include several different approaches. Figure 8-1 shows fund categories by risk/return quadrant.

## RETURN RANKING

One of the most common and easiest approaches to fund selection is the pure return methodology. This approach simply ranks funds by a specific return. Those at the top of the rank are deemed the best funds. This method can be very useful, but only if done properly. As the old saying goes, "if it seems too good to be true, it probably is." Such is the case with return ranking.

**FIGURE 8-1**

Fund Frontier Chart

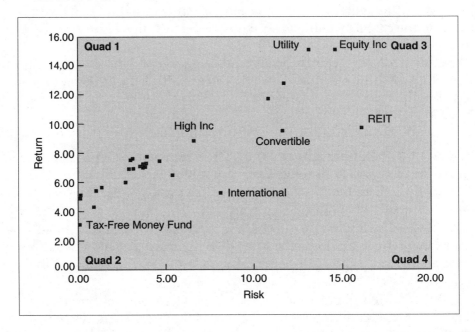

The first problem in simply ranking all funds is that they are not alike. Income funds that do not have similar compositions, quality, and maturity should not be compared to each other. For example, zero coupon funds typically perform far better in declining rate markets and will always be at the top of the income fund return charts. However, this does not make them the best funds to buy, especially if they do not fulfill the investor's particular objective.

The main problem with selecting funds by return alone is that it completely ignores the risk factor. This means you may end up in a fund that historically provided high returns but also ran like a roller coaster.

Another problem arises if the time frames are not representative of varied market conditions. If you were to look at the high income funds over a one-year period in 1990, you would conclude that these are the worst funds ever. In actuality, it was only that one period in the last 10 years that the funds experienced poor performance. You would have missed a great opportunity. Nevertheless, this doesn't mean that using a return ranking can't be useful. It can.

To really get the most out of return ranking, various time periods need to be reviewed, especially if the investment is going to be for a long period of time. In addition, you should be comparing the fund's returns against its peer group and the general market. You want to be sure that the fund can consistently produce acceptable returns through different types of market conditions. Following are three return rank reviews that should be done to identify top returning funds.

- Examine the 1-, 5-, and 10-year annualized return rank of the fund against its peer group.
- Examine the year-by-year annual data to make sure the fund didn't just have one or two superior years, with the rest being duds.
- Examine the fund's performance rank in a bear and a bull market, for example, 1987 for a bear market and 1997 for a bull market.

## RISK RANKING

As mentioned earlier, the fund selection process should be done with a balance of return and risk considerations. While some funds may rise to the top of the return ranks, their associated risks may make them unattractive investments. To properly select funds, a review of risk must be conducted in conjunction with the return ranking.

Similar to the return ranks, funds can be ranked by their risk. Again, it is very important to rank comparable funds. High-income funds should be compared to other high-income funds, not money funds. It's also very helpful to review the comparable risk of all the bond fund sectors. This gives you a good idea where the fund group ranks compared to the general income fund universe. It's a similar exercise to the one suggested using the fund frontier for all fund categories.

One of the standard methods of ranking risk is by measuring the fund's standard deviation (see Chapter 6). The most commonly used period in measuring standard deviation is 36 months. However, data for longer periods is usually available.

If the funds are ranked from highest to lowest, the funds at the top of the rank will be those that have historically exhibited the greatest amount of month-by-month return variability. If the investor is looking for high-risk funds, the funds at the top of this ranking will be the most attractive. For example, funds such as the long-term zero coupon, convertible, international, long-term municipal, corporate, and Treasury will dominate these ranks. Most investors, though, will be looking at the funds at the other end of the spectrum.

Low-risk funds are the most stable and are most often found in money funds and the short-term range (3-year maturity or less). While these funds are the most stable, they also normally offer the lowest returns and yields. These funds will appeal to the more conservative or short-term investor.

Using the risk ranking, a search for funds that offer higher returns or yields but have below-average risk is key. These funds have somehow been managed in a way that favorable return and risk have been achieved.

## YIELD RANKING

Selecting income funds by yield has traditionally been a common and easy approach. The objective is to simply identify the fund that offers the highest yield. If you know the characteristics of the fund category as well as the associated returns and risk, selecting funds by top yield is a great way to develop your "short list" of possible funds for purchase. Even looking at the comparable yields of various fund categories can be very helpful in targeting the funds that will best help you meet your objectives. Like all of the other methods, however, looking only at yield misses some important factors that could lead you down the wrong fund selection path.

*First and foremost, yield is the price of risk.* Those funds at the top of a yield rank will be the most aggressive funds. This means they will typically have the highest associated risk. For high-yield investors, fund selection from the top of this list is ideal, but for investors who are more conservative, it may be completely unsuitable. Again, it goes back to the specific goal of the investment.

Like the other ranking approaches, only comparable funds should be ranked. Otherwise, all the aggressive high-income funds will bubble to the top, and the money funds will land at the bottom. Again, the top fund will be the one that meets the investment goal criteria. This may not be the highest-yielding fund when all the other factors are taken into consideration. For example, if the investor's time horizon is just six months, a money market fund would be a great income fund candidate. Although these funds usually have the lowest yields relative to other income fund alternatives, because of their stable price and high quality, the low yield is an acceptable tradeoff for the added security.

Funds' yields should also be benchmarked against their peer group averages to make sure they are not abnormally high or low. There is usually something wrong with funds at either end of the spectrum. Either they are poorly managed (low yield) or they are taking too many aggressive positions (high yield). Funds at either end should raise a yellow flag of caution.

## RISK-ADJUSTED RETURN AND THE SHARPE RATIO

The major flaw of the fund selection methods discussed thus far is that they don't capture return and risk at the same time. The return and yield ranks ignore risk, and the risk ranks ignore return. In 1966, Stanford University professor (and Nobel Prize winner) Dr. William R. Sharpe developed the Sharpe ratio to help solve this dilemma. It wasn't until the early 1990s, however, that the concept really caught on. *The Sharpe ratio simply describes (quantitatively) how much return you get for a given risk you must accept.* This is called *risk-adjusted return.* The approach is simple, but the results are powerful.

The Sharpe ratio is calculated by dividing a fund's excess return by its standard deviation. The result is the reward per unit of risk. The excess return is calculated by subtracting a risk-free rate of return, which is usually the 3-month Treasury bill, from the fund's three-year average annual return. This shows just how much the fund beats the "safest" investment. The excess return is then divided by the fund's three-year standard deviation.

$$\text{Sharpe Ratio} = \frac{\text{Return} - \text{Risk-free rate}}{\text{Standard deviation}}$$

The higher the Sharpe ratio is, the better the fund's historical risk-adjusted performance. Normally, funds with Sharpe ratios above 1.0 are considered to be attractive because a ratio greater than or equal to 1.0 indicates that return is greater than or proportional to the risk the investor incurred to earn that return. Funds that have Sharpe ratios below 1.0 exhibit more risk than the return would seem to justify and therefore are less attractive. Ranking income funds by their Sharpe ratio (within their proper peer groups) will highlight top funds on a risk/return basis.

When applied to income funds, this approach is most useful for total return income investors rather than yield investors because the ratio does not focus on yields (even though yield is a part of total return). Nevertheless, as a filtering screen for top funds, the Sharpe ratio offers a great way to identify funds that have been managed well with respect to return and risk.

One of the problems with the approach when applied to income funds is that funds with the highest Sharpe ratios may have very low yield. This can occur because short-term, conservative funds (low yield) usually have very low standard deviations. Because the standard deviation is in the denominator, lower numbers can produce higher Sharpe ratios. In the example below, the XYZ fund has twice the return of the ABC fund, but because its standard deviation is much higher, its Sharpe ratio is much lower. This highlights some of the shortcomings of using only the Sharpe ratio in selecting funds.

Short-term fund ABC    Return = 10%; standard deviation = 1%; T-bill = 5%
                       Sharpe = 10% − 1% ÷ 1% = 9%
Fund XYZ               Return = 20%; standard deviation = 5%; T-bill = 5%
                       Sharpe = 20% − 5% ÷ 5% = 3%

The Sharpe ratios of various income fund categories are shown in Figure 8-2.

## OTHER APPROACHES

In addition to the approaches just outlined, there are several others that are worth mentioning. The first is a *blended return approach*. This method combines returns from several different periods, weights them, and then calculates a blended return. Once this is done, all funds are ranked and those at the top are considered the best candidates for purchase. For example, a

## FIGURE 8-2

Income Fund Sharpe Ratio by Category

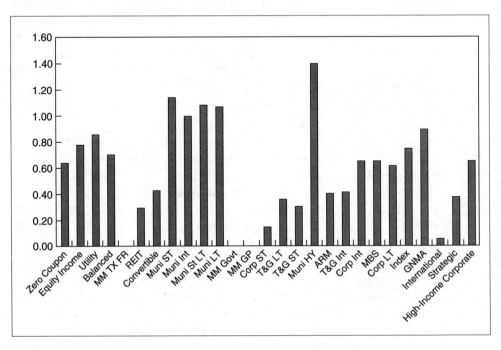

1-month, 6-month, 1-year approach might take the total return for each period and equally weight them. This would capture both the very short-term fund results and returns for the last 12 months. The downside of this approach is that it ignores the risk associated with the return.

Another popular fund selection process is the *momentum approach.* A momentum approach attempts to measure the fund's price activity over a certain period. The assumption is that certain trends are reliable predictors of future price action and that the sentiment of the market is always built into—or is a function of—the price of the fund. The most popular momentum approach is the *moving-average method.* Moving averages are the average price of a fund over a certain period of time, such as the last 150 days. This average is calculated every day and plotted against the fund's NAV. When the fund's NAV rises above its average, it is considered a buying opportunity. When the NAV of the fund drops below its moving average, the fund is a candidate for selling. The downside of this approach is that buy and sell "signals" can occur too frequently in volatile markets, forcing the investor to trade the funds too actively.

## PUTTING IT ALL TOGETHER

As I have mentioned throughout this chapter, you should not rely on just one selection method in choosing your "best" fund. I strongly believe you should incorporate a number of methods into your selection strategy. To do this, you need some good information. There are a number of very good services now available that can provide the information you'll need (see Chapter 13).

Here is a 10-step plan and an alternative scoring method to help you develop a final "short list" of funds to consider for purchase. This process puts equal weight on each of the selection items mentioned previously. However, if your focus is, say, pure income, items such as total return may carry far less importance and may be skipped.

1. *Define your plan.* Once this is accomplished, you will have a good idea of just how much total return or yield you expect and how much risk you are willing to accept. You will also know whether or not you need taxable or tax-free income.
2. *Review all fund categories.* Get the average data for the following items on each income fund category:
   1-, 3-, and 5-year total return
   3-year standard deviation

Current 12-month distribution yield

3-year Sharpe ratio

Expense ratio

Load charges

3. *Review the fund category frontier.* Given your investment parameters in step 1, you can now look at all fund categories to see which are most closely matched to your objectives. From this review, look for fund groups that are closest to quadrant 1 (upper left). Start by choosing at least one fund category.

4. *Rank by return.* Once a category of funds is selected, rank all funds in the category by 3-year total return. (Hold onto the list.)

5. *Rank by risk.* Take the funds in step 3 and rerank by 3-year standard deviation from lowest risk to highest. (Hold onto the list.)

6. *Rank by yield.* Now take the same list and rerank by yield. (Hold onto the list.)

7. *Rank by Sharpe ratio.* Rerank the list again by Sharpe ratio. (Keep this list, too.)

8. *Review the lists in steps 4, 5, 6, and 7.* Look for as many funds as possible that appear toward the top of each list. They don't need to be on every list. If your focus is total return, then the fund should certainly be at the top of the return rankings. Conversely, if your primary goal is yield, make sure the fund is at or near the top of the yield rankings. These funds should constitute your "short list" for review.

9. *Review your short list.* Once you have found funds in step 8, review the load charges for each fund. Those that are no-load should then be at the top of your list.

10. *Review the fund family.* From your final list in step 9, review the fund families. Make sure your final choice is one managed by a fund company you know and are comfortable with for the long term.

## SCORING METHOD

Another combination method I have often used with success in finding good funds is a fund-scoring approach. After completing steps 1 through 3 above, and having one fund category to review, set up a spreadsheet with all the funds in the category and the following data: 1-year and 3-year returns, 3-year standard deviation, Sharpe ratio, 12-month distribution yield, expense ratio, and loads.

Then calculate the category average on each item. If the fund is above the category average, it gets a score of 1 for that data item. On the risk, expense, and load items, a 1 score is applied if the fund has lower-than-average risk, 1 for lower-than-average expenses, and another 1 if it is a no-load fund (I like to give preference to no-loads). After each data item is reviewed with each fund, add up all the scores for each fund. Since there are seven data elements, a perfect score is 7. Now rank all funds by their total scores. Those funds that are better than the peer group average for each item will be at the top of the list, whereas those that underperform their peer group will be at the bottom. In essence, you end up with funds that have lots of positive attributes, but these funds will not necessarily be at the top of any one data category. The highest yielding fund, for instance, may not be at the top of this kind of list, since it might have high risk or other negative attributes that negate the great yield in the scoring process. From this final list, I proceed to step 10, fund family review, and zero in on the final funds for purchase.

# CHAPTER 9

# Income Portfolio Strategies

**O**ne of the most powerful ways to harness the advantages of mutual funds is to put them together in portfolios that capture the best of each fund group, while hopefully reducing those attributes that are not attractive. This is the essence of *asset allocation*. Asset allocation sounds complex, and investors think that somehow the process belongs to the professional. They're wrong. Asset allocation simply involves putting together funds in the right mix to meet your objectives. The combinations of funds and allocations of those funds in a portfolio are almost limitless. Because of the many types of investor objectives, available funds, and allocations, there will never be the "perfect" or "right" asset allocation. It's a matter of what best meets each investor's objectives.

In this section I describe seven allocations that attempt to meet specific income, return, and risk levels. The first, for example, the Conservative Income Investor portfolio, focuses on the safest and highest-yielding strategies for investors who cannot tolerate any risk in their principal, yet they require steady monthly income. At the top of each allocation, I outline the objectives of the portfolio and for whom they are best suited. I also include the expected income, total return, risk, and time horizon for each portfolio. For each allocation, I select some of the top funds for each category based on the methodology described in Chapter 8. A complete list of top funds for each category can be found at the end of the book.

In each of the income investment strategies, I have suggested the use of a small portfolio of income-oriented mutual funds. Each strategy provides a different risk and return profile. The average profile of each portfo-

**FIGURE 9-1**

Allocation Return/Risk Profile

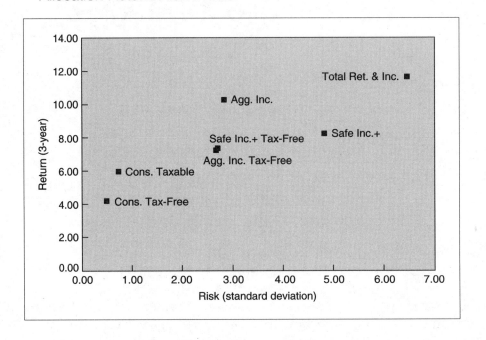

lio can be plotted on the fund frontier that was described in Chapter 8. As you can see from Figure 9-1, greater returns should accompany greater risks. This should make sense, since there is no reason to accept risk without being compensated. Figure 9-2 shows risk for income. The difference here is that portfolio yield is plotted against risk rather than total return versus risk. Again, the greater the risk accepted, the greater the yield that should be expected.

Over time, the risk and return characteristic of each of these portfolios can change because some funds in the portfolio can become more dominant than others. This happens because funds will increase at different rates from each other. For example, if you had a portfolio that was half money funds and half aggressive stock funds, the stock funds would increase in value faster than the money funds, which grow at a very slow rate. What started as a 50/50 split could easily shift to a 70/30 split in favor of the stock fund. In fact, in the last several years, many portfolios have shifted in allocation for this very reason. The bottom line is that no matter which portfolio you use for your own investments, it should be regularly

## FIGURE 9-2

Allocation Yield/Risk Profile

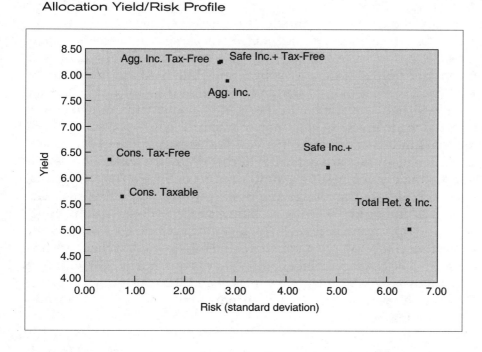

reviewed to make sure it remains consistent with its initial goals and objects.

## DOLLAR COST AVERAGING

Regardless of the strategy you select, at some point you will need to send your money to the fund. There is a natural tendency to be anxious about this process because you are not sure whether you are getting in at the "right" time. Attempting to select just the right point to buy or sell a fund is often called *market timing.* Active traders who believe they can pick the market bottoms and tops usually employ some type of timing strategy based on recent price activity. While some have been successful, market timing requires a lot of luck and a great deal of research. As an investor, your focus should not be on trading or timing the market; rather, you should keep your focus on your long-term goals.

In the greater scheme of things, investing this week or next week won't make that much difference for an investor who has a time horizon of

15 to 20 years. The important thing is to get invested so that your money can start working for you. However, if you still can't get yourself to invest all the money at once, you can utilize a process called *dollar cost averaging*.

*Dollar cost averaging is a method of investing fixed amounts monthly, quarterly, or at some other predefined frequency.* If it is your first investment, you might consider putting a third of your money into the fund immediately, the next third a week or month later, and the last third a week or month after that. This will help you ease into the market without the psychological impact of having to invest all your money at once. It works particularly well with mutual funds because you can invest in shares at any time you desire.

There are many advantages in dollar cost averaging. First, it helps you get over the anxiety of investing a lump sum. Second, on an ongoing basis, it helps you build your account without having to worry about the market's action. If the fund's price is declining and you dollar cost average, you will be buying more shares at lower and lower prices. This lowers your overall cost basis (average cost per share) over the period. If the market is rising, you will be buying at higher and higher prices, but at least your first purchases allowed you to get into the market and start capturing the gains. In fact, if you reinvest dividends of an income fund, you are, in effect, dollar cost averaging because you are buying new shares of the fund at each distribution. Most of us also dollar cost average in our 401(k) programs. After we have made a fund selection with our employer, they automatically make a deduction from our paycheck and add it to our selected funds.

While dollar cost averaging is a great way to get started and invest continuously, the strategy does not insulate your account from market corrections or bear market periods. During these times, you will be buying at lower and lower prices, but your account value will still be falling. In these market environments, the hope is that at some point the market will reverse its course and again move higher.

## HOW MANY FUNDS SHOULD YOU OWN?

When selecting an income investment strategy, one of the common questions asked is how many funds should be included in the portfolio. Unfortunately, there are no set rules on the optimum number of funds to own. The answer really depends on the individual investor's comfort level with the fund, the fund family, and their specific allocation.

As a starting point, funds are not guaranteed in the same way that the FDIC backs a bank savings account or certificate of deposit, or the way the U.S. government guarantees interest and principal on a Treasury bond. There is no FDIC insurance or government backing on any mutual fund.

However, the Securities Investor Protection Corporation (SIPC) does protect a mutual fund investor. All brokers and dealers registered with the Securities and Exchange Commission must be members of SIPC. SIPC insures an investor's account up to a maximum of $500,000 per investor, with a limit of $100,000 for cash accounts, against the failure of the fund company. *SIPC insurance does not cover any loss due to market fluctuations.*

While there is no insurance with fund investing, there is some assurance that the funds are managed properly and that they accurately disclose their risks. The prospectus provides such information. Still, prudent investors should always ask as many questions as they can before sending money to any fund (see Chapter 11).

Most income funds are diversified funds (see Chapter 7), which means they own many securities. For example, the average bond fund holds more than 100 securities, but many funds own in excess of 300. From this perspective, there is enough diversity in the portfolio to help limit the impact of an unforeseen problem in any one holding. In addition, you are paying a fund for its active portfolio management. This means you have a portfolio manager and research group whose job it is to make prudent investment decisions.

Even with active management, diversified portfolios, and SIPC insurance as a last resort, funds can have problems. To help avoid this, using a combination of funds for your asset allocation is a suitable course of action. There are no hard and fast rules on how many funds you should own. Some investment advisors suggest holding a dozen funds, while other suggest just a few. *If you invest with reputable fund families that have proven track records, you do not need to own many funds to properly diversify. It's preferable to own four to six funds to add a degree of diversification and to capture attractive characteristics of different types of funds. There should be little concern in only owning a small number of funds from top fund families.*

In each of the income strategies offered in this chapter, I include just four funds, some from the same fund family. You may want to use more or fewer, depending on your comfort level. Each of the funds selected for the strategies was the result of a review of total return, yield, risk-adjusted return, and management capabilities.

## THE CONSERVATIVE INCOME INVESTOR–TAXABLE

**Objective:** Conservative; safe income with minimum or no impact to principal

**Time horizon:** Short-term or long-term for very conservative investor

**Income level:** Low to moderate

**Total return:** Low

**Risk:** Low

**Investment mix and funds used:** Money funds; short-term bond funds

**Allocation:** 60% money funds; 40% short-term bond funds

***Objective and Time Horizon***   The first income strategy is designed for a conservative income investor who must have high levels of principal protection and reasonable income. This strategy is also well-suited for an investor with a short investment time horizon. For example, the strategy works well for someone who just sold a house and needs the money in a few months to buy another. The two objectives, income and safety, are achieved by using a combination of top-yielding money markets and a well-managed short-term taxable bond fund. The monthly income and possible annual capital gains (from the bond fund) generated from this strategy will be taxable income. It is best used in a conservative tax-qualified account or for someone in a lower tax bracket. If you are in a higher tax bracket, a tax-exempt fund strategy will bring greater income advantages (see Conservative Tax-Exempt Income strategy).

***Income***   The income level with this strategy is generally low to moderate. This means it will normally be less than the yields on long-term bonds but greater than yields found on CDs. However, in a flat interest rate market (flat yield curve), this strategy will produce income levels nearly equal to those of longer-term bonds, including the 30-year Treasury bond. This has been the case in the last few years.

***Total Return***   Because this strategy uses money funds and short-term bond funds, total return will be very low. Money funds have stable NAV, while short-term bond fund NAVs only allow minor price appreciation or loss. Expect total returns to be just a few percentage points higher than the money fund yields in positive years and slightly negative to flat in negative years.

***Risk***   Because of the heavy weight in high-quality money markets and the conservative nature of short-term bond funds, interest-rate risk (duration) and credit risk are extremely minor in this portfolio. Standard deviations should be near or less than 1%.

**Investment Mix and Funds**  To achieve a high degree of stability in principal while maintaining a reasonable income level, the portfolio should hold mostly money market funds. This strategy uses a 60% weighting in money funds. It contains three funds for the money fund component, Vanguard, USAA, and Strong, and each has been given equal weight. Each of these companies has a strong reputation and offers funds with yields at the top of their category. The remaining 40% allocation of the portfolio will be funded with a short-term high-quality corporate bond fund. In this case, I have selected Vanguard's Short-Term Corporate Fund. It offers a nice premium in yield over the money funds and offers some upside in total return if rates decline. However, because it has a maturity of less than three years and a duration of just over two years, its return is less sensitive to rate changes.

**Portfolio Results**  The combination of the four funds provides an annual income of 5.65%. This is about 30 basis points higher than any of the money funds. As you can see, the yield is equal to that of the 30-year Treasury bond but without the interest-rate risk. The portfolio duration of just 0.84 suggests that if rates increased by 1.0% (100 basis points), the portfolio should decline in value by less than 1%. The standard deviation of just 0.85% suggests a less than 1.0% annual return fluctuation. This is indeed a safe income portfolio with a high degree of stability.

**TABLE 9-1**

Conservative Income—Taxable

| Fund | Amount | Yield | Annual Income | 3-Year Return | Standard Deviation | Maturity | Duration |
|------|--------|-------|---------------|---------------|--------------------|----------|----------|
| Vanguard Money Market Prime | $20,000 | 5.31% | $1,062 | 5.43% | 0.06% | 0.41 | 0 |
| USAA Money Market | $20,000 | 5.27% | $1,054 | 5.39% | 0.10% | 0.36 | 0 |
| Strong Heritage Money Market | $20,000 | 5.36% | $1,072 | 5.71% | 0.10% | 0.25 | 0 |
| Vanguard Short-Term Corporate | $40,000 | 6.16% | $2,464 | 6.59% | 1.72% | 2.7 | 2.1 |
| **Total** | **$100,000** | **5.65%** | **$5,652** | **5.94%** | **0.74%** | **1.28** | **0.84** |
| Money Funds | 60% | | | | | | |
| ST Bond Funds | 40% | | | | | | |

## THE CONSERVATIVE INCOME INVESTOR—TAX-FREE

**Objective:** Conservative; safe tax-free income with minimum or no impact to principal

**Time horizon:** Short-term or long-term for very conservative investor

**Income level:** Tax-exempt, low to moderate

**Total return:** Low

**Risk:** Low

**Investment Mix and Funds Used:** National tax-free money funds; short-term municipal bond funds

**Allocation:** 60% money funds; 40% short-term municipal bond funds

*Objective and Time Horizon*    This income strategy is designed for a conservative income investor who requires principal protection and mostly tax-free income. Like the taxable strategy, this strategy is also well-suited for an investor with a short investment time horizon. The two objectives, tax-free income and safety, are achieved by using a combination of top-yielding tax-free money markets and a well-managed short-term municipal bond fund. The monthly income will be exempt from federal taxation, but any annual capital gains (from the bond fund) will be taxable income. This strategy is best for investors in high federal and/or state tax brackets.

*Income*    The income level with this strategy is generally low to moderate. To equate the income to taxable income, a taxable equivalent yield formula should be used (see Chapter 3). In a flat interest rate market (flat yield curve), this strategy will produce income levels nearly equal to those of longer-term bonds.

*Total Return*    Because this strategy uses tax-free money funds and short-term bond funds, total return will be very low. Money funds have stable NAVs, while short-term fund NAVs only allow for minor price appreciation or loss. Expect total returns to be just a few percentage points higher than the money fund yields in positive years and slightly negative to flat in negative years.

*Risk*    Because of the heavy weight in high-quality money markets and the conservative nature of short-term bond funds, interest-rate risk (duration) and credit risk will be extremely minor in this portfolio. Standard deviations should be near or less than 1%.

**Investment Mix and Funds**  To achieve a high degree of stability in principal while maintaining a reasonable tax-free income level, the portfolio should hold mostly money market funds. In this strategy, I have used the same weighting as in the taxable strategy, with 60% in money funds. I have selected three tax-free funds, Vanguard, USAA, and American Century Benham, for the money fund component and have given them equal weight. Each of these companies has a strong reputation and offers funds with yields at the top of their category. The remaining 40% allocation of the portfolio will be funded with a short-term high-quality municipal bond fund managed by USAA, the USAA Tax-Exempt Short-Term. It offers a good premium in yield over the money funds and upside in total return if rates decline. However, because it has a maturity of less than three years and a duration of just over two years, its return is less sensitive to rate changes.

**Portfolio Results**  The combination of these four funds provides an annual tax-free income of 3.85%, which translates into a taxable equivalent yield of 6.27% for an investor in the 39.6% federal tax bracket. This is at least 25 basis points higher than any of the money funds. As you can see, the yield is higher than that of the 30-year Treasury bond, and without the interest rate risk. The portfolio duration of just 0.92 suggests that if rates increased by 1.0% (100 basis points), the portfolio should decline in value by less than 1%. The standard deviation of just 1.34% suggests very minimal annual return fluctuation.

**TABLE 9-2**

Conservative Income—Tax-Free

| Fund | Amount | Yield | Annual Income | 3-Year Return | Standard Deviation | Maturity | Duration |
|------|--------|-------|--------|--------|--------|--------|--------|
| Vanguard Municipal Bond Money Market | $20,000 | 3.40% | $680 | 3.49% | 0.06% | 0.25 | 0 |
| USAA Tax Exempt Money Fund | $20,000 | 3.36% | $672 | 3.44% | 0.07% | 0.38 | 0 |
| American Century/Benham Tax-Free Money | $20,000 | 3.65% | $730 | 3.28% | 0.14% | 0.48 | 0 |
| USAA Tax-Exempt Short-Term | $40,000 | 4.41% | $1,764 | 5.40% | 1.08% | 2.8 | 2.3 |
| **Total** | **$100,000** | **3.85%** | **$3,846** | **4.20%** | **0.49%** | **1.34** | **0.92** |
| TEY Yield @39.6% bracket | | 6.37% | | | | | |
| Money Funds | 60% | | | | | | |
| ST Bond Funds | 40% | | | | | | |

## SAFE TAXABLE INCOME PLUS

> **Objective:** Conservative; safe income with moderate impact to principal
>
> **Time horizon:** Short- to intermediate-term; longer-term for moderate income investors
>
> **Income level:** Moderate
>
> **Total return:** Moderate
>
> **Risk:** Moderate
>
> **Funds used:** Money funds; short-, intermediate-, and long-term bond funds
>
> **Allocation:** 10% money funds; 10% short-term, 40% intermediate-term, and 40% long-term bond funds

***Objective and Time Horizon***   This strategy is designed for a conservative income investor who must have high levels of income and requires only moderate safety in principal. This strategy is also well-suited for an investor with a medium to longer time horizon of at least 5 to 10 years. The two objectives, income and stability, are achieved by using a combination of high-quality money markets and bond funds of various maturities. The monthly income and possible annual capital gains (from the bond funds) will be taxable income. The strategy is best used by someone in a moderately conservative tax-qualified account or for someone in a lower tax bracket.

***Income***   The income level with this strategy will generally be moderate. This means it will normally be greater than yields on money funds but less than those on long-term high-quality bond funds.

***Total Return***   Because this strategy uses a combination of money funds and bond funds, total return will be moderate. The money fund and short-term bond funds will anchor the portfolio's return, while the intermediate- and long-term funds will provide for upside principal gain if rates decline. Expect total returns to be in line with those found on intermediate-term funds.

***Risk***   Owing to the portfolio's balance between the various maturities, it will have moderate interest-rate risk. This means that if rates increase, the fund's return will decline. Considering the portfolio duration of 4.2 years, a 1% rise in rates could produce a loss in principal value of just over 4%. Credit risk should be minimal due to the high quality of the bonds in the portfolios. The portfolio's standard deviations should be expected to hover near or less than 5%.

***Investment Mix and Funds***  To achieve a higher level of income while keeping volatility moderate, the portfolio will balance maturities in a "laddering" strategy. In this portfolio I give 10% weight each to both the money fund and the short-term bond fund. The remaining 80% is split between the intermediate- and long-term bond funds. The intermediate- and long-term funds allow for a higher level of safe income, while the anchor in the money fund and short-term bond fund keep the portfolio fairly stable. I selected all four funds from the Vanguard Group of funds. Each is of high quality and well-managed. Each offers a higher level of yield and return for greater maturity and duration. The combination provides a yield of 6.23%, which is 58 basis points higher than the Conservative Income Fund—Taxable strategy. While the income premium is just over ½%, much of this is due to the existing flat yield curve environment.

***Portfolio Results***  The portfolio's average yield of 6.23% and duration of 4.2 years provide an asset mix that delivers solid income and moderate interest rate risk. With respect to return fluctuation, the fund has an average standard deviation of 4.8%. This is certainly greater than the money fund-oriented portfolio, but it also allows for better total returns. Based on historical performance, this portfolio's total return over the last three years would have been more than 8%.

**TABLE 9-3**

Safe Income Plus—Taxable

| Fund | Amount | Yield | Annual Income | 3-Year Return | Standard Deviation | Maturity | Duration |
|---|---|---|---|---|---|---|---|
| Vanguard Money Market Prime | $10,000 | 5.31% | $531 | 5.43% | 0.60% | 0.41 | 0 |
| Vanguard Short-Term Corporate | $10,000 | 6.16% | $616 | 6.59% | 1.72% | 2.7 | 2.1 |
| Vanguard Intermediate-Term Corp | $40,000 | 6.35% | $2,540 | 7.63% | 4.35% | 7 | 5.3 |
| Vanguard Long-Term Corp | $40,000 | 6.36% | $2,544 | 9.90% | 7.06% | 13 | 6.8 |
| **Total** | **$100,000** | **6.23%** | **$6,231** | **8.21%** | **4.80%** | **8.31** | **4.2** |
| Money Market | 10% | | | | | | |
| Short-Term | 10% | | | | | | |
| Intermediate-Term | 40% | | | | | | |
| Long-Term | 40% | | | | | | |

## SAFE MUNICIPAL INCOME PLUS

**Objective:** Conservative; safe, tax-free income with moderate impact to principal

**Time horizon:** Short- to intermediate-term; longer-term for moderate income investors

**Income level:** Tax-free moderate

**Total return:** Moderate

**Risk:** Moderate

**Funds used:** Tax-free money funds; short-, intermediate-, and long-term bond funds

**Allocation:** 10% money funds; 10% short-term, 40% intermediate-term, 40% long-term bond funds

*Objective and Time Horizon*   This strategy is designed for a moderately conservative tax-free income investor who must have higher levels of income and requires only moderate safety in principal. This strategy is also well-suited for an investor with a medium to longer time horizon of at least 5 to 10 years. The two objectives, tax-free income and moderate stability, are achieved by using a combination of high-quality tax-free money markets and bond funds of various maturities. The monthly income will be exempt from federal tax, but any capital gains (from the bond funds) will be taxable distributions. The strategy is best used by someone in a higher tax bracket.

*Income*   The tax-free income level with this strategy will generally be moderate. This means it will normally be greater than yields on tax-free money funds but less than those of long-term high-quality tax-free bond funds.

*Total Return*   Like the Safe Income—Taxable strategy, this allocation uses a combination of money funds and bond funds, which will achieve moderate total returns. The money fund and short-term bond funds anchor the portfolio's return, while the intermediate- and long-term funds provide for upside principal gain if rates decline. Expect total returns to be in line with those of intermediate-term funds.

*Risk*   Because of the portfolio's balance between the various maturities, it will have moderate interest-rate risk. This means that if rates increase, the fund's return will decline. Long-term municipal bond funds normally have maturities of 15 years or longer, which will make the portfolio a bit more susceptible to interest rate fluctuations than the high-quality taxable bond portfolio. Based on the portfolio duration of 4.3 years, a 1% rise in rates could produce a loss in principal value of just over 4%. Credit risk should be minimal due to the high quality of the municipal bonds in the portfolio. The portfolio's standard deviations should be expected to hover near 2.5%.

***Investment Mix and Funds*** To achieve a higher level of income while keeping volatility moderate, the portfolio balances maturities in a "laddering" strategy in the same manner as the taxable strategy. In this portfolio, I give 10% weight each to both the money fund and the short-term bond fund. The remaining 80% is split between the intermediate- and long-term funds. This allows a higher level of safe income, yet remains fairly stable with anchors in the money fund and short-term bond fund sector. I selected the money fund from Vanguard and the short-, intermediate-, and long-term municipal bond funds from USAA. Each is of high quality and is well-managed. Each offers a higher level of yield and return for greater maturity and duration.

**TABLE 9-4**

Safe Income Plus—Tax-Free

| Fund | Amount | Yield | Annual Income | 3-Year Return | Standard Deviation | Maturity | Duration |
|---|---|---|---|---|---|---|---|
| Vanguard Municipal Bond Money Market | $10,000 | 3.40% | $340 | 3.49% | 0.06% | 0.25 | 0 |
| USAA Tax-Exempt Short-Term | $10,000 | 4.41% | $441 | 5.40% | 1.08% | 2.8 | 2.3 |
| USAA Tax-Exempt Intermediate-Term | $40,000 | 5.14% | $2,056 | 7.67% | 2.84% | 9.6 | 5.3 |
| USAA Tax-Exempt Long-Term | $40,000 | 5.38% | $2,152 | 8.49% | 3.58% | 19.1 | 7 |
| **Total** | **$100,000** | **4.99%** | **$4,989** | **7.35%** | **2.68%** | **11.79** | **4.32** |
| TEY Yield @39.6% bracket | | 8.26% | | | | | |
| Money Market | 10% | | | | | | |
| Short-Term | 10% | | | | | | |
| Intermediate-Term | 40% | | | | | | |
| Long-Term | 40% | | | | | | |

***Portfolio Results*** The municipal fund asset combination provides a tax-free yield of 4.99%, which translates into an 8.26% taxable equivalent yield for someone in the 39.6% federal bracket. The high tax-free yields provide a solid premium over the taxable bond portfolio and over the tax-free money fund portfolio. The duration of the allocation is 4.32 years, and the average standard deviation is 2.68%. Based on historical performance, this portfolio's total return over the last three years would have been 7.35%.

## AGGRESSIVE INCOME—TAXABLE

> **Objective:** High levels of income with moderate to high impact on principal
> **Time horizon:** Intermediate- to long-term
> **Income level:** High
> **Total return:** Moderate to high
> **Risk:** Moderate to high
> **Funds used:** Money market funds; high income bond funds
> **Allocation:** 20% money funds; 80% high-yield bond funds

***Objective and Time Horizon*** The objective of this strategy is to maximize yield and build total return. Since maximum yield is the primary objective, and since yield represents the price of risk in the bond markets, someone using this strategy must be prepared to accept higher levels of risk. However, the strategy utilizes two types of funds, money funds and high-income funds, with very different characteristics. These characteristics can work together to provide much higher levels of income without being 100% exposed to the risks of high-yielding funds.

***Income*** The taxable income level for this strategy will be nearly the highest available without investing 100% in the most speculative types of funds.

***Total Return*** The combination of money funds and high-income funds allows for very solid total returns during periods when rates are falling or steady and the equity markets are moving higher. During these periods, total returns in excess of 10% to 15% can be expected. When rates are rising and the equity markets are falling, this portfolio could experience negative total returns. However, the money fund component in the portfolio should keep downside exposure limited.

**Risk**   Due to the portfolio's exposure to high-income bond funds, there are several types of risks that can be expected. The first is credit risk. If the economy moves into a recession, default rates will increase and the bonds held in the high-income portfolios could lose significant amounts of their value. This was seen in 1990, when the average high-income fund lost more than 9%. Another risk associated with these funds is event risk. Speculative bonds are always susceptible to unexpected events, and sudden defaults or bankruptcies by the issuers are not uncommon. The low standard deviations seen on these funds in the late 1990s may mask the underlying risk associated with these funds in more uncertain economic times. Finally, interest-rate risk is always a possibility with high-income funds, although the high-income rates normally reduce the duration of high-yielding bonds and bond funds. The money fund component of the strategy will act as an anchor for the portfolio and hold down principal volatility.

**Investment Mix and Funds**   To achieve a very high level of income while attempting to maintain some level of security, I have suggested using a combination of money market and high-income junk bond funds. The money market component acts as a stabilizing factor for the portfolio, while the high-income funds offer maximum yield and the possibility of increased total returns. I have suggested a mix of 20% money funds and 80% high-income funds and have used two funds for each asset category. For the money funds, I chose the Vanguard and USAA taxable funds from the Conservative Income strategy. Both are of high quality and are extremely well-managed. For the high-income funds, I selected the Vanguard Corporate High Yield and the T. Rowe Price High Yield. Both invest in low-grade bonds, but both have outstanding fund managers and superb research departments. In addition, each has a low expense ratio that allows for high income levels. In addition, both have high Sharpe ratios, which means they have shown solid returns for their respective risk profiles.

**Portfolio Results**   The 80/20 combination of high-income and money funds produces a yield of 7.88%. This is more than 200 basis points higher than the Conservative Income strategy. If only high-income funds were used, the yield would improve by just more than ½%. What you give up in yield is balanced by the stability the money funds offer. Since the money fund's value will hold steady, it produces a duration of 2.6 and an average standard deviation of 2.82%. This is actually less than the dura-

**TABLE 9-5**

Aggressive Income—Taxable

| Fund | Amount | Yield | Annual Income | 3-Year Return | Standard Deviation | Maturity | Duration |
|------|--------|-------|---------------|---------------|--------------------|----------|----------|
| Vanguard Money Market Prime | $10,000 | 5.31% | $531 | 5.43% | 0.06% | 0.41 | 0 |
| USAA Money Market | $10,000 | 5.27% | $527 | 5.39% | 0.10% | 0.36 | 0 |
| Vanguard Corp. High Yield | $40,000 | 8.37% | $3,348 | 10.98% | 3.32% | 6.6 | 4.6 |
| T. Rowe Price High Yield | $40,000 | 8.69% | $3,476 | 12.10% | 3.69% | 8.4 | 4.2 |
| **Total** | **$100,000** | **7.88%** | **$7,882** | **10.31%** | **2.82%** | **6.08** | **2.60** |
| Money Fund | 20% | | | | | | |
| High Income | 80% | | | | | | |

tion and the standard deviation of the Safe Income Plus strategy. Again, the low volatility in the high-income funds in recent years masks some of the possible volatility these funds can experience. The risk that is not quantified but remains inherent in the strategy is the event risk and the impact the equity market has on these funds. Because high-income funds typically have a higher correlation to the equity market, a correction or bear market in equities can cause the portfolio's value to slide. However, the 20% position in the money funds would help limit a slide, should one occur. The total returns for this portfolio are higher than the other strategies because of the positive impact of the high-income total returns in recent years.

## AGGRESSIVE INCOME—TAX-FREE

**Objective:** High levels of tax-free income with moderate to high impact to principal

**Time Horizon:** Intermediate to long-term

**Income Level:** High

**Total Return:** Moderate to high

**Risk:** Moderate to high

**Funds used:** Tax-free money market funds; high-yield municipal bond funds

**Allocation:** 20% money funds; 80% high-yield bond funds

**Objective and Time Horizon**   The objective of this strategy is to max-imize tax-free yield and build total return. Since maximum yield is the pri-mary objective and yield represents the price of risk in the bond markets, someone using this strategy must be prepared to accept higher levels of risk. However, the strategy utilizes two types of funds with very different characteristics, money funds and high-yield funds. These characteristics can work together to provide much higher levels of income without being 100% exposed to the risks of high-yielding funds.

**Income**   The tax-free income level for this strategy will be nearly the highest available without investing 100% in the most speculative types of funds.

**Total Return**   The combination of tax-free money funds and high-yield bond funds allows for very solid total returns during periods when rates are falling or steady. Unlike the taxable high-income funds, munici-pal high-yield funds are not particularly impacted by equity market action. Instead, they are very sensitive to recession. During recession, speculative municipal issuers tend to have higher default rates, and sig-nificant declines in principal can be expected. For example, in 1994, when rates rose sharply, the average municipal bond fund lost just over 6.5%. Conversely, when rates are declining, the long-term municipal funds can experience solid total returns. This was seen in 1995, when the average long-term municipal fund gained more than 17%. The money fund com-ponent in the portfolio should keep downside and upside returns con-strained.

**Risk**   The 20% money market component of this strategy will have mini-mal risk. Tax-free money funds are highly regulated and normally hold only the highest-quality securities. This significantly reduces any credit risk. In addition, money funds have stable NAVs, which eliminates interest-rate risk. The 80% position in the high-yield municipal bond funds intro-duces several types of risk to the portfolio. The first and most important is interest-rate risk. High-yield municipal funds typically have long maturi-ties and long durations. For example, the average municipal long-term fund has a maturity of just over 17 years and a duration of about 7.5. This makes them far more interest-rate sensitive than high-income taxable bond funds. This normally causes them to have greater fluctuations in their return. The higher standard deviations in fund returns is evidence of this volatility. The other important risk of municipal high-yield funds is credit risk. Since these funds invest in speculative grade bonds, there is a greater possibility of having defaults within the portfolio. While default in a well-diversified fund will typically have only minor impact on the fund as a whole, an increase in municipal defaults can send municipal prices lower, even if they are not directly impacted. Like the previous portfolio, the money fund component of the strategy acts as an anchor, stabilizing the portfolio in times of bond market volatility.

**Investment Mix and Funds**   To achieve a high tax-free yield while attempting to limit risk, I suggest using a combination of tax-free money markets and high-yield municipal bond funds. As mentioned, the money market component acts as a stabilizing factor for the portfolio, while the high-yield funds offer maximum yield and the possibility of increased total returns. I have suggested a mix of 20% money and 80% high-yield funds and have used two funds for each asset category. For the money funds, I use the Vanguard and USAA tax-free money market funds from the Conservative Tax-Free Income strategy. Both are of high quality and are extremely well-managed. For the high-yield funds I selected the Vanguard Municipal High Yield and the T. Rowe Price Tax-Free High Yield funds. Both typically invest in low-grade bonds, but both have outstanding fund managers and superb research departments. In addition, each has a low expense ratio that allows for high income levels. In addition, both have high Sharpe ratios, which means they have shown solid returns for their respective risk profiles.

**Portfolio Results**   The 80/20 combination of high-yield and money funds produces a yield of 4.98% with a taxable equivalent of 8.25%. While this is not significantly above the Safe Income Plus—Tax-Free strategy, it's only because of the flat yield curve seen in 1997. Normally, this portfolio allocation will provide income levels in excess of the more conservative strategy. The duration of the portfolio is 4.26, and the standard deviation is 2.65%. Again, this indicates a higher level of potential return fluctuation and interest-rate risk if the market experiences higher rates, but the 20% money fund buffer will help reduce this downside risk.

**TABLE 9-6**

Aggressive Income—Tax-Free

| Fund | Amount | Yield | Annual Income | 3-Year Return | Standard Deviation | Maturity | Duration |
|------|--------|-------|---------------|---------------|--------------------|----------|----------|
| Vanguard Municipal Bond Money Market | $10,000 | 3.40% | $340 | 3.49% | 0.06% | 0.25 | 0 |
| USAA Tax Exempt Money Fund | $10,000 | 3.36% | $336 | 3.44% | 0.07% | 0.38 | 0 |
| Vanguard Municipal High Yield | $40,000 | 5.35% | $2,140 | 7.98% | 3.44% | 10 | 7.1 |
| T. Rowe Price Tax-Free High Yield | $40,000 | 5.41% | $2,164 | 8.36% | 3.16% | 18.6 | 7.1 |
| **Total** | **$100,000** | **4.98%** | **$4,980** | **7.23%** | **2.65%** | **11.50** | **4.26** |
| TEY Yield @39.6% bracket | | 8.25% | | | | | |
| Money Fund | 20% | | | | | | |
| High Income | 80% | | | | | | |

## TOTAL RETURN AND INCOME

**Objective:** Moderate income with higher levels of conservative total return

**Time horizon:** Long-term

**Income level:** Moderate

**Total return:** Moderate to high

**Risk:** Moderate to high

**Funds used:** Money market; high yield; balanced equity

**Allocation:** 20% money funds; 20% high-yield bond funds; 60% balanced

*Objective and Time Horizon*  The objective of this strategy is to provide conservative total return with moderate levels of income. With total return as a primary objective, an investor must be willing to accept higher levels of risk. However, the fund allocation will be such that return volatility should be far less than that of the general market. In addition to the total return objective, income is, of course, important. The use of two income funds, a money market and a high-income fund, will add significant monthly income to the strategy as well as serve as a stabilizing force in the portfolio. The time horizon for this strategy should be at least three to five years. It is best suited for an investor who wants to maintain an equity market exposure while achieving some income and portfolio stability.

**Income**    The income from this strategy is expected to be moderate, owing to the weighting in money funds and balanced funds, which typically are lower-yielding. The allocation in high-income funds will boost income levels without exposing the fund to too much credit quality and event risk. The income distributions from this strategy will be taxable dividends.

**Total Return**    The allocation to balanced funds is the key to this strategy. Balanced funds typically hold 60% of their portfolios in equities and 40% in fixed income. The equity portion is generally oriented toward higher-yielding established large-cap stocks. These tend to have less overall volatility than the general market. The 60% position in equities provides the strategy with significant total return in positive equity market environments. The average annual total return for all balanced funds over the last 10 years is just under 12.5%. In 1997, the average return was more than 18.5%. The income holdings of balanced funds tend to be corporate bonds, preferreds, convertible bonds, and other taxable income holdings. While these holdings provide income, they can also add to the total return of the fund. The money fund allocation will not add significantly to the total return of the portfolio, but the high-yield allocation will. The high-yield funds not only provide income but in positive equity markets they can show annual total returns in excess of 10% to 15%.

**Risk**    The most significant risk in this portfolio is the risk that the equity markets will decline. Because the portfolio has a heavy weighting in stocks via the balanced funds (60%), a decline in the overall stock market could cause the portfolio to drop in value. However, the bond component of the balanced funds will buffer the downside. The net risk arises from the lower-grade bonds held in the 20% high-income allocation. Since this type of fund buys lower-grade bonds, the credit risk increases. In addition, the high-income funds have a high correlation to the equity market and will lose value if the equity market is moving lower. However, because of the high levels of income derived from the fund, the impact is minimized. Again, the anchor in this portfolio is the money fund allocation (20%). The money fund's value will hold steady while delivering monthly income. This will further minimize portfolio loss in a negative market.

***Investment Mix and Funds*** The 60% balanced fund, 20% high-income fund, and 20% money market fund allocations orient the portfolio toward conservative growth as a primary objective. However, the 20% weight in high-income and 20% in money markets will provide significant amounts of income with only moderate risk. For the money fund, I have again used the Vanguard Money Market Prime Fund because of its high yield and superb management. For the high-income fund, I again tapped the Vanguard Corporate High Yield Fund for its solid management, high yield, and consistent track record of good total return with average risk. The balanced fund allocation is divided between two funds, the Vanguard/Wellesley Income Fund and the INVESCO Balanced Fund. Both have shown excellent and consistent total return records with below-average risk. And both funds have superb management from well-known, reputable fund families.

***Portfolio Results*** The allocation produces a yield of 4.86%. The income is generated by the 8.37% high-income yield and the 5.31% money fund yield. It also gets a nice boost from the 5.06% yield in the Vanguard/Wellesley Income balanced fund. The portfolio's total return in the previous three years was 14.21%. Much of this was derived from the total return generated by the two balanced funds. The moderate standard deviation of 5.49% is about one-third that of the S&P 500. You will notice in Table 9-7 that the duration and maturity average are labelled not applica-

**TABLE 9-7**

Total Return and Income

| Fund | Amount | Yield | Annual Income | 3-Year Return | Standard Deviation | Maturity | Duration |
|------|--------|-------|--------|--------|-----------|----------|----------|
| Vanguard Money Market Prime | $20,000 | 5.28% | $1,056 | 5.42% | 0.06% | 0.41 | 0 |
| Vanguard Corp. High Yield | $20,000 | 8.74% | $1,748 | 9.35% | 4.40% | 6.6 | 4.8 |
| Vanguard/Wellesley Income | $30,000 | 5.17% | $1,551 | 13.72% | 7.58% | Na | Na |
| Invesco Balanced | $30,000 | 2.21% | $663 | 15.27% | 10.87% | Na | Na |
| **Total** | **$100,000** | **5.02%** | **$5,018** | **11.65%** | **6.43%** | **Na** | **Na** |
| Money Fund | 20% | | | | | | |
| High Yield | 20% | | | | | | |
| Balanced Fund | 60% | | | | | | |

ble. This is because the maturity and duration on the balanced equity fund are not directly applicable or comparable to the bond and money fund data. However, you can see that the interest-rate risk should be fairly small.

## THE REVIEW PROCESS—REBALANCING IS KEY

As mentioned at the beginning of this book, prudent investing always starts with an objective and an allocation. The allocations, such as the ones offered previously, are designed to balance various types of investments that have different characteristics with respect to risk, return, diversification, and other attributes. It's simple. The allocation drives the investment plan. If the allocation changes, it also changes the characteristics of the plan. When you have extraordinary performance in the market, your plan may need review, and "rebalancing."

In the best case scenario, your funds and asset allocation would stay in the same proportion for the entire time the plan is in place. In the real world, this seldom occurs, because funds can and do grow at different rates. For example, in a total return and income allocation, a stock fund's performance will normally be far greater than that of the income fund, over time. If you have a portfolio that starts with an even split between stock and money funds, the stock funds will dominate. It's quite possible that after five years of solid equity market returns, your portfolio will look much like a 100% stock portfolio. Could this really be a bad thing?

The answer depends on your objectives. If you started with the goal of maximizing your returns and you have a high tolerance for risk, the equity fund's gain is pure gravy on your way to achieving your objectives. If, however, you have a shorter time frame or need to be very conservative, the growth in the equity portion of your portfolio can be a problem. Let's look at a real example and some real solutions.

Let's assume your goal is conservative growth with income, your time horizon is more than 10 years, and you have $100,000 to invest. To achieve this goal, you set up an allocation in February 1993 that is 50% stock funds and 50% money funds. Your 50/50 split is designed to be conservative, yet allow some participation in the equity markets. For your stock fund, you pick the Legg Mason Value Trust—Primary (LMVTX), and for the money fund, you pick the Vanguard Money Market Prime Portfolio (VMMXX). Here's your portfolio.

| February, 1993 | Allocation | Value |
|---|---|---|
| Legg Mason Value Trust—Primary | 50% | $50,000 |
| Vanguard Money Market Prime | 50% | $50,000 |
| Total | | $100,000 |

## Five-Year Results

It's now five years later and the equity market has been on a roll. This has caused your Legg Mason stock fund to grow at an annualized pace of about 28%. Cumulatively, it has gained 244.75%. The money fund has chugged along at an expected slow pace, averaging about 4.8% with a cumulative return of just 26.39%. You now take a look at your portfolio and see that something wonderful and awful has happened.

The good thing is that your $100,000 grew to $235,570. The bad thing is that the stock fund now makes up 73% of the portfolio, whereas the money fund has declined to just 27% of the portfolio. Even though you have lots more money, the portfolio may be far different than when you started and far too aggressive for your taste.

In addition, the overall risk of the portfolio has increased significantly. At the start, the weighted average standard deviation (a measure of the portfolio's return volatility) was 7.24%. Now it's 10.56%. This means the portfolio's value will move up and down in much wider swings.

| February, 1998 | Allocation | Value | Return |
|---|---|---|---|
| Legg Mason Value Trust Primary | 73% | $172,375 | 244.75% |
| Vanguard Money Market Prime | 27% | $63,195 | 26.39% |
| New Total | | $235,570 | |

If the investor does nothing to this portfolio, it will probably continue to move even further toward a 100% stock portfolio, all because no rebalancing was done. This is a classic example of how a portfolio can move far from its original objective solely due to asset appreciation. And don't forget, this is over just a five-year period!

## Do Nothing or Rebalance

There is absolutely nothing wrong with a portfolio more than doubling in size in just five years. In fact, it's incredible! But the risk and reward characteristics may no longer match the original intent.

According to many financial planners, an annual review of the portfolio should be done. If the allocations have changed and you are not comfortable with the new mix, a shift in assets may be in order. It's important, however, to review both your attitude and objectives. You may be perfectly fine with the way the things are currently. Therefore, no change would be necessary.

Here are a few options in the review process for our 50/50 investor mentioned above. The first is to leave things just as they are. This won't trigger any capital gains and will leave the portfolio open to even greater appreciation. However, the investor must now accept that the portfolio's return can be far more volatile, given the change in allocation.

If, however, the investor feels uncomfortable with such a heavy allocation in equities and decides the portfolio has become far more aggressive than had been expected, a shift in assets is needed.

In this case, it's a simple matter of moving money from the stock fund to the bond fund. To bring the portfolio back to a 50/50 ratio, about $54,600 needs be moved into the money fund from the stock fund. In doing this, the portfolio moves back to the original balance, overall portfolio risk is reduced, and you capture the gains made in the stock fund over the past few years. Taxes will need to be paid on the $54,600, but it should qualify for the 20% capital gain rate. And don't forget to adjust the cost basis higher to reflect all the capital gains and dividend distributions that have been made by the fund in the last five years. This will make the tax bite even smaller.

While most income portfolio allocations are more conservative, there can still be divergence in fund growth rates that would necessitate a portfolio balancing, especially in allocations that include equity funds such as the Total Return and Income portfolio offered earlier in this chapter. Money fund allocations rarely need adjustment, and bond fund allocations usually only need minor shifts over time. Still, the review process is important and should be completed once each year.

## SELLING A FUND

Up to this point, we have talked mostly about selecting good funds and allocations. We haven't focused on when to sell. Hopefully, your careful planning and review will reduce this difficult task, but it's one that will inevitably arise. Selling a fund is one of the toughest investment decisions to make, but with a careful, detailed review, the process should be easier.

It's far easier to buy a fund than to sell one because selling is both a realization of your monetary loss and an admission that you made the wrong investment decision from the start. Admitting defeat in any endeavor is tough, but in the investment world it can be the best response. Holding funds that continually underperform not only impacts short-term results but significantly hinders the positive effects of long-term compounding. But before you pull the plug, it's important to review the action carefully, with respect to both the fund itself and your overall investment plan.

When you sell a fund, it seems only logical to follow the same steps used when you purchased it. Unfortunately, most investors don't apply the same amount of care in the selling process. Selling should be a careful process rather than an impulsive action.

## Resist Impulse Selling

Whenever the market is sliding, there is a natural inclination to take profits. However, if you have a long-term investment horizon that is designed to match a long-term investment objective, selling on impulse due to short-term market volatility is probably the wrong decision. The true test of any real long-term investor is to hold tight and stick to his or her plan during market volatility. If you have carefully selected your funds and allocations, daily or weekly market gyrations should not impact your fund holdings.

It's always a good idea to regularly review your portfolio as mentioned in the last section. An allocation set three years ago could be significantly different today. Make sure your mix of funds remains consistent with your objectives. It's pretty simple, but investors often "let things ride" when times are good, yet are very disappointed when the markets go south. If your allocation is about right but you're having doubts about one or more of the funds, it may be time to take action.

## The Grass Is Always Greener

It's also normal to be frustrated with a fund that is losing value or even moving sideways. But before you sell, make sure it's the fund and not the market sector that's the problem. It's a very common mistake to blame the fund rather than the market.

For example, if you owned a junk bond fund in 1990, you would have experienced a significant decline. However, the entire junk fund sector had difficulty in 1990. This was evidenced by the decline of about 9% in the average fund during the late summer and early fall of that year. If aggressive growth was really your objective, then you should have waited out the sector's general underperformance before you planned to sell. Make sure you compare the fund's performance against its respective benchmark first.

## Peer Group Review

If the fund sector you are targeting is moving higher but your fund is being left behind, it should raise a caution flag during your investment review. For example, through July 1998, the junk funds had scored 12-month returns of more than 9%. If your fund lost money during the same period, it warrants investigation. Either the fund manager has a particular strategy that is on the extreme side for the category, or there has been a significant error in the stock selection. One example of this was with the huge $6.5 billion Brandywine Fund (BRWIX) stock fund, managed by the highly respected Foster Friess. In 1997, the fund produced a return of just 12%, while its peer group gained nearly 22%. The main reason behind the lag was Friess' strategy of increasing the cash position of the portfolio in anticipation of a correction. It didn't happen, and the fund suffered.

The other half of the performance equation is risk. If your fund has had average returns with above-average risk, it should be reviewed. Over the long term, you probably don't want to own a fund that does not compensate you in return for excessive risk when compared to similar funds in the same peer group. Conversely, if your fund has provided average or slightly better-than-average returns but has been able to do it with significantly lower-than-average risk, it should be viewed as a positive.

## Don't Jump Ship Because of Short-Term Problems

After reviewing the fund's recent performance (risk and return) against its peer group, you may find that it is underperforming. Do you sell? The answer is maybe.

If the fund has had a string of outstanding years but has had just one period, say six months, when it has lagged, it doesn't mean you should automatically dump it. In the case of Brandywine, the fund has shown excellent long-term performance and has only had that one poor period.

Every manager makes mistakes. If your manager has proven over several years that she or he can achieve superior returns against their peer group, some leeway should be given.

At a minimum, you should call the fund company and inquire about the poor performance. Ask whether the manager is still in place. If he or she has recently left and the fund returns have dropped, it may be time to leave. But if the manager and the strategy remain in place, consider sticking with it. There are no hard and fast rules on just how long you should stay with a fund that is underperforming, but consider giving the fund at least six months to a year to recover relative to its peers.

### Signals to Sell

If your fund's performance lags its peer group and you have given it an adequate time to recover, it may be time to take action. Here is a checklist of items to review in the selling process:

- First and foremost, make sure the fund's objective is not consistent with your long-term investment plan. Review your original investment plan. If the fund is out of sync with the objective and the plan, it may be time for a change.
- Review the 1-, 3-, and 5-year total returns compared to its peer group. If the fund has consistently underperformed its peer group in each period, consider selling.
- Review the standard deviation and beta (if a stock fund) against the peer group. If the fund shows high standard deviations and/or beta (compared to the peer group), with average or below-average return, consider selling. (The fund's R-squared should be 75 or higher in order to make the beta a reliable indicator.) Also review the fund's Sharpe ratio. Funds with ratios below 1.0 aren't providing adequate return for their risk profile. If the fund falls short on these risk evaluations, consider selling.
- If the fund you are reviewing is a bond or other income fund, compare the risk and return measures suggested above, but also compare yield, maturity, and duration. Since yield is a prime objective in a fixed-income fund, it should measure up. Again, compare the peer group's yield against your fund's yield. If yours falls significantly short, there may be a problem. High durations or maturities on a fund that is supposed to be conservative should also be a caution sign.

■ If your fund has a high expense ratio yet does not produce solid returns, some suggest you should look elsewhere. Check the average expense ratio of the peer group for comparison, because some fund sectors are more expensive to run than others. For example, bond index funds are typically less expensive to manage than high income.

### One Last Consideration—Taxes

If you have owned a fund for many years, you may have built up a significant capital gain. When you sell the fund, you will end up paying taxes on that gain. Fortunately, the long-term capital gains tax is now 20% (for a 12-month or more holding period), so the burden has at least been eased. However, paying taxes reduces the earning power of your fund investment by at least 20% (the taxes). If the fund is only lagging its peers by a small amount, the tax implication alone may be the decisive factor. The tax upside is that if you are selling the fund at a loss, you can use that loss to offset capital gains in other investments. If your fund is in a qualified account such as a 401(k), the tax question is moot and you should make changes as they are needed.

## BOND FUND INVESTING WHEN RATES ARE RISING

While rates have been declining in recent years, that's not always the norm. At some point interest rates will rise again, and bond prices will fall. This is often a perplexing situation for income investors. On the one hand, increasing yields will generate more cash flow. On the other hand, an increase in rates will cause the price of income funds (excluding money funds) to decline. Sometimes, the decline in the price of the fund can wipe out any increase in income. What can you do—what should you do—during these periods?

First, if you have a good investment strategy and your time horizon is long-term, small changes in the market should not impact your perspective. You must expect some peaks and valleys in the market and your funds over time. In most cases your best action is to simply "hold the course." However, if you become very nervous over market conditions or are in the process of shifting your allocation for other reasons, there are several strategies you can use to deal with declining bond fund prices and rising rates.

## Opportunity in Corrections

There are several strategies you can use to maintain your income and protect your portfolio in uncertain market environments and get it ready for the next lowering in rates.

## 1994–1995—Lessons Learned

In 1994, the yield on the 30-year Treasury bond moved from an all-time low of 5.78% to more than 8.0%. Investors who were not invested in bonds during that time were lucky, or smart. Nearly all longer-maturity bond funds had negative total returns in 1994. That meant that rising rates ate away the entire income of the average fund. There were, however, some income funds which ended up with positive total returns.

Many investors thought it would take years to recover from the losses in 1994. But guess what, it only took the first few months of 1995 to make it all back. Savvy bond fund investors turned a disastrous 1994 into a phenomenal 1995. How did they do it? They had the insight to see an opportunity presenting itself and knew the actions to take to make the most of it. The bond market rebound in 1995 is one of the best examples of why you should view any correction as a chance to improve your bond fund portfolio returns.

## The First Step

The first thing you should consider when rates are on the rise is if you really want to take action. The answer to this question depends on your investment time horizon. As mentioned at the start of this section, staying put can be the best course of action. This in itself is a market strategy. Staying in a long-term fund through an interest-rate cycle allows you to "dollar cost average" your share purchases. As prices decline, your reinvested income will buy more shares at lower prices and thus give you greater income accumulation. If you go this route, you must have the discipline to stick it out all the way through.

The last thing you want to do is panic and sell just as prices are bottoming. If you'd rather play a more proactive role in your investment strategy and take steps to modify your portfolio, you need to consider your investment options. These steps should include identifying funds that offer safety and income as rates rise.

## Taking Proactive Steps

If you can call the market just right (probably the hardest thing to do in the financial markets), the simplest way to take advantage of a rising rate market is to get to the sidelines. While this is the simplest strategy to understand, the implementation is the hardest. Knowing when rates are bottoming and peaking is very difficult at best, takes a good amount of work, and sometimes lots of luck.

As an alternative to this "timing" strategy, you can modify your portfolio with funds that offer advantages as rates rise. The question one may immediately ask is, "Do *any* income funds fare well when rates increase?" The answer is yes.

## Thinking Short

Let's assume that for some reason you can't bear to have your money "sitting" in a money fund, and you are too risk-averse to use a junk bond fund or some "contra" equity fund. What are your next choices?

If 1994 taught us any lesson, it was that going with short-maturity, short-duration bond funds can pay off in rising rate markets. Short-term bond funds are those which usually have maturities under three years.

The only traditional bond fund categories that, on average, produced positive returns in 1994 were the corporate and municipal short-term funds. Even though the returns were relatively small, compared to the 5.4% decline in the long-term government funds and the 6.25% decline in the long-term municipals, they fared very well and truly served their purpose. Many consider these funds as money fund surrogates because they have minimal interest-rate risk. In addition, the quality of most portfolios tends to be very high.

As rates rise, these funds can offer several advantages. The first is a significant protection of principal. The second is an income that will normally be higher than a money fund. Third is the opportunity to be well positioned when the market turns around.

## Principal Protection

When rates are on the rise, the funds with the greatest exposure to principal loss are those with longer maturities and higher duration's (price sensitivity to a change in rates). As you move to shorter and shorter maturity and duration funds, a given change in interest rates will have less impact on principal. In addition, as rates advance, the manager of the fund typically becomes more defensive, even in the short-maturity funds. This means the manager will buy securities that are less rate-sensitive to help protect the share price of the fund. For example, in 1994, the average duration on a government short-term bond fund stood at 2.25 years at the start of the year. By September, the average duration had moved to 2.0 years, an 11.1% decline in rate sensitivity. This is exactly the "value-added" investors should expect from good fund managers.

## Income

The normal rule of thumb for the bond markets is that the safer your investment, the less income you'll receive. However, how much less income you receive by going to safer investments is the key question. For example, in recent years, the yield curve has been flat, meaning rates on various maturities have been similar. Moving from a more interest-rate sensitive fund to a shorter maturity, less sensitive fund does not necessarily mean a significant reduction in income. This can be a great choice in a rising rate market. You are able to maintain almost all the income advantage with significantly less price volatility.

## Upside Potential

If the principal and income advantages haven't swayed you, this last point should. As mentioned earlier, adjusting your portfolio when rates are rising is a proactive way to maintain your principal and income. Also mentioned was that being able to take advantage of the market when it turns for the better is essential. However, one would think that with all the safety of short durations and maturities, short-term funds would severely limit your upside total return potential when rates move back lower. The answer here is also a bit surprising.

If you don't happen to catch the beginning of a market rally, some opportunity will be lost if you're not in a fund that maximizes total returns. For most of us, catching the very start of a rally is nearly impossible. Typically, once a rally begins, we wait for it to develop and sustain itself before we consider shifting our portfolios. This normally causes us to miss the first "burst" higher in prices. The nice thing about using short-term bond funds is that even if you aren't able get in at the start of a market rally, you don't give up much in total return. Let's look at an example.

## An All-Weather Choice?

Let's say you were smart and moved to short-term bond funds in 1994, when rates were rising. You would have protected your principal and maintained your income. However, you happened to go on vacation in early 1995 and held your short-term fund for the entire year. When you got back and reviewed your portfolio, you would have been pleasantly surprised. In 1995, the average total return of the government short-term funds was 10.6%. The average for the high-quality corporate short-term funds was 9.9%, and the short-term municipal funds gained just over 6.5%. These returns compared quite favorably to those on long-term funds.

## Adjusting Your Portfolio

The final step in preparing your portfolio for higher rates is making the necessary changes with the funds that you have identified to meet your goals in your allocation. You can start by identifying those funds you own which are at most principal risk or may not present enough income value for their given volatility, such as long-maturity, long-duration funds.

Review both the income level and the duration of each fund you own and match it against a shorter-maturity bond fund. If the income is nearly identical, the durations are significantly lower (2 to 3 times), and you aren't investing for big total return, consider making a shift. Also, don't forget the tax consequences. Even if you are selling a municipal bond fund, you may have capital gains taxes to pay, and this may play into your decision.

# CHAPTER 10

# Keeping Track of Your Investments and the Market

The investment process does not end after you have selected a strategy and purchased the funds. In many ways, its has just begun. Throughout your investment lifetime, you'll need to monitor your accounts to make sure they remain in line with your plan, and you'll need to keep good records.

## MONITORING YOUR PORTFOLIO

One of the easiest ways to keep in touch with your portfolio is to keep good records from your mutual fund company. Keeping good records on your funds is not only easy, it also helps you make future investment decisions and properly calculate your tax liabilities.

The first step to keeping good records is to store all of your records in one place. This may seem very simple, but if you own funds from several different fund families or have a second residence, it's likely your records may get separated. The simple solution is to go out and buy a three-ringed notebook. Each time something is mailed from the fund, add it to the book. Most fund families punch standard holes in their statements for this very purpose.

You will probably also want to keep a list of all fund family phone numbers, along with personal IDs, social security numbers, and account numbers. Most funds want all this before they let you make a transaction. If you are on a vacation or are away from home, you can take your account book with you in case you need to make an exchange or redemption. Make sure your spouse or other important people know where your records are in case of emergency. Since these items are the keys to your money, make sure you keep them in a secure place. Don't leave them out on an open desk or on a hotel room table. Be safe; lock them up if you can.

## DAILY AND MONTHLY RECORDS

Many fund families now have the ability to send you a monthly statement, but quarterly statements are the norm. To help out between cycles, you can keep a simple spreadsheet on your PC that tallies current shares, price, and value for each fund. Also add to the spreadsheet a total of all your fund assets and a simple pie chart showing your allocation. Daily information on your fund can be obtained from most newspapers. It covers the current price (NAV) of the fund, along with some return data. The fund families themselves also offer daily information about the funds in the form of NAVs and returns. In addition, most fund families provide some form of shareholder newsletter or magazine on a regular basis. These can be very helpful in keeping in touch with the viewpoints of the fund and its managers.

Another way to track your fund values through the month or even daily is to use one of the online Internet services that allows you to track portfolios. Most tracking programs update your fund prices each day and calculate a value based on the number of shares in the portfolio. For those who like to see how their fund did on the most recent jump or decline in market price, the daily updating really comes in handy. This also gives you a sense of just how sensitive your funds are to general market movements. Most of the fund families now have Internet sites that offer price and return data along with lots of other information about the funds and investing.

## CONFIRMS AND REPORTS

Each time you add money to your account, your fund company is required to send you a confirmation. The confirmation statement includes the date of the purchase, the purchase price, including any commissions, and the number of shares bought. Again, make sure these all go into your investment notebook. You will need these confirmation statements to calculate a cost basis if you sell your fund in the future. At the end of the year, your fund will send you a 1099-DIV, as well as a year-end statement. The 1099-DIV is used to report dividend and capital gains, and the year-end report is a good reference for your accounts. It usually includes all the dates of fund activity, such as redemptions and exchanges. You may also get a 1099-B, which reports the sale of funds. These distribution records help you calculate your capital gains or losses.

As a fund shareholder, you will receive annual and semiannual reports. You'll also receive any updated prospectus for your fund. All of these are useful. The annual and semiannual reports contain the current investment strategy of the fund, and most provide an interview with the manager. The semiannual report usually contains the fund's holdings. Both reports are a great way to keep up-to-date on what your fund manager is doing and what's going on in the portfolio. Finally, there are a number of other resources to keep track of your funds, from investment newsletters and magazines to Internet services. They all can be useful in getting different opinions and information on your fund.

## WHAT MOVES THE MARKET

There are hundreds of factors that impact the income markets on a daily basis. To follow all of these items each day would force an individual investor to spend the entire day in front of a computer screen or buried in research papers. Fortunately, owning mutual funds removes much of the day-to-day work, but there are still items that all income investors should be aware of, because they impact the value of their investments. The three key factors are interest rates, the economy, and the Federal Reserve.

### Interest Rates

As mentioned in many chapters, a change in interest rates will have a direct impact on the price of a bond or a bond fund's return and yield. Many consider interest rates as the most important determinate of the direction of all the financial markets. As rates increase, bond fund prices decline, stock prices usually move lower, and money fund yields increase. Conversely, a decline in rates helps bond and stock prices but causes money fund yields to drop.

*The most watched indicator of interest rates is the 30-year Treasury bond yield.* The 30-year bond yield can be found each day in most newspapers and on financial radio and television programs. The 30-year bond is considered the key indicator for all U.S. rates. In fact, most other rates, such as corporate and municipal bond rates, are based on the activity in Treasury bonds. There are also other important interest rates to track, including the federal funds rates.

*One of the primary factors that causes rates to move up and down is infla-tion.* As inflation increases, it normally forces interest rates higher. Market rates need to be higher in order to compensate investors for the loss due to an increase in the cost of living. If bread prices go up 50 cents, that's 50 cents more income investors need to squeeze out of their monthly checks to make ends meet. There are two significant pieces of economic data that help you track inflation, the consumer price index and the producer price index. The *consumer price index* (CPI) measures the prices of a fixed basket of goods bought by the average consumer. These goods include food, transportation, shelter, utilities, clothing, medical care, and entertainment. The CPI is reported by the Bureau of Labor Statistics once per month. The *producer price index* (PPI) measures the change in wholesale prices. It tracks the prices of food, metals, lumber, oil, and gas, as well as many other com-modities. It does not measure the price of services. The PPI is also reported monthly by the Bureau of Labor Statistics. If either the PPI or CPI increases more than the market expects for a given month, bond prices will fall and yields will increase. Tracking these indicators and what the market expects of them will greatly enhance your understanding of yield changes in the market.

## The Economy

In addition to inflation, the trend in economic growth is critical in deter-mining interest rates and the value of income fund investments. The reason economic growth and rates are so interdependent has much to do with expectations of inflation. Usually, when the economy is growing, price increases lead the way. This, in turn, causes the PPI and CPI to rise and bond prices to fall. These events often occur simultaneously. As the econ-omy grows, the Federal Reserve will often counter the expansion and the potential for inflation. They do this by raising rates. As you might guess, higher rates mean lower bond fund prices and higher fund yields. This was most evident in 1994, when the Federal Reserve raised rates several times to slow the economy and keep inflation under control. Conversely, as the economy slows or is heading into a recession, the Fed will attempt to stim-ulate growth by lowering rates.

*One of the key economic indicators is the quarterly gross domestic product (GDP) report.* GDP is the broadest measure of the value of all goods and ser-vices that are provided inside the borders of any nation within a year. The U.S. GDP is reported quarterly by the Commerce Department. Because GDP measures national output, and strong output is indicative of a healthy economy, bond prices react negatively to strong GDP data. A strong economy ignites inflationary fears, which is a negative for bond prices. Equities, on the other hand, tend to perform well when GDP is rising, since earnings growth prospects are better during economic expansions. Again, this data is widely available when it is released.

## The Federal Reserve

The Federal Reserve, or the "Fed" as it is called on Wall Street, is probably the most powerful governmental institution in the world. The Federal Reserve is the center of the U.S. federal banking system and consists of 12 independent reserve banks: Atlanta, Boston, Chicago, Cleveland, Dallas, Kansas City, Minneapolis, New York, Philadelphia, Richmond, San Francisco, and St. Louis. Within the system are these 12 member banks, a board of governors, and the Federal Open Market Committee.

The primary functions of the system include issuing currency, conducting monetary policy, and providing regulation to the banking system. Monetary policy is carried out through the adjustment of the discount rate, the federal funds rate, and the required reserve level placed on banks. The Federal Open Market Committee is the decision-making entity when it comes to monetary policy, the goal of which is to promote price stability and dampen swings in the business cycle. In its regular meetings, the FOMC decides whether to influence interest rates to help slow or speed up the economy.

The Fed normally carries out their interest-rate policy by buying and selling government securities (Treasury bonds, notes, and bills). Such adjustments affect the cost of borrowing and the availability of funds through the lending community. Generally, a tightening of monetary policy pushes interest rates higher, making variable rate loans and credit cards more costly. A loosening of monetary policy normally brings these rates down, which allows for mortgage refinancings and lower interest payments on credit cards.

The Federal Reserve chairman is the most visible and most watched member of the Fed. Twice annually, he delivers his Humphrey-Hawkins address to Congress. Economists, politicians, and the investment community pay careful attention to this testimony, as it can be a critical indicator of the Fed's intentions.

Tracking the Fed's movements is done on a daily basis on Wall Street. Economists spend a good part of their professional lives trying to anticipate the Fed's next move. The Fed bases its interest rate decisions on the levels of inflation, the economy, the dollar's level against other currencies, and the financial markets. Most watched are the FOMC meetings. Once each meeting is over, there is typically an announcement of the Fed's new policy in which they indicate a change in rates if any.

The following is a table of indicators to watch and their impact on the income fund markets.

| Item | Action | Impact |
| --- | --- | --- |
| 30-year Treasury bonds | Trend higher | Bond fund NAVs lower |
| 30-year Treasury bonds | Trend lower | Bond fund NAVs higher |
| CPI and PPI | Trend higher | Bond and stock NAVs lower |
| CPI and PPI | Trend lower | Bond and stock NAVs higher |
| GDP | Growth strong | Bond NAVs often lower; stock NAVs usually higher |
| GDP | Growth weaker | Bond NAV's usually higher; stock NAVs usually lower |
| Fed policy | Raising rates | Bond and stock NAVs lower |
| Fed policy | Lowering rates | Bond and stock NAVs higher |

# 26 Key Questions to Ask Before You Invest in an Income Fund

1. **Does the fund match your objective with respect to your investment time horizon?**

   Match return and risk expectation with your ultimate investment objective. Don't buy an aggressive fund if you have only a few months before you need the money. Conversely, don't invest in safe, low-returning funds if you have a far higher expectation for return.

2. **Does the fund match your objectives with respect to return and risk?**

   Make sure you fully understand how much return and risk the fund has exhibited over the years. If you are a conservative investor, don't buy a risky stock fund.

3. **How long has the manager been running the fund?**

   If the manager does not have much experience, consider a comparable fund with a more seasoned professional at the helm. Look for managers with at least five years' experience.

4. **What is the background of the manager—education, previous jobs, etc.?**

   While education does not guarantee success, it's nice to see that the fund manager has advanced degrees in business or related fields. Also, prior experience with other funds or fund families is a plus.

5. **How much does the fund manager manage in total assets? The company?**

   While not always the case, managers who handle large funds are usually considered higher on the skill scale than those who run very small or new funds. Also, consider sticking with those funds that have a large amount of assets under management. Funds don't grow assets and shareholders unless they are doing something right.

6. **How big is the fund company in terms of funds, assets, and employees? How long has it been in business?**

   Big, successful companies are usually those that are leaders among their peers. Larger fund families have more resources to hire top managers and pay for superior research. Funds that have been around for more than 10 or 15 years have been able to weather many financial environments and are probably doing something right.

7. **What is the average quality of bonds in the fund?**

   Make sure you know what's in the portfolio. If you think you are buying a high-quality fund, make sure the bulk of the securities are rated AA or better.

8. **What is the current average maturity of the fund?**

   Longer maturities mean potentially greater price volatility. In other words, funds with long maturities are more sensitive to rate changes.

9. **What is the duration of the fund?**

   Similar to maturity, duration is an indicator of the sensitivity of the fund to changes in rates. If you are looking for a stable, more conservative fund, make sure durations are short. If you want lots of return in a declining rate market, high duration funds should do the trick.

10. **Have the duration and/or maturity been consistent over time? Do they fluctuate?**

    Be careful with funds that have had lots of variability in their maturity and/or duration. This is a sign that the fund manager has lots of leeway in managing the portfolio. Is this really what you want? If not, look for consistent duration and maturity numbers over the years.

11. **What are the expenses—expense ratio, 12-b fee, etc.?**

    High expense with mediocre returns is not a good sign. In funds with low returns and yields (money funds), expenses can be very important. Try to stick with funds that have low expenses compared to their peer group.

12. **Are there transaction fees for exchanges or for other services such as check writing?**

    The best funds offer the most flexibility. Make sure your fund offers ways to get at your money easily and inexpensively. Know the cost before you have to make the transaction.

13. **Does the fund have a front-end or back-end load charge?**

   How much the fund will cost is key. No-loads are preferable, but many load funds offer great returns. Again, know the costs before you send your money.

14. **What type of bonds does the fund own? Can they hold others?**

   Does the fund own junk bonds, high-quality, low-quality? What can they buy, and how is the portfolio restricted? Knowing this information in advance can remove surprises later.

15. **What has been the 1-, 3-, 5-, and 10-year total return of the fund? How does it compare to its peers?**

   How does the fund stack up against its peers. Don't buy funds that never beat the averages. The better funds are those that do well consistently.

16. **What are the risks of the fund? How much volatility should you expect? What are the standard deviations and how do they compare with peers?**

   Don't forget that risk is the other half of the investment equation. Does the risk match your objectives and expectations for the fund? Funds with standard deviations that are lower than the fund's peer group are usually more advantageous.

17. **What is the fund's current Sharpe ratio? How does it compare to the peer group?**

   How has the fund done on a risk-adjusted basis? The Sharpe ratio helps identify those that do well. Funds with Sharpe ratios above 1.0 are more preferable.

18. **What is the fund's yield—12-month distribution and 30-day SEC?**

   In the income world, yield is key. Make sure the fund offers as much yield as others in its peer group. For maximum income, seek funds with top yields. Don't forget that yield is the price of risk. Higher-yielding funds normally carry greater risks.

19. **Has the fund had a consistent income payout?**

   Review the 12-month distribution yield over the last few years. Ask the fund company for the dividend-per-month payout. Do they look consistent? Greater consistency is a positive attribute. If not, the fund may shift its focus more often. This should be viewed as a negative.

**20. Does the fund own any derivatives?**

Usually, derivatives signal possible risk. Ask how the derivatives are used and their allocation in the portfolio. Some funds that hedge currency risk need derivatives to reduce risk. Funds that use derivatives to leverage return should be considered much more aggressive.

**21. Has the fund distributed an annual capital gain in recent years? How much?**

Be aware ahead of time what taxable distribution the fund may be distributing. Large capital gains mean greater tax liability.

**22. When does the fund pay its monthly dividend, capital gain?**

If you expect a monthly check, make sure the fund distributes monthly. Some funds, especially equity-oriented income funds, distribute only quarterly.

**23. What flexibility options does the fund offer—exchange, wire, checkwriting, etc.?**

If you want to make a change, make sure your fund can handle the transaction. Look for funds with telephone exchange, wire redemption, and automatic withdrawal or investment options.

**24. What other funds does the fund family offer?**

If your investment objectives change, make sure the fund family can accommodate your new plan. Do they have a variety of other funds with solid returns? Fund families that have lots of funds with good results are more favorable.

**25. Does the fund own any foreign investments? Are they hedged?**

Many domestic funds own foreign securities, which adds another dimension of risk. Does the fund you are considering control this risk? If it doesn't, it should sound an alarm. Ask what type of hedging it does to reduce risk. If they don't hedge, ask how much additional return volatility can be expected.

**26. Is there an incentive for the broker to sell you this fund versus others?**

Many funds are aggressively "sold" because a broker needs to make a commission. This can lead to inappropriate sales tactics and funds that are inconsistent with your investment objectives. If the fund pitch sounds too good to be true, it probably is.

# Tables of Top Funds by Category

**TABLE B-1**

Balanced Funds

| Fund Name | Ticker | 3-Year Return | 5-Year Return | Standard Deviation | 12-Month Yield | Sharpe Ratio | Asset | Expense Ratio | Front Load | Back Load | Initial Purchase | Telephone No. |
|---|---|---|---|---|---|---|---|---|---|---|---|---|
| Pax World | PAXWX | 17.80 | 13.81 | 9.57 | 2.53 | 1.49 | 712 | 0.91 | 0.00 | 0.00 | 250 | 800-767-1729 |
| Dreyfus Premier Balanced A | PRBAX | 17.76 | — | 10.58 | 2.36 | 1.35 | 34 | 1.25 | 5.75 | 0.00 | 1000 | 800-554-4611 |
| Vanguard/Wellesley Income | VWINX | 13.72 | 10.68 | 7.58 | 5.17 | 1.28 | 7896 | 0.31 | 0.00 | 0.00 | 3000 | 800-662-7447 |
| Founders Balanced | FRINX | 15.32 | 13.64 | 8.98 | 2.75 | 1.28 | 1151 | 0.99 | 0.00 | 0.00 | 1000 | 800-525-2440 |
| Idex Balanced A | IBALX | 17.34 | — | 11.40 | 1.04 | 1.21 | 22 | 1.85 | 5.50 | 0.00 | 500 | 888-233-4339 |
| Gabelli Westwood Bal Ret | WEBAX | 15.58 | 14.45 | 9.84 | 2.41 | 1.20 | 124 | 1.25 | 0.00 | 0.00 | 1000 | 800-937-8966 |
| MFS Total Return A | MSFRX | 14.51 | 11.62 | 9.04 | 3.48 | 1.17 | 3621 | 0.93 | 4.75 | 0.00 | 1000 | 800-637-2929 |
| Idex Balanced C | IBACX | 16.73 | — | 11.32 | 0.54 | 1.16 | 4 | 2.40 | 0.00 | 0.00 | 500 | 888-233-4339 |
| Janus Balanced | JABAX | 16.79 | 14.15 | 11.64 | 2.09 | 1.13 | 584 | 1.10 | 0.00 | 0.00 | 2500 | 800-525-8983 |
| Atlas Balanced A | ATBAX | 14.05 | — | 9.08 | 3.20 | 1.11 | 74 | 1.20 | 0.00 | 0.00 | 2500 | 800-933-2852 |
| BlackRock Balanced Inv A | PCBAX | 16.58 | 12.96 | 11.78 | 1.88 | 1.10 | 93 | 1.24 | 4.50 | 0.00 | 500 | 800-441-7762 |
| Victory Balanced A | SBALX | 14.66 | — | 9.89 | 2.52 | 1.09 | 390 | 1.25 | 5.75 | 0.00 | 500 | 800-539-3863 |
| Montag & Caldwell Balanced | MOBAX | 17.92 | — | 13.36 | 1.60 | 1.08 | 132 | 1.25 | 0.00 | 0.00 | 2500 | 800-992-8151 |
| Federated Stock & Bond A | FSTBX | 14.34 | 11.48 | 9.65 | 3.37 | 1.08 | 176 | 1.21 | 5.50 | 0.00 | 500 | 800-341-7400 |
| Vanguard/Wellington | VWELX | 15.65 | 13.70 | 11.32 | 3.83 | 1.05 | 24560 | 0.29 | 0.00 | 0.00 | 3000 | 800-662-7447 |
| Regions Balanced Invmt | FPBLX | 13.86 | — | 9.36 | 2.63 | 1.05 | 96 | 1.13 | 0.00 | 3.00 | 1000 | 800-433-2829 |

| Fund Name | Ticker | 3-Year Return | 5-Year Return | Standard Deviation | 12-Month Yield | Sharpe Ratio | Asset | Expense Ratio | Front Load | Back Load | Initial Purchase | Telephone No. |
|---|---|---|---|---|---|---|---|---|---|---|---|---|
| Invesco Balanced | IMABX | 15.27 | — | 10.87 | 2.21 | 1.05 | 193 | 1.29 | 0.00 | 0.00 | 1000 | 800-525-8085 |
| Columbia Balanced | CBALX | 13.71 | 11.61 | 9.21 | 3.44 | 1.05 | 942 | 0.68 | 0.00 | 0.00 | 1000 | 800-547-1707 |
| Delaware A | DELFX | 15.23 | 12.08 | 11.06 | 2.28 | 1.03 | 597 | 0.97 | 4.75 | 0.00 | 1000 | 800-523-4640 |
| American Balanced | ABALX | 13.29 | 11.51 | 9.04 | 3.47 | 1.02 | 5592 | 0.65 | 5.75 | 0.00 | 500 | 800-421-4120 |
| Mentor Income & Growth A | MIGAX | 13.60 | 12.43 | 9.40 | 2.27 | 1.01 | 95 | 1.36 | 5.75 | 0.00 | 1000 | 800-382-0016 |
| Evergreen Balanced B | EKBBX | 14.38 | 10.84 | 10.40 | 2.08 | 1.00 | 566 | 1.35 | 0.00 | 4.00 | 1000 | 800-343-2898 |
| Vanguard Balanced Index | VBINX | 14.40 | 12.32 | 10.84 | 3.27 | 0.96 | 1687 | 0.20 | 0.00 | 0.00 | 3000 | 800-662-7447 |
| Hotchkis & Wiley Balanced | HWBAX | 11.05 | 10.33 | 6.94 | 4.57 | 0.96 | 102 | 0.98 | 0.00 | 0.00 | 10000 | 800-346-7301 |
| George Putnam of Boston A | PGEOX | 14.18 | 12.35 | 10.64 | 3.28 | 0.96 | 3375 | 1.06 | 5.75 | 0.00 | 500 | 800-225-1581 |
| Chase Vista Balanced A | VBALX | 13.38 | 11.74 | 9.71 | 2.56 | 0.96 | 89 | 1.25 | 5.75 | 0.00 | 2500 | 800-348-4782 |
| STI Classic Balanced Inv | STBLX | 14.08 | — | 10.65 | 2.04 | 0.95 | 9 | 1.25 | 3.75 | 0.00 | 2000 | 800-428-6970 |
| Flag Inv Value Builder D | FVBDX | 16.16 | 14.00 | 13.16 | 2.13 | 0.94 | 18 | 1.62 | 0.00 | 4.00 | — | 800-767-3524 |
| T. Rowe Price Balanced | RPBAX | 13.34 | 11.43 | 10.19 | 3.23 | 0.91 | 1484 | 0.81 | 0.00 | 0.00 | 2500 | 800-638-5660 |
| George Putnam of Boston M | PGEMX | 13.61 | — | 10.59 | 2.81 | 0.90 | 279 | 1.56 | 3.50 | 0.00 | 500 | 800-225-1581 |

Source: Morningstar, Inc.

**TABLE B-2**

Utility Funds

| Fund Name | Ticker | 3-Year Return | 5-Year Return | Standard Deviation | 12-Month Yield | Sharpe Ratio | Asset | Expense Ratio | Front Load | Back Load | Initial Purchase | Telephone No. |
|---|---|---|---|---|---|---|---|---|---|---|---|---|
| Prudential Utility A | PRUAX | 17.73 | 10.72 | 13.49 | 2.63 | 1.05 | 2612 | 0.82 | 5.00 | 0.00 | 1000 | 800-225-1852 |
| MSDW Utilities B | UTLBX | 14.80 | 8.62 | 11.71 | 2.53 | 0.93 | 2429 | 1.67 | 0.00 | 5.00 | 1000 | 800-869-3863 |
| Franklin Utilities I | FKUTX | 13.76 | 7.25 | 12.54 | 4.67 | 0.77 | 2021 | 0.75 | 4.25 | 0.00 | 1000 | 800-342-5236 |
| Fidelity Utilities | FIUIX | 17.42 | 11.55 | 14.76 | 1.94 | 0.94 | 1589 | 0.85 | 0.00 | 0.00 | 2500 | 800-544-8888 |
| IDS Utilities Income A | INUTX | 18.69 | 11.77 | 13.41 | 2.99 | 1.14 | 966 | 0.89 | 5.00 | 0.00 | 2000 | 800-328-8300 |
| Putnam Util Growth & Inc A | PUGIX | 16.67 | 11.20 | 10.64 | 3.46 | 1.22 | 746 | 1.05 | 5.75 | 0.00 | 500 | 800-225-1581 |
| Vanguard Spec Utilities Inc | VGSUX | 15.28 | 9.75 | 10.91 | 3.78 | 1.05 | 744 | 0.44 | 0.00 | 0.00 | 3000 | 800-662-7447 |
| Federated Utility A | LBUTX | 15.63 | 9.78 | 11.59 | 2.60 | 1.02 | 719 | 1.14 | 5.50 | 0.00 | 1500 | 800-341-7400 |
| Eaton Vance Utilities A | EVTMX | 12.91 | 5.74 | 12.15 | 3.29 | 0.72 | 350 | 1.13 | 5.75 | 0.00 | 1000 | 800-225-6265 |
| Fidelity Sel Utilities Grth | FSUTX | 20.44 | 12.42 | 15.04 | 0.76 | 1.15 | 341 | 1.46 | 3.00 | 0.00 | 2500 | 800-544-8888 |
| Merrill Lynch Global Util B | MBGUX | 16.89 | 10.39 | 14.72 | 1.58 | 0.90 | 319 | 1.59 | 0.00 | 4.00 | 1000 | 800-637-3863 |
| Colonial Utilities A | CUTLX | 16.55 | 9.52 | 12.81 | 3.29 | 1.01 | 316 | 1.22 | 4.75 | 0.00 | 1000 | 800-426-3750 |
| Franklin Global Utilities I | FRGUX | 14.25 | 10.73 | 17.04 | 1.59 | 0.60 | 226 | 1.00 | 5.75 | 0.00 | 1000 | 800-342-5236 |
| American Cent Utilities | BULIX | 18.70 | 10.88 | 15.60 | 2.20 | 0.98 | 208 | 0.72 | 0.00 | 0.00 | 2500 | 800-345-2021 |

| Fund Name | Ticker | 3-Year Return | 5-Year Return | Standard Deviation | 12-Month Yield | Sharpe Ratio | Asset | Expense Ratio | Front Load | Back Load | Initial Purchase | Telephone No. |
|---|---|---|---|---|---|---|---|---|---|---|---|---|
| IDS Utilities Income B | IUTBX | 17.77 | — | 13.14 | 2.18 | 1.08 | 207 | 1.65 | 0.00 | 5.00 | 2000 | 800-328-8300 |
| MFS Utilities A | MMUFX | 20.89 | 15.27 | 13.53 | 2.62 | 1.31 | 195 | 1.10 | 4.75 | 0.00 | 1000 | 800-637-2929 |
| Strong American Utilities | SAMUX | 17.47 | 12.48 | 12.98 | 2.32 | 1.07 | 183 | 1.10 | 0.00 | 0.00 | 1000 | 800-368-1030 |
| AIM Global Utilities A | AUTLX | 15.38 | 8.26 | 12.80 | 2.58 | 0.90 | 172 | 1.13 | 5.50 | 0.00 | 500 | 800-347-4246 |
| Colonial Global Utilities A | CGUAX | 12.90 | 7.76 | 14.30 | 1.77 | 0.61 | 156 | 1.31 | 5.75 | 0.00 | 1000 | 800-426-3750 |
| America's Utility | AMUTX | 13.91 | 7.41 | 11.83 | 2.93 | 0.84 | 156 | 1.21 | 0.00 | 0.00 | 1000 | 800-487-3863 |
| Invesco Strat Utilities | FSTUX | 15.28 | 9.14 | 13.71 | 2.13 | 0.83 | 151 | 1.22 | 0.00 | 0.00 | 1000 | 800-525-8085 |
| Global Utility A | GLUAX | 14.69 | 10.39 | 12.45 | 2.61 | 0.87 | 129 | 1.21 | 5.00 | 0.00 | 1000 | 800-225-1852 |
| First Invest Utilities Inc A | FIUTX | 13.33 | 8.04 | 12.64 | 2.41 | 0.73 | 113 | 1.20 | 6.25 | 0.00 | 1000 | 800-423-4026 |
| Evergreen Utility A | EVUAX | 13.00 | — | 13.32 | 3.58 | 0.66 | 97 | 0.99 | 4.75 | 0.00 | 1000 | 800-343-2898 |
| Principal Utilities A | PUTLX | 17.15 | 8.82 | 13.28 | 3.20 | 1.02 | 75 | 1.15 | 4.75 | 0.00 | 1000 | 800-451-5447 |
| Van Kampen Utility A | VKUAX | 16.79 | 9.52 | 11.98 | 2.50 | 1.10 | 61 | 1.41 | 5.75 | 0.00 | 500 | 800-421-5666 |
| Lindner Utility Inv | LDUTX | 9.02 | — | 20.59 | 2.63 | 0.21 | 40 | 0.89 | 0.00 | 0.00 | 3000 | 314-727-5305 |
| Countrywide Utility A | CUTAX | 15.68 | 9.98 | 12.77 | 2.69 | 0.93 | 38 | 1.25 | 4.00 | 0.00 | 1000 | 800-543-8721 |
| Franklin Utilities II | FRUSX | 13.17 | — | 12.44 | 4.19 | 0.73 | 34 | 1.27 | 1.00 | 0.99 | 1000 | 800-342-5236 |
| Merrill Lynch Utility Inc B | MBUTX | 11.84 | — | 12.11 | 4.60 | 0.62 | 31 | 1.34 | 0.00 | 4.00 | 1000 | 800-637-3863 |

Source: Morningstar, Inc.

**TABLE B-3**

Equity Income Funds

| Fund Name | Ticker | 3-Year Return | 5-Year Return | Standard Deviation | 12-Month Yield | Sharpe Ratio | Asset | Expense Ratio | Front Load | Back Load | Initial Purchase | Telephone No. |
|---|---|---|---|---|---|---|---|---|---|---|---|---|
| Ameristock | AMSTX | 26.65 | — | 16.67 | 0.68 | 1.45 | 12 | 0.56 | 0.00 | 0.00 | 1000 | 800-394-5064 |
| Capital Income Builder | CAIBX | 16.41 | 12.96 | 10.17 | 4.84 | 1.25 | 8734 | 0.65 | 5.75 | 0.00 | 1000 | 800-421-4120 |
| American Cent Equity Inc Inv | TWEIX | 17.21 | — | 11.56 | 3.38 | 1.18 | 267 | 1.00 | 0.00 | 0.00 | 2500 | 800-345-2021 |
| Vanguard Equity-Income | VEIPX | 19.21 | 14.83 | 13.57 | 3.00 | 1.17 | 2530 | 0.45 | 0.00 | 0.00 | 3000 | 800-662-7447 |
| T. Rowe Price Equity—Income | PRFDX | 17.26 | 15.66 | 12.68 | 2.52 | 1.08 | 13390 | 0.79 | 0.00 | 0.00 | 2500 | 800-638-5660 |
| First American Equity—Inc A | FFEIX | 17.33 | 13.96 | 12.86 | 2.70 | 1.07 | 11 | 1.00 | 4.50 | 0.00 | 1000 | 800-637-2548 |
| Evergreen Fund for Tot Ret A | EKTAX | 18.99 | 13.77 | 15.46 | 0.65 | 1.01 | 54 | 1.22 | 4.75 | 0.00 | 1000 | 800-343-2898 |
| Oppenheimer Equity-Income A | OPPEX | 16.97 | 13.49 | 13.38 | 3.40 | 1.00 | 2892 | 0.88 | 5.75 | 0.00 | 1000 | 800-525-7048 |
| Pioneer Equity-Income A | PEQIX | 17.23 | 13.67 | 13.82 | 1.91 | 0.99 | 572 | 1.11 | 5.75 | 0.00 | 1000 | 800-225-6292 |
| Van Kampen Equity—Income A | ACEIX | 16.48 | 14.23 | 13.07 | 2.08 | 0.98 | 775 | 0.86 | 5.75 | 0.00 | 500 | 800-421-5666 |
| Dreyfus Premier Lrg Co Stk A | DRDEX | 21.24 | — | 18.76 | 0.77 | 0.97 | 19 | 1.15 | 5.75 | 0.00 | 1000 | 800-554-4611 |
| Chase Vista Equity Income A | VEQIX | 18.40 | 13.88 | 15.49 | 1.28 | 0.97 | 71 | 1.50 | 4.50 | 0.00 | 2500 | 800-348-4782 |
| One Group Income Equity A | OIEIX | 18.55 | 15.14 | 15.77 | 1.07 | 0.96 | 103 | 1.25 | 4.50 | 0.00 | 1000 | 800-480-4111 |
| Delaware Decatur Income A | DELDX | 17.28 | 14.39 | 14.22 | 2.37 | 0.96 | 1983 | 0.88 | 4.75 | 0.00 | 1000 | 800-523-4640 |

| Fund Name | Ticker | 3-Year Return | 5-Year Return | Standard Deviation | 12-Month Yield | Sharpe Ratio | Asset | Expense Ratio | Front Load | Back Load | Initial Purchase | Telephone No. |
|---|---|---|---|---|---|---|---|---|---|---|---|---|
| Gabelli Equity-Income | GABEX | 16.41 | 13.85 | 13.38 | 1.59 | 0.95 | 77 | 1.78 | 0.00 | 0.00 | 1000 | 800-422-3554 |
| Montgomery Equity Income R | MNEIX | 16.17 | — | 13.28 | 2.45 | 0.94 | 31 | 0.86 | 0.00 | 0.00 | 1000 | 800-572-3863 |
| Smith Barney Prem Tot Ret A | SOPAX | 14.85 | 12.66 | 11.93 | 3.62 | 0.92 | 952 | 1.11 | 5.00 | 0.00 | 1000 | 800-451-2010 |
| Pioneer Equity— Income B | PBEQX | 16.36 | — | 13.71 | 1.18 | 0.92 | 272 | 1.88 | 0.00 | 4.00 | 1000 | 800-225-6292 |
| Oppenheimer Equity—Income B | OPEBX | 15.99 | 12.55 | 13.28 | 2.63 | 0.92 | 635 | 1.69 | 0.00 | 5.00 | 1000 | 800-525-7048 |
| One Group Income Equity B | OGIBX | 17.69 | — | 15.48 | 0.39 | 0.92 | 149 | 2.00 | 0.00 | 5.00 | 1000 | 800-480-4111 |
| Marshall Equity— Income | MREIX | 16.66 | — | 14.24 | 2.09 | 0.91 | 461 | 1.22 | 0.00 | 0.00 | 1000 | 800-236-8560 |
| Federated Equity— Income A | LEIFX | 16.85 | 13.48 | 14.59 | 2.03 | 0.91 | 753 | 1.09 | 5.50 | 0.00 | 1500 | 800-341-7400 |
| Putnam Equity Income A | PEYAX | 16.59 | 14.89 | 14.38 | 1.84 | 0.90 | 1059 | 1.06 | 5.75 | 0.00 | 500 | 800-225-1581 |
| Galaxy Equity Income Ret A | GAEIX | 16.05 | 13.80 | 13.71 | 1.36 | 0.90 | 188 | 1.39 | 3.75 | 0.00 | 2500 | 800-628-0414 |
| Franklin Equity Income I | FISEX | 14.20 | 11.54 | 11.44 | 3.40 | 0.89 | 434 | 0.97 | 5.75 | 0.00 | 1000 | 800-342-5236 |
| Amana Income | AMANX | 15.51 | 10.41 | 13.09 | 1.23 | 0.89 | 19 | 1.36 | 0.00 | 0.00 | 100 | 800-728-8762 |
| United Income A | UNCMX | 18.43 | 16.45 | 17.05 | 0.65 | 0.88 | 6405 | 0.84 | 5.75 | 0.00 | 500 | 800-366-5465 |
| Smith Barney Prem Tot Ret O | SPTCX | 14.52 | 12.25 | 11.97 | 3.41 | 0.88 | 121 | 1.56 | 0.00 | 1.00 | 1000 | 800-451-2010 |
| U.S. Global Inv Income | USINX | 14.12 | 7.91 | 11.82 | 1.55 | 0.86 | 11 | 2.19 | 0.00 | 0.00 | 5000 | 800-873-8637 |
| Invesco Industrial Income | FIIIX | 15.11 | 12.68 | 13.20 | 2.40 | 0.85 | 4326 | 0.95 | 0.00 | 0.00 | 1000 | 800-525-8085 |

Source: Morningstar, Inc.

**T A B L E  B-4**

REIT Funds

| Fund Name | Ticker | 3-Year Return | 5-Year Return | Standard Deviation | 12-Month Yield | Sharpe Ratio | Asset | Expense Ratio | Front Load | Back Load | Initial Purchase | Telephone No. |
|---|---|---|---|---|---|---|---|---|---|---|---|---|
| Columbia Real Estate Equity | CREEX | 16.58 | — | 15.39 | 5.03 | 0.84 | 159 | 1.02 | 0.00 | 0.00 | 1000 | 800-547-1707 |
| GrandView Realty Growth | GVRGX | 16.72 | — | 16.99 | 1.13 | 0.77 | 2 | 2.00 | 4.50 | 0.00 | 1000 | 800-525-3863 |
| Van Kampen Real Estate Sec A | ACREX | 13.54 | — | 14.72 | 3.03 | 0.64 | 51 | 1.77 | 4.75 | 0.00 | 500 | 800-421-5666 |
| Davis Real Estate A | RPFRX | 13.93 | — | 15.60 | 4.01 | 0.64 | 186 | 1.18 | 4.75 | 0.00 | 1000 | 800-279-0279 |
| UAM Heitman Real Estate Adv | HTREX | 13.12 | — | 14.62 | 3.34 | 0.61 | 67 | 1.73 | 4.75 | 0.00 | 5000 | 800-638-7983 |
| CGM Realty | CGMRX | 14.75 | — | 17.82 | 5.49 | 0.61 | 569 | 1.00 | 0.00 | 0.00 | 2500 | 800-345-4048 |
| Franklin Real Estate Sec I | FREEX | 11.35 | — | 13.73 | 3.00 | 0.51 | 355 | 1.00 | 5.75 | 0.00 | 1000 | 800-342-5236 |
| Munder Real Estate Eq Invt A | MURAX | 11.56 | — | 15.32 | 4.88 | 0.47 | 4 | 1.35 | 5.50 | 0.00 | 500 | 800-438-5789 |
| Cohen & Steers Realty Shares | CSRSX | 11.58 | 9.52 | 15.84 | 4.59 | 0.46 | 2499 | 1.05 | 0.00 | 0.00 | 10000 | 800-437-9912 |
| Fidelity Real Estate Invmnt | FRESX | 11.17 | 7.85 | 14.89 | 4.99 | 0.45 | 1632 | 0.90 | 0.00 | 0.00 | 2500 | 800-544-8888 |
| Crabbe Huson Real Est Prim | CHREX | 10.88 | — | 14.22 | 3.99 | 0.45 | 19 | 1.50 | 0.00 | 0.00 | 2000 | 800-541-9732 |
| Franklin Real Estate Sec II | FRRSX | 10.52 | — | 13.60 | 2.45 | 0.44 | 138 | 1.75 | 1.00 | 1.00 | 1000 | 800-342-5236 |
| Flag Inv Real Estate Secs A | FLREX | 10.64 | — | 15.93 | 4.83 | 0.39 | 38 | 1.25 | 4.50 | 0.00 | 2000 | 800-767-3524 |
| Phoenix Real Estate Secs A | PHRAX | 10.45 | — | 15.82 | 3.58 | 0.38 | 29 | 1.30 | 4.75 | 0.00 | 500 | 800-243-4361 |
| U.S. Global Inv Real Estate | UNREX | 9.34 | 4.57 | 14.44 | 4.36 | 0.32 | 11 | 1.80 | 0.00 | 0.00 | 5000 | 800-873-8637 |
| Phoenix Real Estate Secs B | PHRBX | 9.60 | — | 15.72 | 2.77 | 0.32 | 21 | 2.05 | 0.00 | 5.00 | 500 | 800-243-4361 |
| Pioneer Real Estate A | PWREX | 9.39 | — | 16.27 | 4.04 | 0.29 | 89 | 1.69 | 5.75 | 0.00 | 1000 | 800-225-6292 |
| AIM Adv Real Estate C | IARCX | 9.13 | — | 16.08 | 2.59 | 0.28 | 36 | 2.40 | 0.00 | 1.00 | 500 | 800-554-1156 |
| GrandView S&P REIT Index | GVRIX | 7.48 | — | 14.19 | 5.61 | 0.18 | 1 | 1.04 | 3.00 | 0.00 | 1000 | 800-525-3863 |
| Stratton Monthly Div REIT | STMDX | 6.12 | 1.75 | 10.58 | 7.87 | 0.09 | 92 | 1.02 | 0.00 | 0.00 | 2000 | 800-634-5726 |

Source: Morningstar, Inc.

## TABLE B–5

Money Market Funds

| Top-Performing Government Retail M | 7-Day Yield | 7-Day Compounded | Telephone No. |
|---|---|---|---|
| Lake Forest Money Market Fund | 5.49 | 5.64 | 800-295-5707 |
| Monetta Government MMF | 5.27 | 5.41 | 800-666-3882 |
| Vanguard MMR/Federal Port | 5.24 | 5.38 | 800-662-7447 |
| ABN AMRO Govt MMF/Common Cl | 5.23 | 5.37 | 800-443-4725 |
| John Hancock US Govt Cash Res | 5.22 | 5.36 | 800-225-5291 |
| USAA Treasury MM Trust | 5.21 | 5.35 | 800-382-8722 |
| US Govt Securities Savings Fund | 5.20 | 5.33 | 800-873-8637 |
| Zweig Ser Tr/Zweig Cash Fund/Cl M | 5.19 | 5.32 | 800-272-2700 |
| Fidelity US Govt Reserves | 5.18 | 5.31 | 800-544-8888 |
| SSgA US Govt MMF/Cl A | 5.18 | 5.31 | 800-647-7327 |
| Amer AAdvntge US Govt/Plan Ahead Cl | 5.17 | 5.30 | 800-388-3344 |
| Northern US Govt MMF | 5.16 | 5.29 | 800-595-9111 |
| Victory US Govt Oblig/Inv A | 5.15 | 5.28 | 800-362-5365 |
| Norwest US Government Fund | 5.15 | 5.28 | 800-363-3301 |
| Fidelity Spartan US Govt MMF | 5.14 | 5.27 | 800-544-8888 |
| JP Morgan Federal MMF | 5.14 | 5.27 | 800-847-9487 |
| Vanguard Admiral/US Treas MMP | 5.14 | 5.27 | 800-662-7447 |
| Zurich Government Money Fund | 5.13 | 5.26 | 800-523-4140 |
| Lindner Government MMF | 5.13 | 5.26 | 800-733-3769 |
| SouthTrust Treas Obligs MMF | 5.13 | 5.26 | 800-245-0242 |
| Dreyfus BASIC US Government MMF | 5.12 | 5.25 | 800-782-6620 |
| Nations Treasury Fund/Investor B | 5.12 | 5.25 | 800-321-7854 |
| Nations Treasury Fund/Investor C | 5.12 | 5.25 | 800-321-7854 |
| Pacific Hrzn Treas Fund/PacHrzn Shr | 5.10 | 5.23 | 800-332-3863 |
| Amer AAdvntge US Govt MM Mlge Fun | 5.09 | 5.22 | 800-388-3344 |

Source: IBC Financial Data, Inc.

**TABLE B-6**

Top-Performing Nongovernment Retail Money Funds

|  | 7-Day Yield | 7-Day Compound | Telephone No. |
|---|---|---|---|
| Strong Investors Money Fund | 5.64 | 5.80 | 800-368-3863 |
| Scudder Premium Money Market Shares | 5.48 | 5.63 | 800-854-8525 |
| OLDE Premium Plus MM Series | 5.45 | 5.60 | 800-872-6533 |
| Kiewit Mutual Fund/MMP | 5.42 | 5.57 | 800-254-3948 |
| Aon Funds/Money Market Fund | 5.39 | 5.53 | 800-266-3637 |
| Transamerica Premier Cash Res/Inv | 5.37 | 5.51 | 800-892-7587 |
| TIAA-CREF Money Market Fund | 5.34 | 5.48 | 800-223-1200 |
| Fremont Money Market Fund | 5.32 | 5.46 | 800-548-4539 |
| Marshall MMF/Class A | 5.32 | 5.46 | 800-236-3863 |
| MFS Money Market Fund | 5.32 | 5.46 | 800-225-2606 |
| Putnam Money Market Fund/Cl A | 5.32 | 5.46 | 800-225-1581 |
| ABN AMRO MMF/Common Cl | 5.32 | 5.46 | 800-443-4725 |
| Zurich YieldWise Money Fund | 5.31 | 5.45 | 800-523-4140 |
| Strong Heritage Money Fund | 5.31 | 5.45 | 800-368-3863 |
| Schwab Value Advantage MF | 5.27 | 5.41 | 800-435-4000 |
| SSgA Money Market Fund/Cl A | 5.27 | 5.41 | 800-647-7327 |
| Vanguard MMR/Prime Port/Retail | 5.27 | 5.41 | 800-662-7447 |
| USAA Money Market Fund | 5.25 | 5.39 | 800-382-8722 |
| Flex-fund Money Market Fund | 5.24 | 5.38 | 800-325-3539 |
| Dreyfus BASIC MMF | 5.23 | 5.37 | 800-782-6620 |
| McM Principal Preservation Fund | 5.23 | 5.37 | 800-788-9485 |
| Nicholas-Applegate MMP | 5.23 | 5.37 | 800-551-8045 |
| Norwest Cash Investment Fund | 5.23 | 5.37 | 800-363-3301 |
| Amer AAdvntge MMF/Plan Ahead Cl | 5.21 | 5.35 | 800-388-3344 |
| Fidelity Spartan MMF | 5.21 | 5.35 | 800-544-8888 |
| Preferred Money Market Fund | 5.21 | 5.35 | 800-2-GROW |
| T. Rowe Price Summit Cash Reserves | 5.21 | 5.35 | 800-638-5660 |

Source: IBC Financial Data, Inc.

## TABLE B-7

Top-Performing Tax-Free Retail Money Funds

|  | 7-Day Yield | 7-Day Compound | Telephone No. |
|---|---|---|---|
| Strong Municipal MMF | 3.31 | 3.36 | 800-368-3863 |
| ABN AMRO T-E MMF/Common CI | 3.30 | 3.35 | 800-443-4725 |
| USAA Tax Exempt MMF | 3.23 | 3.28 | 800-382-8722 |
| Benham Tax-Free MMF | 3.18 | 3.23 | 800-345-2021 |
| Zurich Tax-Free Money Fund | 3.18 | 3.23 | 800-523-4140 |
| Vanguard Muni Bond/MMP | 3.16 | 3.21 | 800-662-7447 |
| Vanguard OH Tax-Free/MMP | 3.15 | 3.20 | 800-662-7447 |
| Vanguard PA Tax-Free/MMP | 3.13 | 3.18 | 800-662-7447 |
| Eaton Vance Tax-Free Reserves | 3.12 | 3.17 | 800-225-6265 |
| Dreyfus BASIC Muni MM Portfolio | 3.10 | 3.15 | 800-782-6620 |
| Hough/The FL TaxFree MMF | 3.09 | 3.14 | 800-557-7555 |
| USAA Tax Exempt VA MMF | 3.09 | 3.14 | 800-382-8722 |
| T. Rowe Price Summit Muni MMF | 3.06 | 3.11 | 800-638-5660 |
| Vanguard NY Tax-Free MMP | 3.06 | 3.11 | 800-662-7447 |
| Janus T-E MMF/Retail Shrs | 3.05 | 3.10 | 800-525-3713 |
| ABN AMRO T-E MMF/Investor CI | 3.05 | 3.10 | 800-443-4725 |
| Fidelity Spartan Municipal MF | 3.01 | 3.05 | 800-544-8888 |
| USAA FL Tax-Free MMF | 3.01 | 3.05 | 800-382-8722 |
| USAA TX Tax-Free MMF | 3.01 | 3.05 | 800-382-8722 |
| Montgomery Federal T-F MMF/CI R | 3.00 | 3.04 | 800-572-3863 |
| Boston 1784 Tax Free MMF | 3.00 | 3.04 | 800-252-1784 |
| WPG Tax-Free MMF | 2.98 | 3.02 | 800-223-3332 |
| Calvert T-F Reserves/CA MMP | 2.96 | 3.00 | 800-368-2748 |
| SAFECO Tax-Free MMF | 2.95 | 2.99 | 800-426-6730 |
| Excelsior S-T T-E Money Fund | | | |

Source: IBC Financial Data, Inc.

**TABLE B-8**

Treasury and Government Short-Term Funds

| Fund Name | Ticker | 3-Year Return | 5-Year Return | Standard Deviation | 12-Month Yield | Sharpe Ratio | Asset | Expense Ratio | Front Load | Back Load | Initial Purchase | Telephone No. |
|---|---|---|---|---|---|---|---|---|---|---|---|---|
| Smith Breeden Sht Dur US Gov | SBSHX | 5.96 | 5.55 | 0.58 | 4.94 | 1.29 | 66 | 0.78 | 0.00 | 0.00 | 1000 | 800-221-3138 |
| Montgomery Sh Dur Govt Bd R | MNSGX | 7.03 | 6.28 | 1.64 | 5.68 | 1.23 | 100 | 0.60 | 0.00 | 0.00 | 1000 | 800-572-3863 |
| Oppenheimer Ltd-Term Govt A | OPGVX | 6.70 | 5.61 | 1.61 | 6.82 | 1.02 | 621 | 0.87 | 3.50 | 0.00 | 1000 | 800-525-7048 |
| Vanguard F/I Short-Trm Fed | VSGBX | 6.53 | 5.53 | 1.66 | 5.86 | 0.86 | 1541 | 0.27 | 0.00 | 0.00 | 3000 | 800-662-7447 |
| Vanguard F/I Short-Trm US Tr | VFISX | 6.49 | 5.63 | 1.79 | 5.51 | 0.78 | 1066 | 0.27 | 0.00 | 0.00 | 3000 | 800-662-7447 |
| T. Rowe Price Sh-Term U.S. | PRARX | 6.37 | 5.28 | 1.95 | 5.71 | 0.64 | 115 | 0.70 | 0.00 | 0.00 | 2500 | 800-638-5660 |
| AIM Ltd Mat Treasury Ret | SHTIX | 5.86 | 5.18 | 1.15 | 5.22 | 0.57 | 360 | 0.54 | 1.00 | 0.00 | 500 | 800-347-4246 |
| Payden & Rygel US Govt R | PYUSX | 6.71 | — | 3.00 | 5.06 | 0.55 | 75 | 0.45 | 0.00 | 0.00 | 5000 | 800-572-9336 |
| Asset Mgmt Short US Gov Secs | ASITX | 5.96 | 5.32 | 1.73 | 5.91 | 0.45 | 105 | 0.49 | 0.00 | 0.00 | 10000 | 800-527-3713 |
| Franklin Sh-Intrm Govt I | FRGVX | 5.89 | 4.69 | 1.55 | 5.53 | 0.44 | 190 | 0.78 | 2.25 | 0.00 | 1000 | 800-342-5236 |
| BT Investment Lim-Term U.S. | BTLGX | 5.80 | 5.04 | 1.34 | 4.95 | 0.43 | 55 | 0.60 | 0.00 | 0.00 | 2500 | 800-730-1313 |
| Excelsior Short-Term Govt | UMGVX | 5.79 | 5.15 | 1.34 | 5.23 | 0.42 | 45 | 0.62 | 0.00 | 0.00 | 500 | 800-446-1012 |

| Fund Name | Ticker | 3-Year Return | 5-Year Return | Standard Deviation | 12-Month Yield | Sharpe Ratio | Asset | Expense Ratio | Front Load | Back Load | Initial Purchase | Telephone No. |
|---|---|---|---|---|---|---|---|---|---|---|---|---|
| American Cent-Ben S/T Trs Iv | BSTAX | 5.76 | 5.02 | 1.34 | 5.15 | 0.40 | 48 | 0.61 | 0.00 | 0.00 | 2500 | 800-345-2021 |
| MSDW Short-Term US Treas | DWSHX | 5.91 | 4.74 | 1.91 | 5.35 | 0.37 | 244 | 0.83 | 0.00 | 0.00 | 10000 | 800-869-3863 |
| Wright U.S. Govt Near Term | WNTBX | 5.75 | 4.48 | 1.50 | 5.61 | 0.35 | 100 | 0.87 | 0.00 | 0.00 | 1000 | 800-888-9471 |
| GE Short-Term Government A | GGVAX | 5.67 | — | 1.31 | 5.28 | 0.33 | 9 | 0.95 | 2.50 | 0.00 | 500 | 800-242-0134 |
| Columbia U.S. Govt Secs | CUGGX | 5.78 | 4.92 | 1.79 | 4.72 | 0.31 | 39 | 0.87 | 0.00 | 0.00 | 1000 | 800-547-1707 |
| STI Classic Sh-Trm US TryInv | STSFX | 5.60 | 4.85 | 1.20 | 4.95 | 0.29 | 3 | 0.80 | 1.00 | 0.00 | 2000 | 800-428-6970 |
| CitiFunds Short-Tm U.S. Gov | CFSUX | 5.59 | 4.67 | 1.72 | 5.13 | 0.20 | 30 | 0.80 | 0.00 | 0.00 | 1000 | 800-721-1899 |
| Van Kampen Limited Mat Gov A | ACFMX | 5.49 | 4.75 | 1.48 | 5.40 | 0.15 | 31 | 1.32 | 3.25 | 0.00 | 500 | 800-421-5666 |
| Bernstein Govt Short Dur | SNGSX | 5.42 | 4.80 | 1.12 | 5.17 | 0.12 | 131 | 0.69 | 0.00 | 0.00 | 25000 | 212-756-4097 |
| Regions Limited Mat Govt Inv | FPLGX | 5.42 | — | 1.66 | 4.75 | 0.09 | 88 | 1.01 | 0.00 | 3.00 | 1000 | 800-433-2829 |
| Reynolds U.S. Govt Bond | RUSGX | 5.21 | 3.50 | 1.36 | 5.14 | −0.08 | 3 | 0.90 | 0.00 | 0.00 | 1000 | 800-773-9665 |
| Permanent Port Treasury Bill | PRTBX | 4.23 | 4.05 | 0.12 | 3.96 | −11.74 | 94 | 1.20 | 0.00 | 0.00 | 1000 | 800-531-5142 |

Source: Morningstar, Inc.

## TABLE B-9

Treasury and Government Intermediate-Term Funds

| Fund Name | Ticker | 3-Year Return | 5-Year Return | Standard Deviation | 12-Month Yield | Sharpe Ratio | Asset | Expense Ratio | Front Load | Back Load | Initial Purchase | Telephone No. |
|---|---|---|---|---|---|---|---|---|---|---|---|---|
| Colonial Sh Dur US Govt A | — | 6.46 | 5.49 | 1.14 | 5.89 | 1.19 | 7 | 0.50 | 3.25 | 0.00 | 1000 | 800-426-3750 |
| Sit U.S. Government Secs | SNGVX | 7.20 | 6.51 | 2.00 | 5.56 | 1.10 | 125 | 0.80 | 0.00 | 0.00 | 2000 | 800-332-5580 |
| Enterprise Government Secs A | ENGVX | 8.28 | 6.27 | 3.34 | 5.77 | 1.04 | 68 | 1.30 | 4.75 | 0.00 | 1000 | 800-432-4320 |
| Oppenheimer U.S. Govt A | OUSGX | 8.03 | 6.52 | 3.29 | 6.11 | 0.96 | 567 | 1.06 | 4.75 | 0.00 | 1000 | 800-525-7048 |
| Merrill Lynch Federal Secs A | MAFSX | 7.45 | — | 2.63 | 6.15 | 0.95 | 267 | 0.65 | 4.00 | 0.00 | 1000 | 800-637-3863 |
| State St Research Govt Inc A | SSGIX | 8.10 | 6.57 | 3.54 | 6.10 | 0.92 | 497 | 1.08 | 4.50 | 0.00 | 2500 | 800-882-0052 |
| AARP GNMA & U.S. Treasury | AGNMX | 7.04 | 5.66 | 2.22 | 6.67 | 0.91 | 4485 | 0.65 | 0.00 | 0.00 | 500 | 800-322-2282 |
| Fidelity Intermediate Govt | FSTGX | 7.15 | 6.02 | 2.50 | 6.59 | 0.86 | 701 | 0.54 | 0.00 | 0.00 | 10000 | 800-544-8888 |
| Nationwide Intm U.S. Govt D | NAUGX | 8.08 | 6.64 | 3.88 | 5.38 | 0.83 | 47 | 1.07 | 4.50 | 0.00 | 1000 | 800-848-0920 |
| Sentinel Short Mat Govt A | SSIGX | 6.42 | — | 1.65 | 5.80 | 0.79 | 63 | 1.00 | 1.00 | 0.00 | 1000 | 800-282-3863 |
| Putnam American Govt Inc A | PAGVX | 7.95 | 6.08 | 3.89 | 5.90 | 0.79 | 1436 | 0.97 | 4.75 | 0.00 | 500 | 800-225-1581 |
| Fidelity Spartan Govt Income | SPGVX | 7.94 | 6.22 | 3.85 | 5.85 | 0.79 | 430 | 0.60 | 0.00 | 0.00 | 25000 | 800-544-8888 |
| Tower U.S. Government Income | TWRGX | 7.25 | 5.86 | 2.93 | 5.76 | 0.77 | 84 | 0.88 | 3.00 | 0.00 | 1000 | — |
| Gradison Govt Income | GGIFX | 7.29 | 6.02 | 3.02 | 5.84 | 0.77 | 136 | 0.90 | 0.00 | 0.00 | 1000 | 800-869-5999 |

| Fund Name | Ticker | 3-Year Return | 5-Year Return | Standard Deviation | 12-Month Yield | Sharpe Ratio | Asset | Expense Ratio | Front Load | Back Load | Initial Purchase | Telephone No. |
|---|---|---|---|---|---|---|---|---|---|---|---|---|
| Galaxy II U.S. Treas Idx Ret | IUTIX | 7.99 | 6.27 | 4.11 | 5.84 | 0.76 | 146 | 0.40 | 0.00 | 0.00 | 2500 | 800-628-0414 |
| Hancock Interm Mat Govt A | TAUSX | 7.35 | 5.87 | 3.19 | 6.19 | 0.75 | 160 | 0.75 | 3.00 | 0.00 | 1000 | 800-225-5291 |
| American Cent-Ben Int Trs Iv | CPTNX | 7.55 | 5.94 | 3.54 | 5.27 | 0.74 | 400 | 0.51 | 0.00 | 0.00 | 2500 | 800-345-2021 |
| United Government Secs A | UNGVX | 7.77 | 6.08 | 3.91 | 5.91 | 0.73 | 131 | 0.89 | 4.25 | 0.00 | 500 | 800-366-5465 |
| Security Income U.S. Govt A | SIUSX | 7.93 | 5.82 | 4.26 | 6.03 | 0.72 | 11 | 1.10 | 4.75 | 0.00 | 100 | 800-888-2461 |
| Fortis U.S. Govt Secs A | FIUAX | 7.53 | — | 3.59 | 5.24 | 0.72 | 52 | 1.06 | 4.50 | 0.00 | 500 | 800-800-2638 |
| Colonial Int U.S. Govt A | CUSGX | 7.43 | 6.08 | 3.45 | 6.34 | 0.72 | 651 | 1.13 | 4.75 | 0.00 | 1000 | 800-426-3750 |
| Vanguard F/I Interm-Trm US | VFITX | 8.18 | 6.61 | 4.70 | 5.80 | 0.71 | 1746 | 0.27 | 0.00 | 0.00 | 3000 | 800-662-7447 |
| Heartland U.S. Govt Secs | HRUSX | 8.45 | 5.14 | 5.19 | 5.75 | 0.70 | 53 | 0.87 | 0.00 | 0.00 | 1000 | 800-432-7856 |
| Hancock Government Income A | JHGIX | 7.79 | — | 4.13 | 6.52 | 0.70 | 335 | 1.13 | 4.50 | 0.00 | 1000 | 800-225-5291 |
| AIM Intermediate Govt A | AGOVX | 7.46 | 5.84 | 3.56 | 6.58 | 0.70 | 196 | 1.00 | 4.75 | 0.00 | 500 | 800-347-4246 |
| Value Line U.S. Government | VALBX | 7.40 | 4.15 | 3.58 | 6.12 | 0.68 | 185 | 0.65 | 0.00 | 0.00 | 1000 | 800-223-0818 |
| U.S. Government Securities | AMUSX | 7.35 | 5.29 | 3.48 | 6.46 | 0.68 | 1133 | 0.80 | 4.75 | 0.00 | 1000 | 800-421-4120 |
| T. Rowe Price US Treas Intrm | PRTIX | 7.42 | 6.09 | 3.60 | 5.39 | 0.68 | 224 | 0.61 | 0.00 | 0.00 | 2500 | 800-638-5660 |
| Fidelity Government Secs | FGOVX | 7.59 | 5.73 | 3.98 | 5.60 | 0.67 | 1247 | 0.72 | 0.00 | 0.00 | 2500 | 800-544-8888 |
| Dreyfus US Treas Int Term | DRGIX | 6.96 | 5.37 | 3.65 | 6.82 | 0.53 | 186 | 0.80 | 0.00 | 0.00 | 2500 | 800-373-9387 |

Source: Morningstar, Inc.

**TABLE B-10**

Treasury and Government Long-Term Funds

| Fund Name | Ticker | 3-Year Return | 5-Year Return | Standard Deviation | 12-Month Yield | Sharpe Ratio | Asset | Expense Ratio | Front Load | Back Load | Initial Purchase | Telephone No. |
|---|---|---|---|---|---|---|---|---|---|---|---|---|
| PaineWebber Pace Govt Secs | PCGTX | 7.74 | — | 2.94 | 5.59 | 0.96 | 162 | — | 0.00 | 0.00 | 25000 | 800-647-1568 |
| Vanguard Admiral LngTm US Tr | VALGX | 11.17 | 8.41 | 8.50 | 5.68 | 0.80 | 433 | 0.15 | 0.00 | 0.00 | 50000 | 800-662-7447 |
| Pacific Advisors Govt Secs A | PADGX | 9.49 | 7.94 | 6.04 | 3.26 | 0.80 | 4 | 1.65 | 4.75 | 0.00 | 0 | 800-989-6693 |
| Vanguard F/I L/T U.S. Treas | VUSTX | 11.05 | 8.25 | 8.56 | 5.65 | 0.77 | 1260 | 0.27 | 0.00 | 0.00 | 3000 | 800-662-7447 |
| American Cent-Ben L/T Trs Iv | BLAGX | 10.97 | 7.46 | 8.58 | 5.33 | 0.76 | 137 | 0.60 | 0.00 | 0.00 | 2500 | 800-345-2021 |
| T. Rowe Price US Treas Lg-Tm | PRULX | 10.79 | 8.26 | 8.85 | 5.27 | 0.72 | 289 | 0.67 | 0.00 | 0.00 | 2500 | 800-638-5660 |
| Dreyfus US Treas Long-Term | DRGBX | 9.55 | 6.49 | 6.96 | 5.19 | 0.70 | 138 | 0.80 | 0.00 | 0.00 | 2500 | 800-373-9387 |
| New England Govt Secs A | NEFUX | 8.36 | 6.09 | 5.20 | 5.37 | 0.68 | 100 | 1.36 | 4.50 | 0.00 | 2500 | 800-225-7670 |
| Invesco U.S. Govt Securities | FBDGX | 8.88 | 6.30 | 6.12 | 4.96 | 0.68 | 74 | 1.01 | 0.00 | 0.00 | 1000 | 800-525-8085 |
| Flag Inv Tot Ret US Treas A | FLTSX | 8.93 | 6.91 | 6.21 | 6.02 | 0.68 | 120 | 0.83 | 4.50 | 0.00 | 2000 | 800-767-3524 |
| Federated US Govt Bond | FEDBX | 9.30 | 7.19 | 6.86 | 4.97 | 0.68 | 114 | 0.85 | 0.00 | 0.00 | 25000 | 800-341-7400 |
| Norwest Advant Interm Govt I | NVGIX | 7.34 | — | 3.53 | 6.04 | 0.67 | 415 | — | 0.00 | 0.00 | 1000 | 800-338-1348 |
| SunAmerica U.S. Govt Secs A | SGTAX | 7.06 | — | 3.20 | 5.09 | 0.64 | 96 | 1.63 | 4.75 | 0.00 | 500 | 800-858-8850 |
| Rushmore U.S. Govt Bond | RSGVX | 10.28 | 6.96 | 8.97 | 4.67 | 0.64 | 18 | 0.80 | 0.00 | 0.00 | 2500 | 800-343-3355 |
| Colonial Federal SecuritiesA | CFSAX | 8.09 | 6.21 | 5.07 | 6.44 | 0.64 | 818 | 1.19 | 4.75 | 0.00 | 1000 | 800-426-3750 |

| Fund Name | Ticker | 3-Year Return | 5-Year Return | Standard Deviation | 12-Month Yield | Sharpe Ratio | Asset | Expense Ratio | Front Load | Back Load | Initial Purchase | Telephone No. |
|---|---|---|---|---|---|---|---|---|---|---|---|---|
| Sentinel Government Secs | SEGSX | 7.43 | 5.97 | 4.01 | 5.92 | 0.62 | 75 | 0.98 | 4.00 | 0.00 | 1000 | 800-282-3863 |
| MFS Government Securities A | MFGSX | 7.41 | 6.20 | 4.08 | 6.10 | 0.60 | 288 | 0.94 | 4.75 | 0.00 | 1000 | 800-637-2929 |
| Phoenix U.S. Govt Secs A | PHGBX | 7.27 | 5.98 | 4.01 | 6.07 | 0.57 | 171 | 0.98 | 4.75 | 0.00 | 500 | 800-243-4361 |
| Star U.S. Govt Income A | STUGX | 7.32 | 5.59 | 4.27 | 5.51 | 0.55 | 138 | 0.92 | 3.50 | 0.00 | 1000 | 800-677-3863 |
| Nations Govt Secs Inv A | NGVAX | 7.08 | 5.25 | 3.93 | 5.18 | 0.53 | 22 | 1.10 | 0.00 | 0.00 | 1000 | 800-321-7854 |
| STI Classic US Govt Secs Inv | SCUSX | 7.03 | — | 4.00 | 5.36 | 0.50 | 3 | 1.15 | 3.75 | 0.00 | 2000 | 800-428-6970 |
| PaineWebber U.S. Govt Inc A | PUGAX | 7.05 | 3.98 | 4.10 | 5.82 | 0.49 | 276 | 0.94 | 4.00 | 0.00 | 1000 | 800-647-1568 |
| Nations Govt Secs Inv C | NGVSX | 6.65 | 4.77 | 3.91 | 4.59 | 0.40 | 0 | 1.58 | 0.00 | 0.50 | 1000 | 800-321-7854 |
| MFS Government Securities B | MFGBX | 6.67 | 5.34 | 4.05 | 5.43 | 0.39 | 123 | 1.59 | 0.00 | 4.00 | 1000 | 800-637-2929 |
| Nations Govt Secs Inv B | NGVTX | 6.58 | 4.77 | 3.91 | 4.59 | 0.38 | 32 | 1.63 | 0.00 | 4.00 | 1000 | 800-321-7854 |
| PaineWebber U.S. Govt Inc C | PWGDX | 6.54 | 3.50 | 4.16 | 5.43 | 0.35 | 25 | 1.44 | 0.00 | 0.75 | 1000 | 800-647-1568 |
| Phoenix U.S. Govt Secs B | PUSBX | 6.47 | — | 3.99 | 5.49 | 0.34 | 7 | 1.71 | 0.00 | 5.00 | 500 | 800-243-4361 |
| Stagecoach US Govt Inc A | OEGIX | 6.44 | 5.23 | 4.05 | 5.51 | 0.33 | 189 | 0.88 | 4.50 | 0.00 | 1000 | 800-776-0179 |
| Rydex U.S. Government Bond | RYGBX | 8.81 | — | 12.19 | 0.33 | 0.33 | 42 | 1.49 | 0.00 | 0.00 | 25000 | 800-820-0888 |
| PaineWebber U.S. Govt Inc B | PUGBX | 6.25 | 3.22 | 4.10 | 5.04 | 0.27 | 26 | 1.69 | 0.00 | 5.00 | 1000 | 800-647-1568 |

Source: Morningstar, Inc.

## TABLE B-11

General Mortgage Funds

| Fund Name | Ticker | 3-Year Return | 5-Year Return | Standard Deviation | 12-Month Yield | Sharpe Ratio | Asset | Expense Ratio | Front Load | Back Load | Initial Purchase | Telephone No. |
|---|---|---|---|---|---|---|---|---|---|---|---|---|
| Cardinal Government Oblg Inv | CGOGX | 7.61 | 6.51 | 2.03 | 6.89 | 1.32 | 109 | 1.01 | 4.50 | 0.00 | 1000 | 800-848-7734 |
| Franklin Strategic Mortgage | FSMIX | 7.91 | 6.78 | 2.43 | 6.60 | 1.25 | 13 | 0.00 | 4.25 | 0.00 | 1000 | 800-342-5236 |
| Parkstone Govt Income Inv A | PKGAX | 7.32 | 6.19 | 2.09 | 6.24 | 1.13 | 49 | 1.00 | 4.00 | 0.00 | 1000 | 800-451-8377 |
| IDS Federal Income A | IFINX | 7.47 | 6.15 | 2.25 | 5.74 | 1.12 | 1429 | 0.90 | 5.00 | 0.00 | 2000 | 800-328-8300 |
| Franklin U.S. Govt Secs I | FKUSX | 7.73 | 6.53 | 2.60 | 6.63 | 1.09 | 8920 | 0.64 | 4.25 | 0.00 | 1000 | 800-342-5236 |
| Victory Fund for Income | IPFIX | 7.33 | 6.21 | 2.17 | 6.17 | 1.08 | 29 | 0.99 | 2.00 | 0.00 | 500 | 800-539-3863 |
| Smith Breeden Interm Dur Gov | SBIDX | 7.49 | 6.46 | 2.42 | 5.34 | 1.05 | 48 | 0.88 | 0.00 | 0.00 | 1000 | 800-221-3138 |
| SunAmerica Federal Secs A | SFSAX | 8.50 | — | 3.60 | 4.84 | 1.03 | 32 | 1.47 | 4.75 | 0.00 | 500 | 800-858-8850 |
| Accessor Mortgage Securities | AMSFX | 7.82 | 6.71 | 2.91 | 5.61 | 1.01 | 136 | 0.84 | 0.00 | 0.00 | 5000 | 800-759-3504 |
| Advantus Mortgage Secs Inc A | ADMSX | 7.94 | 6.33 | 3.15 | 6.34 | 0.97 | 31 | 1.26 | 5.00 | 0.00 | 250 | 800-665-6005 |
| Federated Income Instl | FICMX | 7.43 | 6.26 | 2.69 | 6.16 | 0.92 | 712 | 0.58 | 0.00 | 0.00 | 25000 | 800-341-7400 |
| Alliance Mortgage Secs Inc A | ALMSX | 7.33 | 5.31 | 2.58 | 6.58 | 0.92 | 411 | 1.41 | 4.25 | 0.00 | 250 | 800-227-4618 |
| Victory Government Mortgage | SIGOX | 7.31 | 6.10 | 2.63 | 5.79 | 0.89 | 103 | 0.85 | 5.75 | 0.00 | 500 | 800-539-3863 |
| Putnam Interm U.S. Govt IncA | PBLGX | 7.33 | 6.02 | 2.78 | 5.65 | 0.85 | 142 | 1.15 | 3.25 | 0.00 | 500 | 800-225-1581 |

| Fund Name | Ticker | 3-Year Return | 5-Year Return | Standard Deviation | 12-Month Yield | Sharpe Ratio | Asset | Expense Ratio | Front Load | Back Load | Initial Purchase | Telephone No. |
|---|---|---|---|---|---|---|---|---|---|---|---|---|
| Putnam U.S. Govt Income A | PGSIX | 7.44 | 6.12 | 3.03 | 6.31 | 0.82 | 2048 | 0.89 | 4.75 | 0.00 | 500 | 800-225-1581 |
| Franklin U.S. Govt Secs II | FRUGX | 7.16 | — | 2.64 | 6.11 | 0.82 | 199 | 1.20 | 1.00 | 0.99 | 1000 | 800-342-5236 |
| Pacific Horizon U.S. Govt A | PHGVX | 7.14 | 5.30 | 2.68 | 6.46 | 0.80 | 69 | 0.75 | 5.50 | 0.00 | 500 | 800-332-3863 |
| Kemper U.S. Govt Secs A | KUSAX | 7.47 | 6.27 | 3.20 | 6.81 | 0.79 | 3285 | 0.78 | 4.50 | 0.00 | 1000 | 800-621-1048 |
| Atlas U.S. Govt & Mortgage A | ASGMX | 6.96 | 5.75 | 2.45 | 6.37 | 0.79 | 200 | 1.03 | 0.00 | 0.00 | 2500 | 800-933-2852 |
| Federated Fund for US Govt A | FUSGX | 7.13 | 5.83 | 2.76 | 6.27 | 0.77 | 1094 | 0.94 | 4.50 | 0.00 | 1500 | 800-341-7400 |
| Asset Mgmt US Govt Mort Secs | ASMTX | 7.60 | 6.26 | 3.46 | 6.92 | 0.77 | 80 | 0.53 | 0.00 | 0.00 | 10000 | 800-527-3713 |
| Principal Govt Secs Income A | PRGVX | 7.98 | 6.41 | 4.09 | 6.01 | 0.76 | 248 | 0.84 | 4.75 | 0.00 | 1000 | 800-451-5447 |
| Wright Current Income Stnd | WCIFX | 7.24 | 6.15 | 3.00 | 6.09 | 0.75 | 86 | 0.89 | 0.00 | 0.00 | 1000 | 800-888-9471 |
| Marshall Government Income | MRGIX | 7.40 | 6.06 | 3.28 | 6.31 | 0.74 | 280 | 0.86 | 0.00 | 0.00 | 1000 | 800-236-8560 |
| Van Kampen US Govt A | VKMGX | 7.15 | 5.63 | 3.00 | 6.86 | 0.71 | 2155 | 0.90 | 4.75 | 0.00 | 500 | 800-421-5666 |
| Kemper U.S. Mortgage A | KUMAX | 7.31 | 6.01 | 3.32 | 6.68 | 0.70 | 1791 | 0.96 | 4.50 | 0.00 | 1000 | 800-621-1048 |
| Smith Barney U.S. Govt SecsA | SBCGX | 7.41 | 6.49 | 3.87 | 6.27 | 0.63 | 262 | 0.80 | 4.50 | 0.00 | 1000 | 800-451-2010 |
| MFS Government Mortgage A | MGMTX | 6.81 | 5.84 | 2.87 | 6.40 | 0.61 | 655 | 1.09 | 4.75 | 0.00 | 1000 | 800-637-2929 |
| Asset Mgmt Interm Mort Secs | ASCPX | 6.78 | 5.60 | 2.79 | 6.63 | 0.61 | 94 | 0.49 | 0.00 | 0.00 | 10000 | 800-527-3713 |
| North American U.S. Govt A | NAGVX | 6.74 | 5.91 | 2.92 | 5.74 | 0.57 | 49 | 1.25 | 4.75 | 0.00 | 1000 | 800-872-8037 |

Source: Morningstar, Inc.

**T A B L E  B-12**

Bond Index Funds

| Fund Name | Ticker | 3-Year Return | 5-Year Return | Standard Deviation | 12-Month Yield | Sharpe Ratio | Asset | Expense Ratio | Front Load | Back Load | Initial Purchase | Telephone No. |
|---|---|---|---|---|---|---|---|---|---|---|---|---|
| Vanguard Bond Idx Total | VBMFX | 8.25 | 6.77 | 3.71 | 6.16 | 0.92 | 6619 | 0.20 | 0.00 | 0.00 | 3000 | 800-662-7447 |
| Vanguard Bond Idx Short-Term | VBISX | 6.82 | — | 1.96 | 5.80 | 0.90 | 625 | 0.20 | 0.00 | 0.00 | 3000 | 800-662-7447 |
| Vanguard Bond Idx Long-Term | VBLTX | 10.89 | — | 8.19 | 5.93 | 0.79 | 162 | 0.20 | 0.00 | 0.00 | 3000 | 800-662-7447 |
| Vanguard Bond Idx Intrm-Term | VBIIX | 8.36 | — | 4.61 | 6.21 | 0.77 | 959 | 0.20 | 0.00 | 0.00 | 3000 | 800-662-7447 |
| Galaxy II U.S. Treas Idx Ret | IUTIX | 7.99 | 6.27 | 4.11 | 5.84 | 0.76 | 146 | 0.40 | 0.00 | 0.00 | 2500 | 800-628-0414 |
| Firstar Short-Term Bond Ret | FRSBX | 6.06 | — | 1.26 | 5.79 | 0.70 | 70 | 0.75 | 2.00 | 0.00 | 1000 | 800-228-1024 |
| Schwab Short-Term Bd Mkt Idx | SWBDX | 6.33 | 4.73 | 1.87 | 5.73 | 0.64 | 153 | 0.49 | 0.00 | 0.00 | 1000 | 800-435-4000 |
| Schwab Total Bond Market Idx | SWLBX | 8.03 | 6.05 | 5.37 | 5.92 | 0.59 | 275 | 0.20 | 0.00 | 0.00 | 1000 | 800-435-4000 |

Source: Morningstar, Inc.

**TABLE B-13**

Convertible Securities Bond Funds

| Fund Name | Ticker | 3-Year Return | 5-Year Return | Standard Deviation | 12-Month Yield | Sharpe Ratio | Asset | Expense Ratio | Front Load | Back Load | Initial Purchase | Telephone No. |
|---|---|---|---|---|---|---|---|---|---|---|---|---|
| Calamos Convertible A | CCVIX | 14.52 | 11.77 | 11.57 | 3.40 | 0.91 | 68 | 1.50 | 4.75 | 0.00 | 500 | 800-823-7386 |
| Davis Convertible Secs A | RPFCX | 14.96 | 11.84 | 12.85 | 3.19 | 0.86 | 128 | 1.07 | 4.75 | 0.00 | 1000 | 800-279-0279 |
| Victory Convertible Secs | SBFCX | 10.86 | 8.93 | 10.04 | 4.15 | 0.64 | 107 | 1.34 | 5.75 | 0.00 | 500 | 800-539-3863 |
| Nicholas-Apple Convertible A | NIGAX | 13.41 | 10.57 | 14.76 | 2.33 | 0.63 | 51 | 1.60 | 5.25 | 0.00 | 2000 | 800-551-8043 |
| Value Line Convertible | VALCX | 11.07 | 8.85 | 11.13 | 4.99 | 0.60 | 74 | 0.98 | 0.00 | 0.00 | 1000 | 800-223-0818 |
| Putnam Convert Income-Grth A | PCONX | 10.95 | 10.21 | 12.04 | 4.53 | 0.54 | 1153 | 1.03 | 5.75 | 0.00 | 500 | 800-225-1581 |
| Oppenheimer Convertible SecA | RCVAX | 8.83 | — | 9.71 | 5.48 | 0.42 | 212 | 0.95 | 5.75 | 1.00 | 1000 | 800-525-7048 |
| Smith Barney Convertible A | SCRAX | 8.02 | 7.08 | 8.94 | 4.58 | 0.35 | 37 | 1.27 | 5.00 | 0.00 | 1000 | 800-451-2010 |
| Fidelity Convertible Secs | FCVSX | 9.72 | 9.19 | 15.44 | 3.13 | 0.33 | 914 | 0.73 | 0.00 | 0.00 | 2500 | 800-544-8888 |
| MSDW Convertible B | CNSBX | 7.97 | 8.56 | 10.59 | 4.39 | 0.29 | 319 | 1.84 | 0.00 | 5.00 | 1000 | 800-869-3863 |
| Phoenix Convertible A | PHCVX | 7.34 | 6.85 | 9.72 | 3.23 | 0.24 | 179 | 1.12 | 4.75 | 0.00 | 500 | 800-243-4361 |
| Franklin Convertible Secs I | FISCX | 7.45 | 8.73 | 11.56 | 5.16 | 0.22 | 207 | 1.01 | 5.75 | 0.00 | 1000 | 800-342-5236 |
| Van Kampen Harbor A | ACHBX | 7.18 | 6.44 | 13.53 | 4.90 | 0.16 | 388 | 1.04 | 5.75 | 0.00 | 500 | 800-421-5666 |
| Merrill Lynch Convertible A | MACFX | 6.87 | 5.66 | 11.78 | 2.44 | 0.15 | 68 | — | 5.25 | 0.00 | 1000 | 609-282-2800 |
| Vanguard Convertible Secs | VCVSX | 6.71 | 6.68 | 13.06 | 4.70 | 0.13 | 189 | 0.67 | 0.00 | 0.00 | 3000 | 800-662-7447 |
| Lexington Convertible Secs | CNCVX | 2.46 | 5.03 | 14.53 | 0.61 | -0.23 | 11 | 2.38 | 0.00 | 0.00 | 1000 | 800-526-0056 |
| Gabelli Glob Convert Secs | GAGCX | 2.65 | — | 11.28 | 1.34 | -0.27 | 7 | 2.48 | 0.00 | 0.00 | 1000 | 800-422-3554 |

Source: Morningstar, Inc.

**TABLE B-14**

Adjustable Rate Mortgage Funds

| Fund Name | Ticker | 3-Year Return | 5-Year Return | Standard Deviation | 12-Month Yield | Sharpe Ratio | Asset | Expense Ratio | Front Load | Back Load | Initial Purchase | Telephone No. |
|---|---|---|---|---|---|---|---|---|---|---|---|---|
| Asset Mgmt Adjustable Rate | ASARX | 6.19 | 5.55 | 0.51 | 5.84 | 2.07 | 877 | 0.50 | 0.00 | 0.00 | 10000 | 800-527-3713 |
| Evergreen Cap Pres & IncomeA | EKPAX | 6.22 | — | 0.55 | 5.68 | 1.95 | 17 | 0.90 | 3.25 | 0.00 | 1000 | 800-343-2898 |
| Franklin Adj Rate Secs | FIARX | 6.44 | 5.15 | 0.91 | 5.53 | 1.46 | 23 | 0.81 | 2.25 | 0.00 | 1000 | 800-342-5236 |
| One Group Ultra Sh-Term A | ONUAX | 6.08 | 5.02 | 0.62 | 5.53 | 1.45 | 22 | 0.70 | 3.00 | 0.00 | 1000 | 800-480-4111 |
| Goldman Sachs Adj Rt Gov A | GSAMX | 5.91 | — | 0.53 | 5.68 | 1.35 | 56 | 0.74 | 1.50 | 0.00 | 1000 | 800-526-7384 |
| Franklin Adj U.S. Govt Secs | FISAX | 6.23 | 4.39 | 1.01 | 5.67 | 1.07 | 304 | 0.75 | 2.25 | 0.00 | 1000 | 800-342-5236 |
| New England Adj Rate US GovA | NEFAX | 5.83 | 4.99 | 0.87 | 5.71 | 0.69 | 161 | 0.70 | 1.00 | 0.00 | 2500 | 800-225-7670 |
| Countrywide Adj Rt U.S. Govt | CARAX | 5.57 | 4.79 | 0.73 | 5.47 | 0.43 | 11 | 0.75 | 2.00 | 0.00 | 1000 | 800-543-8721 |
| Federated Adj Rate US Govt F | FADJX | 5.55 | 4.58 | 0.70 | 5.31 | 0.42 | 154 | 1.10 | 0.00 | 1.00 | 1500 | 800-341-7400 |

| Fund Name | Ticker | 3-Year Return | 5-Year Return | Standard Deviation | 12-Month Yield | Sharpe Ratio | Asset | Expense Ratio | Front Load | Back Load | Initial Purchase | Telephone No. |
|---|---|---|---|---|---|---|---|---|---|---|---|---|
| Smith Barney Adj Rate Govt A | ARMGX | 5.72 | 5.00 | 1.26 | 5.25 | 0.39 | 121 | 1.58 | 0.00 | 0.00 | 1000 | 800-451-2010 |
| Merrill Lynch Adj Rate Sec B | MBAJX | 5.44 | 4.51 | 0.68 | 5.07 | 0.24 | 81 | 1.65 | 0.00 | 4.00 | 1000 | 800-637-3863 |
| Van Kampen Limited Mat Gov A | ACFMX | 5.49 | 4.75 | 1.48 | 5.40 | 0.15 | 31 | 1.32 | 3.25 | 0.00 | 500 | 800-421-5666 |
| Kemper Adj Rate U.S. Govt A | KADAX | 4.98 | 4.20 | 0.89 | 5.12 | -0.42 | 61 | 1.25 | 3.50 | 0.00 | 1000 | 800-621-1048 |
| Van Kampen Limited Mat Gov C | ACFWX | 4.75 | 3.98 | 1.49 | 4.60 | -0.43 | 3 | 2.10 | 0.00 | 1.00 | 500 | 800-421-5666 |
| Stagecoach Var Rate Govt A | OEVGX | 4.96 | 3.36 | 0.87 | 5.20 | -0.46 | 162 | 0.81 | 3.00 | 0.00 | 1000 | 800-222-8222 |
| First American Adj Rte Mrt A | FJARX | 3.40 | 2.56 | 4.80 | 5.60 | -0.46 | 146 | 0.81 | 2.00 | 0.00 | 250 | 800-637-2548 |

Source: Morningstar, Inc.

## TABLE B-15

Corporate Short-Term Funds

| Fund Name | Ticker | 3-Year Return | 5-Year Return | Standard Deviation | 12-Month Yield | Sharpe Ratio | Asset | Expense Ratio | Front Load | Back Load | Initial Purchase | Telephone No. |
|---|---|---|---|---|---|---|---|---|---|---|---|---|
| Hotchkis & Wiley Sh-Tm Invmt | HWSTX | 6.45 | 6.42 | 0.51 | 6.22 | 2.60 | 30 | 0.48 | 0.00 | 0.00 | 10000 | 800-346-7301 |
| Strong Advantage | STADX | 6.32 | 6.07 | 0.61 | 6.09 | 1.96 | 2623 | 0.80 | 0.00 | 0.00 | 2500 | 800-368-1030 |
| First American Ltd-Trm Inc A | FALTX | 6.06 | 5.40 | 0.56 | 5.34 | 1.56 | 5 | 0.60 | 2.00 | 0.00 | 1000 | 800-637-2548 |
| Strong Short-Term Bond | SSTBX | 7.05 | 5.85 | 1.47 | 6.78 | 1.39 | 1366 | 0.90 | 0.00 | 0.00 | 2500 | 800-368-1030 |
| American Perform Sh-Term Inc | APSTX | 6.98 | — | 1.78 | 6.12 | 1.10 | 32 | 0.33 | 2.00 | 0.00 | 1000 | 800-762-7085 |
| USAA Short-Term Bond | USSBX | 6.88 | 6.00 | 1.81 | 6.16 | 1.01 | 177 | 0.50 | 0.00 | 0.00 | 3000 | 800-382-8722 |
| Janus Short-Term Bond | JASBX | 6.80 | 5.22 | 1.76 | 6.09 | 0.99 | 92 | 0.65 | 0.00 | 0.00 | 2500 | 800-525-8983 |
| Homestead Short-Term Bond | HOSBX | 6.33 | 5.56 | 1.24 | 5.61 | 0.97 | 129 | 0.75 | 0.00 | 0.00 | 500 | 800-258-3030 |
| Vanguard F/I Short-Tm Corp | VFSTX | 6.71 | 5.99 | 1.74 | 6.12 | 0.94 | 5205 | 0.28 | 0.00 | 0.00 | 3000 | 800-662-7447 |
| Vanguard Bond Idx Short-Term | VBISX | 6.82 | — | 1.96 | 5.80 | 0.90 | 625 | 0.20 | 0.00 | 0.00 | 3000 | 800-662-7447 |
| Marshall Short-Term Income | MSINX | 6.11 | 5.35 | 1.15 | 6.37 | 0.82 | 133 | 0.49 | 0.00 | 0.00 | 1000 | 800-236-8560 |
| Firstar Short-Term Bond Ret | FRSBX | 6.06 | — | 1.26 | 5.79 | 0.70 | 70 | 0.75 | 2.00 | 0.00 | 1000 | 800-228-1024 |
| Fidelity Short-Term Bond | FSHBX | 6.03 | 4.51 | 1.25 | 6.04 | 0.68 | 803 | 0.70 | 0.00 | 0.00 | 2500 | 800-544-8888 |
| Federated Ltd Term A | LTDFX | 6.32 | 5.33 | 1.75 | 5.97 | 0.68 | 109 | 1.10 | 1.00 | 0.00 | 500 | 800-341-7400 |
| Parnassus Income Fixed-Inc | PRFIX | 7.95 | 6.31 | 4.65 | 4.79 | 0.66 | 10 | 0.82 | 0.00 | 0.00 | 2000 | — |

| Fund Name | Ticker | 3-Year Return | 5-Year Return | Standard Deviation | 12-Month Yield | Sharpe Ratio | Asset | Expense Ratio | Front Load | Back Load | Initial Purchase | Telephone No. |
|---|---|---|---|---|---|---|---|---|---|---|---|---|
| Boston 1784 Short-Term Inc | SESTX | 6.27 | — | 1.84 | 5.55 | 0.61 | 185 | 0.64 | 0.00 | 0.00 | 1000 | 800-252-1784 |
| Fidelity Adv Sh Fix-Inc T | FASFX | 5.94 | 4.63 | 1.29 | 5.90 | 0.58 | 315 | 0.89 | 1.50 | 0.00 | 2500 | 800-522-7297 |
| AmSouth Limited Mat Classic | AOLMX | 6.28 | 5.24 | 2.10 | 5.61 | 0.54 | 4 | 0.77 | 3.00 | 0.00 | 1000 | 800-451-8379 |
| Managers Short & Interm Bond | MGSIX | 6.11 | 4.22 | 1.90 | 5.42 | 0.50 | 18 | 1.40 | 0.00 | 0.00 | 2000 | 800-835-3879 |
| Stagecoach Sh-Term Govt Corp | OSTGX | 5.64 | — | 0.85 | 5.70 | 0.47 | 11 | 0.39 | 3.00 | 0.00 | 1000 | 800-222-8222 |
| Pioneer Short-Term Income A | PSTTX | 5.83 | 5.19 | 1.34 | 6.01 | 0.46 | 45 | 0.85 | 2.50 | 0.00 | 5000 | 800-225-6292 |
| Bernstein Short Dur Plus | SNSDX | 5.74 | 5.00 | 1.11 | 5.82 | 0.46 | 581 | 0.65 | 0.00 | 0.00 | 25000 | 212-756-4097 |
| WM Sh-Tm Hi-Qual A | SRHQX | 5.97 | — | 1.72 | 5.63 | 0.45 | 34 | 0.82 | 3.50 | 0.00 | 250 | 800-543-8072 |
| T. Rowe Price Sh-Term Bond | PRWBX | 5.91 | 4.32 | 1.63 | 5.70 | 0.44 | 321 | 0.72 | 0.00 | 0.00 | 2500 | 800-638-5660 |
| Diversified Inv High-Quality | DVHQX | 5.82 | — | 1.42 | 2.77 | 0.42 | 212 | 0.98 | 0.00 | 0.00 | 5000 | 914-697-8779 |
| Accessor Short-Interm F/I | ASIFX | 5.89 | 4.90 | 1.95 | 5.12 | 0.35 | 47 | 0.86 | 0.00 | 0.00 | 5000 | 800-759-3504 |
| DG Limited-Term Govt Income | DGLTX | 5.57 | 4.87 | 1.23 | 5.19 | 0.26 | 30 | 0.68 | 2.00 | 0.00 | 1000 | 800-748-8500 |
| State Farm Interim | SFITX | 5.95 | 5.20 | 3.32 | 5.76 | 0.23 | 120 | 0.22 | 0.00 | 0.00 | 50 | 309-766-2311 |
| Vintage Limited Term Bond | AFTRX | 5.62 | — | 2.90 | 5.33 | 0.13 | 52 | 1.40 | 0.00 | 0.00 | 1000 | 800-438-6375 |
| Franklin Invmnt Grad Inc I | FIGPX | 5.26 | 4.47 | 1.58 | 4.73 | -0.03 | 53 | 1.05 | 4.25 | 0.00 | 1000 | 800-342-5236 |

Source: Morningstar, Inc.

## TABLE B-16

Corporate Intermediate-Term Funds

| Fund Name | Ticker | 3-Year Return | 5-Year Return | Standard Deviation | 12-Month Yield | Sharpe Ratio | Asset | Expense Ratio | Front Load | Back Load | Initial Purchase | Telephone No. |
|---|---|---|---|---|---|---|---|---|---|---|---|---|
| Hotchkis & Wiley Low Dur | HWLDX | 7.60 | 7.88 | 1.35 | 6.43 | 1.98 | 277 | 0.00 | 0.58 | 0.00 | 10000 | 800-346-7301 |
| SSgA Yield Plus | SSYPX | 5.60 | 5.29 | 0.23 | 5.68 | 1.54 | 674 | 0.00 | 0.38 | 0.00 | 1000 | 800-647-7327 |
| Warburg Pincus FixedInc Comm | CUFIX | 8.14 | 7.03 | 2.89 | 5.71 | 1.14 | 406 | 0.00 | 0.75 | 0.00 | 2500 | 800-927-2874 |
| Pegasus Bond A | PGBOX | 9.12 | 6.93 | 3.91 | 5.78 | 1.13 | 240 | 4.50 | 0.86 | 0.00 | 1000 | 800-688-3350 |
| Invesco Select Income | FBDSX | 9.04 | 8.23 | 4.05 | 6.30 | 1.07 | 515 | 0.00 | 1.03 | 0.00 | 1000 | 800-525-8085 |
| Fremont Bond | FBDFX | 9.28 | 7.38 | 4.48 | 5.94 | 1.03 | 176 | 0.00 | 0.61 | 0.00 | 2000 | 800-548-4539 |
| Harbor Short Duration | HASDX | 6.32 | 5.62 | 1.23 | 6.31 | 0.96 | 197 | 0.00 | 0.36 | 0.00 | 2000 | 800-422-1050 |
| Oppenheimer Bond A | OPIGX | 8.01 | 6.20 | 3.41 | 6.70 | 0.92 | 232 | 4.75 | 1.26 | 0.00 | 1000 | 800-525-7048 |
| First American Int-Tm Inc A | FAIIX | 7.18 | 6.00 | 2.55 | 5.20 | 0.85 | 50 | 3.75 | 0.70 | 0.00 | 1000 | 800-637-2548 |
| Columbia Fixed-Income Secs | CFISX | 8.04 | 6.50 | 3.75 | 6.20 | 0.85 | 416 | 0.00 | 0.66 | 0.00 | 1000 | 800-547-1707 |
| Chicago Trust Bond | CHTBX | 7.84 | — | 3.46 | 5.94 | 0.85 | 132 | 0.00 | 0.80 | 0.00 | 2500 | 800-992-8151 |
| Bond Fund of America | ABNDX | 7.77 | 6.25 | 3.41 | 7.18 | 0.84 | 9180 | 4.75 | 0.68 | 0.00 | 1000 | 800-421-4120 |
| Babson Bond S | BBDSX | 7.04 | 5.77 | 2.43 | 5.98 | 0.83 | 38 | 0.00 | 0.67 | 0.00 | 500 | 800-422-2766 |
| Calvert Income A | CFICX | 8.26 | 6.11 | 4.20 | 5.65 | 0.82 | 40 | 3.75 | 1.07 | 0.00 | 2000 | 800-368-2748 |
| Fidelity Spartan Invmt Gr Bd | FSIBX | 7.75 | 5.89 | 3.57 | 6.07 | 0.80 | 998 | 0.00 | 0.48 | 0.00 | 10000 | 800-544-8888 |

| Fund Name | Ticker | 3-Year Return | 5-Year Return | Standard Deviation | 12-Month Yield | Sharpe Ratio | Asset | Expense Ratio | Front Load | Back Load | Initial Purchase | Telephone No. |
|---|---|---|---|---|---|---|---|---|---|---|---|---|
| McM Intermediate Fixed-Inc | MCMNX | 7.28 | — | 2.91 | 5.64 | 0.79 | 122 | 0.00 | 0.50 | 0.00 | 5000 | 800-788-9485 |
| First American Fixed-Inc A | FAFIX | 7.84 | 6.40 | 3.90 | 4.99 | 0.76 | 409 | 3.75 | 0.95 | 0.00 | 1000 | 800-637-2548 |
| Stein Roe Intermediate Bond | SRBFX | 7.61 | 6.34 | 3.58 | 6.60 | 0.75 | 424 | 0.00 | 0.73 | 0.00 | 2500 | 800-338-2550 |
| Intermediate Bond Fd America | AIBAX | 6.70 | 5.26 | 2.17 | 6.34 | 0.75 | 1412 | 4.75 | 0.82 | 0.00 | 1000 | 800-421-4120 |
| Armada Enhanced Income Ret | AINRX | 6.10 | — | 1.25 | 5.48 | 0.74 | 1 | 2.75 | 0.31 | 0.00 | 500 | 800-622-3863 |
| American Cent-Ben Ltd Bd Inv | ABLIX | 6.22 | — | 1.44 | 5.50 | 0.74 | 19 | 0.00 | 0.69 | 0.00 | 2500 | 800-345-2021 |
| William Blair Income | WBRRX | 6.85 | 6.01 | 2.46 | 6.23 | 0.73 | 181 | 0.00 | 0.71 | 0.00 | 5000 | 800-742-7272 |
| Legg Mason Investment Gr Pr | LMIGX | 7.82 | 6.30 | 4.03 | 5.94 | 0.73 | 148 | 0.00 | 0.88 | 0.00 | 1000 | 800-577-8589 |
| Government Street Bond | GVSBX | 7.02 | 5.77 | 2.78 | 6.20 | 0.72 | 38 | 0.00 | 0.75 | 0.00 | 5000 | 800-443-4249 |
| Federated Intrm Inc InstlSvc | INISX | 7.76 | — | 3.93 | 5.77 | 0.72 | 7 | 0.00 | 0.80 | 0.00 | 25000 | 800-341-7400 |
| Thornburg Ltd-Term Inc A | THIFX | 6.81 | 5.80 | 2.47 | 5.87 | 0.71 | 34 | 2.50 | 1.00 | 0.00 | 5000 | 800-847-0200 |
| SG Cowen Interm Fixed-Inc A | CFIAX | 7.07 | 5.82 | 2.90 | 5.05 | 0.71 | 9 | 2.35 | 0.65 | 0.00 | 1000 | 800-262-7116 |
| Fidelity Invmnt Grade Bond | FBNDX | 7.42 | 5.50 | 3.56 | 5.90 | 0.69 | 1913 | 0.00 | 0.75 | 0.00 | 2500 | 800-544-8888 |
| Vanguard F/I Interm-Trm Corp | VFICX | 7.81 | — | 4.32 | 6.31 | 0.67 | 1070 | 0.00 | 0.26 | 0.00 | 3000 | 800-662-7447 |
| Bernstein Interm Duration | SNIDX | 7.32 | 5.87 | 3.31 | 5.96 | 0.71 | 2361 | 0.00 | 0.62 | 0.00 | 25000 | 212-756-4097 |

Source: Morningstar, Inc.

**TABLE B-17**

Corporate Long-Term Funds

| Fund Name | Ticker | 3-Year Return | 5-Year Return | Standard Deviation | 12-Month Yield | Sharpe Ratio | Asset | Expense Ratio | Front Load | Back Load | Initial Purchase | Telephone No. |
|---|---|---|---|---|---|---|---|---|---|---|---|---|
| Strong Corporate Bond | STCBX | 9.97 | 9.49 | 4.63 | 6.52 | 1.17 | 783 | 1.00 | 0.00 | 0.00 | 2500 | 800-368-1030 |
| Norwest Advant Stable Inc I | NVSIX | 6.17 | — | 0.88 | 5.49 | 1.16 | 158 | — | 0.00 | 0.00 | 1000 | 800-338-1348 |
| Harbor Bond | HABDX | 9.27 | 7.12 | 4.25 | 5.68 | 1.08 | 447 | 0.67 | 0.00 | 0.00 | 2000 | 800-422-1050 |
| PaineWebber Invmt Grade IncA | PIGAX | 9.00 | 6.72 | 4.30 | 6.99 | 1.00 | 218 | 1.03 | 4.00 | 0.00 | 1000 | 800-647-1568 |
| Elfun Income | EINFX | 8.27 | 6.88 | 3.53 | 6.21 | 0.98 | 250 | 0.20 | 0.00 | 0.00 | 500 | 800-242-0134 |
| Target Total Return Bond | TATBX | 8.80 | 7.07 | 4.29 | 4.87 | 0.94 | 62 | 0.91 | 0.00 | 0.00 | 25000 | 800-442-8748 |
| Federated Bond A | FDBAX | 8.72 | — | 4.24 | 7.15 | 0.93 | 195 | 1.05 | 4.50 | 0.00 | 500 | 800-341-7400 |
| Hancock Sovereign Bond A | JHNBX | 8.07 | 6.74 | 3.63 | 6.76 | 0.89 | 1320 | 1.11 | 4.50 | 0.00 | 1000 | 800-225-5291 |
| Crabbe Huson Income Prim | CHINX | 9.14 | 6.71 | 5.06 | 8.00 | 0.88 | 6 | 0.80 | 0.00 | 0.00 | 2000 | 800-541-9732 |
| WPG Core Bond | WPGVX | 7.15 | 4.12 | 2.56 | 5.44 | 0.84 | 119 | 0.86 | 0.00 | 0.00 | 25000 | 800-223-3332 |
| IDS Bond A | INBNX | 8.05 | 7.00 | 3.97 | 6.86 | 0.81 | 2757 | 0.84 | 5.00 | 0.00 | 2000 | 800-328-8300 |
| Dodge & Cox Income | DODIX | 8.10 | 6.89 | 4.14 | 5.84 | 0.79 | 842 | 0.49 | 0.00 | 0.00 | 2500 | 800-621-3979 |
| WM Income A | CMPIX | 8.36 | 6.83 | 4.59 | 6.55 | 0.77 | 219 | 1.03 | 4.00 | 0.00 | 1000 | 800-543-8072 |
| JP Morgan Bond | PPBDX | 7.62 | 6.34 | 3.53 | 6.22 | 0.76 | 224 | 0.68 | 0.00 | 0.00 | 2500 | 800-221-7930 |
| Northern Fixed-Income | NOFIX | 7.98 | — | 4.21 | 5.31 | 0.74 | 228 | 0.90 | 0.00 | 0.00 | 2500 | 800-595-9111 |

| Fund Name | Ticker | 3-Year Return | 5-Year Return | Standard Deviation | 12-Month Yield | Sharpe Ratio | Asset | Expense Ratio | Front Load | Back Load | Initial Purchase | Telephone No. |
|---|---|---|---|---|---|---|---|---|---|---|---|---|
| IAI Bond | IAIBX | 7.91 | 5.73 | 4.08 | 6.14 | 0.74 | 57 | 1.10 | 0.00 | 0.00 | 5000 | 800-945-3863 |
| Principal Bond A | PRBDX | 8.39 | 7.10 | 5.05 | 6.16 | 0.71 | 141 | 0.95 | 4.75 | 0.00 | 1000 | 800-451-5447 |
| Galaxy High-Qual Bond Ret A | GAHQX | 7.94 | 5.99 | 4.34 | 5.26 | 0.70 | 40 | 1.07 | 3.75 | 0.00 | 2500 | 800-628-0414 |
| USAA Income Strategy | USICX | 9.77 | — | 7.57 | 3.82 | 0.68 | 44 | 1.00 | 0.00 | 0.00 | 3000 | 800-382-8722 |
| Preferred Fixed-Income | PFXIX | 7.35 | 6.24 | 3.55 | 6.08 | 0.67 | 154 | 0.74 | 0.00 | 0.00 | 1000 | 800-662-4769 |
| Ivy Bond A | MCFIX | 7.97 | 6.49 | 4.75 | 7.13 | 0.65 | 114 | 1.47 | 4.75 | 0.00 | 1000 | 800-456-5111 |
| Sentinel Bond A | SNBDX | 7.53 | 5.91 | 4.04 | 6.14 | 0.64 | 90 | 0.97 | 4.00 | 0.00 | 1000 | 800-282-3863 |
| Accessor Intermediate F/I | AIFIX | 7.56 | 5.67 | 4.08 | 5.52 | 0.64 | 46 | 0.84 | 0.00 | 0.00 | 5000 | 800-759-3504 |
| Guardian Invest Qual Bond A | GUIQX | 7.30 | 5.39 | 3.78 | 5.37 | 0.62 | 135 | 0.75 | 4.50 | 0.00 | 1000 | 800-221-3253 |
| Babson Bond L | BABIX | 7.17 | 5.88 | 3.50 | 5.98 | 0.62 | 126 | 0.97 | 0.00 | 0.00 | 500 | 800-422-2766 |
| Aquinas Fixed-Income | AQFIX | 7.20 | — | 3.58 | 5.29 | 0.62 | 40 | 0.99 | 0.00 | 0.00 | 500 | 800-423-6369 |
| Dreyfus A Bonds Plus | DRBDX | 7.26 | 5.58 | 3.96 | 5.92 | 0.58 | 622 | 0.95 | 0.00 | 0.00 | 2500 | 800-373-9387 |
| Van Kampen Corp Bond A | ACCBX | 7.61 | 6.26 | 4.83 | 6.83 | 0.56 | 185 | 1.13 | 4.75 | 0.00 | 500 | 800-421-5666 |
| T. Rowe Price New Income | PRCIX | 6.77 | 5.89 | 4.07 | 6.28 | 0.42 | 2113 | 0.71 | 0.00 | 0.00 | 2500 | 800-638-5660 |
| MFS Bond A | MFBFX | 7.39 | 6.50 | 4.50 | 6.71 | 0.54 | 774 | 0.98 | 4.75 | 0.00 | 1000 | 800-637-2929 |

Source: Morningstar, Inc.

**TABLE B-18**

Corporate High-Income Funds

| Fund Name | Ticker | 3-Year Return | 5-Year Return | Standard Deviation | 12-Month Yield | Sharpe Ratio | Asset | Expense Ratio | Front Load | Back Load | Initial Purchase | Telephone No. |
|---|---|---|---|---|---|---|---|---|---|---|---|---|
| Legg Mason High-Yield Prim | LMHYX | 13.24 | — | 5.14 | 8.43 | 1.77 | 493 | 1.30 | 0.00 | 0.00 | 1000 | 800-577-8589 |
| Value Line Aggressive Income | VAGIX | 13.17 | 10.20 | 6.82 | 9.58 | 1.33 | 151 | 0.95 | 0.00 | 0.00 | 1000 | 800-223-0818 |
| Idex Income Plus A | IHIYX | 9.28 | 7.77 | 3.59 | 6.52 | 1.28 | 65 | 1.27 | 4.75 | 0.00 | 500 | 888-233-4339 |
| Summit High-Yield Ret | SUMHX | 13.57 | — | 7.68 | 9.27 | 1.24 | 53 | 1.60 | 4.50 | 0.00 | 1000 | 800-272-3442 |
| Pilgrim America High-Yield A | PIHYX | 11.26 | 9.43 | 5.71 | 9.70 | 1.20 | 91 | 1.00 | 4.75 | 0.00 | 1000 | 800-334-3444 |
| United High-Income A | UNHIX | 10.66 | 9.00 | 5.23 | 8.66 | 1.18 | 1023 | 0.84 | 5.75 | 0.00 | 500 | 800-366-5465 |
| Columbia High-Yield | CMHYX | 9.83 | — | 4.46 | 7.87 | 1.17 | 51 | 1.00 | 0.00 | 0.00 | 1000 | 800-547-1707 |
| United High-Income II A | UNHHX | 10.41 | 8.75 | 5.34 | 8.79 | 1.10 | 411 | 0.93 | 5.75 | 0.00 | 500 | 800-366-5465 |
| Vanguard F/I High-Yield Corp | VWEHX | 9.35 | 8.63 | 4.40 | 8.74 | 1.07 | 4954 | 0.28 | 0.00 | 0.00 | 3000 | 800-662-7447 |
| First Invest Fund for Inc A | FIFIX | 10.07 | 9.68 | 5.20 | 9.23 | 1.06 | 408 | 1.15 | 6.25 | 0.00 | 1000 | 800-423-4026 |
| T. Rowe Price High-Yield | PRHYX | 10.12 | 7.59 | 5.31 | 9.15 | 1.05 | 1761 | 0.81 | 0.00 | 0.00 | 2500 | 800-638-5660 |
| Northeast Investors | NTHEX | 10.99 | 11.20 | 6.50 | 8.89 | 1.01 | 2604 | 0.64 | 0.00 | 0.00 | 1000 | 800-225-6704 |
| Invesco High-Yield | FHYPX | 11.55 | 9.13 | 7.49 | 9.06 | 0.96 | 653 | 1.00 | 0.00 | 0.00 | 1000 | 800-525-8085 |
| Delaware Delchester A | DETWX | 9.73 | 7.77 | 5.32 | 9.45 | 0.96 | 955 | 1.04 | 4.75 | 0.00 | 1000 | 800-523-4640 |
| Eaton Vance Income of Boston | EVIBX | 10.71 | 9.35 | 6.73 | 9.55 | 0.93 | 225 | 1.05 | 4.75 | 0.00 | 1000 | 800-225-6265 |

| Fund Name | Ticker | 3-Year Return | 5-Year Return | Standard Deviation | 12-Month Yield | Sharpe Ratio | Asset | Expense Ratio | Front Load | Back Load | Initial Purchase | Telephone No. |
|---|---|---|---|---|---|---|---|---|---|---|---|---|
| Colonial High-Yield Secs A | COLHX | 10.26 | 9.49 | 6.18 | 9.60 | 0.93 | 550 | 1.20 | 4.75 | 0.00 | 1000 | 800-426-3750 |
| Seligman High-Yield Bond A | SHYBX | 10.78 | 10.75 | 6.86 | 9.71 | 0.92 | 934 | 1.14 | 4.75 | 0.00 | 1000 | 800-221-2783 |
| Federated High-Income Bond A | FHIIX | 9.93 | 9.21 | 5.96 | 8.96 | 0.90 | 705 | 1.21 | 4.50 | 0.00 | 500 | 800-341-7400 |
| SunAmerica High-Income A | SHNAX | 10.36 | 6.43 | 6.66 | 9.45 | 0.88 | 62 | 1.52 | 4.75 | 0.00 | 500 | 800-858-8850 |
| Federated High-Yield | FHYTX | 9.81 | 8.83 | 6.02 | 9.29 | 0.87 | 1016 | 0.88 | 0.00 | 0.00 | 25000 | 800-341-7400 |
| Smith Barney High-Income A | SHIAX | 9.54 | 8.05 | 5.71 | 9.92 | 0.86 | 500 | 1.06 | 4.50 | 0.00 | 1000 | 800-451-2010 |
| Northstar High-Yield A | NHYAX | 9.17 | — | 5.34 | 8.76 | 0.84 | 21 | 1.20 | 4.75 | 0.00 | 2500 | 800-595-7827 |
| Executive Investors Hi-Yield | EIHYX | 9.50 | 8.77 | 5.87 | 9.28 | 0.83 | 219 | 1.22 | 4.75 | 0.00 | 1000 | 800-423-4026 |
| Oppenheimer High-Yield A | OPPHX | 9.51 | 8.35 | 6.10 | 9.16 | 0.80 | 1139 | 1.00 | 4.75 | 0.00 | 1000 | 800-525-7048 |
| First Invest High-Yield A | FIHYX | 9.05 | 9.29 | 5.45 | 9.09 | 0.80 | 192 | 1.29 | 6.25 | 0.00 | 1000 | 800-423-4026 |
| Fidelity High-Income | SPHIX | 10.26 | 10.82 | 8.62 | 9.10 | 0.66 | 3309 | 0.80 | 0.00 | 0.00 | 10000 | 800-544-8888 |
| Safeco High-Yield No Load | SAFHX | 8.84 | 7.67 | 5.50 | 9.06 | 0.74 | 80 | 0.91 | 0.00 | 0.00 | 1000 | 800-426-6730 |
| AIM High-Yield A | AMHYX | 9.35 | 8.50 | 6.25 | 9.74 | 0.75 | 1868 | 0.90 | 4.75 | 0.00 | 500 | 800-347-4246 |
| IDS Extra Income A | INEAX | 9.48 | 8.23 | 6.12 | 9.53 | 0.79 | 3136 | 0.89 | 5.00 | 0.00 | 2000 | 800-328-8300 |
| Federated High-Income Bond B | FHBBX | 9.09 | — | 5.86 | 8.16 | 0.75 | 1004 | 1.97 | 0.00 | 5.50 | 1500 | 800-341-7400 |

Source: Morningstar, Inc.

**TABLE B-19**

Municipal Short-Term Funds

| Fund Name | Ticker | 3-Year Return | 5-Year Return | Standard Deviation | 12-Month Yield | Sharpe Ratio | Asset | Expense Ratio | Front Load | Back Load | Initial Purchase | Telephone No. |
|-----------|--------|---------------|---------------|--------------------|----------------|--------------|-------|---------------|------------|-----------|------------------|---------------|
| Strong Short-Term Muni Bond | STSMX | 5.69 | 4.15 | 1.18 | 4.81 | 0.38 | 203 | 0.70 | 0.00 | 0.00 | 2500 | 800-368-1030 |
| USAA Tax-Exempt Short-Term | USSTX | 5.30 | 4.78 | 1.06 | 4.56 | −0.01 | 972 | 0.41 | 0.00 | 0.00 | 3000 | 800-382-8722 |
| Federated Ltd Term Muni F | LMFSX | 4.77 | 4.34 | 1.06 | 4.29 | −0.59 | 28 | 0.65 | 0.00 | 1.00 | 1500 | 800-341-7400 |
| Dreyfus Short-Intrm Muni Bd | DSIBX | 4.82 | 4.18 | 0.96 | 4.20 | −0.59 | 290 | 0.76 | 0.00 | 0.00 | 2500 | 800-373-9387 |
| Federated Ltd Term Muni A | LMINX | 4.51 | 4.11 | 1.05 | 4.04 | −0.88 | 83 | 0.90 | 1.00 | 0.00 | 1500 | 800-341-7400 |
| Kent Limited Term T/F Invmt | KLTIX | 4.25 | — | 1.36 | 3.60 | −0.91 | 0 | 0.87 | 0.00 | 0.00 | 1000 | 800-633-5368 |
| Nations Short-Trm Muni Inv A | NSMMX | 4.44 | — | 1.02 | 3.94 | −0.99 | 31 | 0.60 | 0.00 | 0.00 | 1000 | 800-321-7854 |
| Excelsior Short-Tm T/E Secs | USSSX | 4.23 | 3.91 | 1.15 | 3.72 | −1.08 | 40 | 0.58 | 0.00 | 0.00 | 500 | 800-446-1012 |

| Fund Name | Ticker | 3-Year Return | 5-Year Return | Standard Deviation | 12-Month Yield | Sharpe Ratio | Asset | Expense Ratio | Front Load | Back Load | Initial Purchase | Telephone No. |
|---|---|---|---|---|---|---|---|---|---|---|---|---|
| Payden & Rygel Sh Dur T/E R | PYSDX | 4.08 | — | 1.07 | 4.07 | -1.34 | 17 | 0.45 | 0.00 | 0.00 | 5000 | 800-572-9336 |
| Merrill Lynch Muni Ltd Mat A | MALMX | 4.24 | 3.97 | 0.75 | 3.85 | -1.66 | 291 | 0.39 | 1.00 | 0.00 | 1000 | 800-637-3863 |
| Vanguard Muni Short-Term | VWSTX | 4.06 | 3.90 | 0.56 | 3.92 | -2.60 | 1595 | 0.18 | 0.00 | 0.00 | 3000 | 800-662-7447 |
| Stagecoach Sh-Term Muni Inc | OVSIX | 3.73 | — | 0.62 | 3.74 | -2.96 | 5 | 0.40 | 3.00 | 0.00 | 1000 | 800-222-8222 |
| Bernstein Short Dur Div Muni | SDDMX | 3.84 | — | 0.58 | 3.49 | -2.97 | 137 | 0.72 | 0.00 | 0.00 | 25000 | 212-756-4097 |
| Calvert Tax-Fr Res Lim-TermA | CTFLX | 4.09 | 3.97 | 0.41 | 3.78 | -3.44 | 498 | 0.69 | 1.00 | 0.00 | 2000 | 800-368-2748 |
| Strong Municipal Advantage | SMUAX | — | — | — | 4.32 | — | 1321 | 0.00 | 0.00 | 0.00 | 2500 | 800-368-1030 |

Source: Morningstar, Inc.

**TABLE B-20**

Municipal Intermediate-Term Funds

| Fund Name | Ticker | 3-Year Return | 5-Year Return | Standard Deviation | 12-Month Yield | Sharpe Ratio | Asset | Expense Ratio | Front Load | Back Load | Initial Purchase | Telephone No. |
|---|---|---|---|---|---|---|---|---|---|---|---|---|
| USAA Tax-Exempt Interm-Term | USATX | 7.50 | 6.22 | 2.85 | 5.30 | 0.89 | 2090 | 0.37 | 0.00 | 0.00 | 3000 | 800-382-8722 |
| Tax-Exempt Bond of America | AFTEX | 7.72 | 6.29 | 3.20 | 4.94 | 0.88 | 1751 | 0.68 | 4.75 | 0.00 | 1000 | 800-421-4120 |
| Strong Municipal Bond | SXFIX | 8.04 | 5.61 | 3.78 | 5.07 | 0.84 | 268 | 0.80 | 0.00 | 0.00 | 2500 | 800-368-1030 |
| Goldman Sachs Muni Inc A | GSMIX | 8.21 | 6.31 | 4.06 | 4.15 | 0.83 | 90 | 0.85 | 4.50 | 0.00 | 1000 | 800-526-7384 |
| Oppenheimer Insured Muni A | OPISX | 8.03 | 5.71 | 3.96 | 4.66 | 0.80 | 100 | 0.95 | 4.75 | 0.00 | 1000 | 800-525-7048 |
| New England Municipal Inc A | NEFTX | 7.42 | 5.54 | 3.09 | 5.05 | 0.80 | 175 | 0.93 | 4.50 | 0.00 | 2500 | 800-225-7670 |
| Boston 1784 T/E Med-Term Inc | SETMX | 7.30 | 6.19 | 3.14 | 4.45 | 0.74 | 317 | 0.80 | 0.00 | 0.00 | 1000 | 800-252-1784 |
| Putnam Tax Exempt Income A | PTAEX | 7.66 | 5.34 | 3.78 | 5.03 | 0.73 | 1985 | 0.78 | 4.75 | 0.00 | 500 | 800-225-1581 |
| Nuveen Flagship Interm A | FINTX | 7.50 | 6.26 | 3.49 | 4.59 | 0.73 | 44 | 0.79 | 3.00 | 0.00 | 3000 | 800-351-4100 |
| Scudder Managed Muni Bonds | SCMBX | 7.67 | 6.06 | 3.85 | 4.90 | 0.71 | 728 | 0.64 | 0.00 | 0.00 | 2500 | 800-225-2470 |
| Dreyfus Basic Interm Muni Bd | DBIMX | 7.16 | — | 3.08 | 4.58 | 0.70 | 92 | 0.24 | 0.00 | 0.00 | 10000 | 800-373-9387 |
| Franklin Fed Int-Trm T/F Inc | FKITX | 6.78 | 6.10 | 2.50 | 4.72 | 0.69 | 149 | 0.75 | 2.25 | 0.00 | 1000 | 800-342-5236 |
| Fidelity Spartan Interm Muni | FLTMX | 6.90 | 5.71 | 2.70 | 4.74 | 0.69 | 1113 | 0.55 | 0.00 | 0.00 | 10000 | 800-544-8888 |
| Van Kampen Int-Term Muni A | VKLMX | 6.81 | 6.14 | 2.56 | 4.52 | 0.68 | 20 | 1.52 | 3.25 | 0.00 | 500 | 800-421-5666 |
| T. Rowe Price Summit MuniInt | PRSMX | 6.88 | — | 2.81 | 4.45 | 0.65 | 71 | 0.50 | 0.00 | 0.00 | 25000 | 800-638-5660 |

| Fund Name | Ticker | 3-Year Return | 5-Year Return | Standard Deviation | 12-Month Yield | Sharpe Ratio | Asset | Expense Ratio | Front Load | Back Load | Initial Purchase | Telephone No. |
|---|---|---|---|---|---|---|---|---|---|---|---|---|
| Thornburg Interm Muni A | THIMX | 6.35 | 5.67 | 2.14 | 4.63 | 0.57 | 369 | 1.00 | 3.50 | 0.00 | 5000 | 800-847-0200 |
| Galaxy Tax-Exempt Bond Ret A | GABDX | 7.01 | 5.56 | 3.50 | 4.34 | 0.57 | 24 | 0.93 | 3.75 | 0.00 | 2500 | 800-628-0414 |
| Colonial Intermediate T/E A | CIXAX | 6.78 | 5.70 | 3.03 | 5.12 | 0.56 | 13 | 0.60 | 3.25 | 0.00 | 1000 | 800-426-3750 |
| Babson Tax-Free Income L | BALTX | 6.91 | 5.12 | 3.51 | 4.37 | 0.53 | 27 | 1.01 | 0.00 | 0.00 | 1000 | 800-422-2766 |
| Putnam Tax Exempt Income B | PTBEX | 6.98 | 4.69 | 3.79 | 4.43 | 0.52 | 247 | 1.43 | 0.00 | 5.00 | 500 | 800-225-1581 |
| New England Municipal Inc B | NETBX | 6.61 | — | 3.06 | 4.31 | 0.50 | 14 | 1.68 | 0.00 | 5.00 | 2500 | 800-225-7670 |
| WPG Intermediate Muni Bond | WPGMX | 6.40 | 5.43 | 2.59 | 4.23 | 0.49 | 25 | 0.85 | 0.00 | 0.00 | 2500 | 800-223-3332 |
| Limited Term Tax-Ex Bd Amer | LTEBX | 6.20 | — | 2.12 | 4.40 | 0.49 | 227 | 0.75 | 4.75 | 0.00 | 1000 | 800-421-4120 |
| WM Tax-Exempt Bond A | CMTEX | 6.81 | 5.44 | 3.80 | 4.77 | 0.46 | 305 | 0.75 | 4.00 | 0.00 | 1000 | 800-543-8072 |
| Delaware Tax-Free USA Int A | DMUSX | 6.09 | 5.34 | 1.97 | 4.54 | 0.46 | 23 | 0.43 | 2.75 | 0.00 | 1000 | 800-523-4640 |
| Scudder Medium-Term Tax-Free | SCMTX | 6.37 | 5.70 | 2.90 | 4.48 | 0.43 | 666 | 0.74 | 0.00 | 0.00 | 2500 | 800-225-2470 |
| Fidelity Adv Interm Muni T | FALRX | 6.31 | 4.98 | 2.75 | 4.13 | 0.43 | 59 | 1.00 | 2.75 | 0.00 | 2500 | 800-522-7297 |
| Calvert Natl Muni Interm A | CINMX | 6.37 | 5.91 | 2.86 | 4.34 | 0.43 | 71 | 0.69 | 2.75 | 0.00 | 2000 | 800-368-2748 |
| Vanguard Muni Intermed-Term | VWITX | 6.24 | 5.79 | 2.66 | 4.89 | 0.41 | 7505 | 0.18 | 0.00 | 0.00 | 3000 | 800-662-7447 |
| Dreyfus Intermediate Muni | DITEX | 6.30 | 5.38 | 2.89 | 4.79 | 0.40 | 1338 | 0.74 | 0.00 | 0.00 | 2500 | 800-373-9387 |
| Stein Roe Intermediate Munis | SRIMX | 6.27 | 5.34 | 2.93 | 4.63 | 0.39 | 194 | 0.70 | 0.00 | 0.00 | 2500 | 800-338-2550 |

**TABLE B-21**

Municipal Long-Term Funds

| Fund Name | Ticker | 3-Year Return | 5-Year Return | Standard Deviation | 12-Month Yield | Sharpe Ratio | Asset | Expense Ratio | Front Load | Back Load | Initial Purchase | Telephone No. |
|---|---|---|---|---|---|---|---|---|---|---|---|---|
| Sit Tax-Free Income | SNTIX | 8.11 | 6.80 | 2.32 | 5.07 | 1.41 | 648 | 0.79 | 0.00 | 0.00 | 2000 | 800-332-5580 |
| Davis Tax-Free High Income A | VMPAX | 6.70 | — | 1.28 | 6.27 | 1.28 | 250 | 1.25 | 4.75 | 0.00 | 1000 | 800-279-0279 |
| T. Rowe Price Summit MuniInc | PRINX | 9.16 | — | 3.81 | 4.82 | 1.17 | 56 | 0.50 | 0.00 | 0.00 | 25000 | 800-638-5660 |
| Eaton Vance Natl Municipal A | EANAX | 9.84 | — | 4.76 | 5.58 | 1.10 | 133 | 0.97 | 4.75 | 0.00 | 1000 | 800-225-6265 |
| USAA Tax-Exempt Long-Term | USTEX | 8.61 | 6.19 | 3.63 | 5.48 | 1.06 | 2094 | 0.37 | 0.00 | 0.00 | 3000 | 800-382-8722 |
| Dreyfus Basic Muni Bond | DRMBX | 8.97 | — | 4.08 | 4.86 | 1.04 | 188 | 0.26 | 0.00 | 0.00 | 10000 | 800-373-9387 |
| Nuveen Flagship All-Amer A | FLAAX | 8.41 | 6.42 | 3.61 | 5.07 | 1.00 | 250 | 0.81 | 4.20 | 0.00 | 3000 | 800-621-7227 |
| Merrill Lynch Muni Natl A | MANLX | 8.18 | 6.13 | 3.44 | 5.46 | 0.97 | 960 | 0.55 | 4.00 | 0.00 | 1000 | 800-637-3863 |
| Franklin Fed Tax-Free Inc I | FKTIX | 7.50 | 6.23 | 2.63 | 5.48 | 0.97 | 7083 | 0.58 | 4.25 | 0.00 | 1000 | 800-342-5236 |
| Oppenheimer Municipal Bond A | OPTAX | 8.23 | 5.80 | 3.56 | 5.02 | 0.96 | 590 | 0.87 | 4.75 | 0.00 | 1000 | 800-525-7048 |
| United Municipal Bond A | UNMBX | 8.31 | 6.50 | 3.67 | 4.86 | 0.95 | 989 | 0.67 | 4.25 | 0.00 | 500 | 800-366-5465 |
| Norwest Advant Tax-Fr Inc A | NWTFX | 8.50 | 6.49 | 3.93 | 4.95 | 0.94 | 41 | 0.60 | 4.00 | 0.00 | 1000 | 800-338-1348 |
| Fidelity Spartan Muni Inc | FHIGX | 8.24 | 5.94 | 3.63 | 4.68 | 0.94 | 2416 | 0.55 | 0.00 | 0.00 | 10000 | 800-544-8888 |
| CitiFunds Natl Tax-Free Inc | CFNIX | 8.81 | — | 4.32 | 4.78 | 0.94 | 47 | 0.14 | 0.00 | 0.00 | 0 | 800-721-1899 |
| Alliance Muni Income Natl A | ALTHX | 8.57 | 6.40 | 4.03 | 5.21 | 0.94 | 357 | 0.69 | 4.25 | 0.00 | 250 | 800-227-4618 |

| Fund Name | Ticker | 3-Year Return | 5-Year Return | Standard Deviation | 12-Month Yield | Sharpe Ratio | Asset | Expense Ratio | Front Load | Back Load | Initial Purchase | Telephone No. |
|---|---|---|---|---|---|---|---|---|---|---|---|---|
| Smith Barney Muni National A | SBBNX | 8.23 | 6.55 | 3.74 | 5.50 | 0.91 | 382 | 0.70 | 4.00 | 0.00 | 1000 | 800-451-2010 |
| Executive Investors Ins T/E | EIITX | 8.89 | 7.47 | 4.56 | 4.48 | 0.91 | 1181 | 0.75 | 4.75 | 0.00 | 1000 | 800-423-4026 |
| Principal Tax-Exempt Bond A | PTBDX | 7.75 | 5.84 | 3.17 | 4.86 | 0.90 | 202 | 0.79 | 4.75 | 0.00 | 1000 | 800-451-5447 |
| Lord Abbett T/F Inc Natl A | LANSX | 8.10 | 5.60 | 3.65 | 4.66 | 0.89 | 598 | 0.87 | 4.75 | 0.00 | 1000 | 800-874-3733 |
| Hancock Tax-Free Bond A | TAMBX | 8.42 | 5.96 | 4.17 | 5.10 | 0.87 | 589 | 0.85 | 4.50 | 0.00 | 1000 | 800-225-5291 |
| Alliance Muni Insured Natl A | CABTX | 8.63 | 6.35 | 4.46 | 4.67 | 0.87 | 176 | 1.02 | 4.25 | 0.00 | 250 | 800-227-4618 |
| Seligman Municipal Natl A | SNXEX | 8.30 | 5.55 | 4.03 | 4.77 | 0.86 | 101 | 0.80 | 4.75 | 0.00 | 1000 | 800-221-2783 |
| Nations Muni Income Inv A | NMUIX | 7.90 | 6.06 | 3.61 | 4.53 | 0.84 | 22 | 0.80 | 0.00 | 0.00 | 1000 | 800-321-7854 |
| AAL Municipal Bond A | AAMBX | 8.51 | 6.60 | 4.55 | 4.41 | 0.82 | 245 | 0.89 | 4.00 | 0.00 | 1000 | 800-553-6319 |
| Vanguard Muni Long-Term | VWLTX | 7.98 | 6.50 | 3.83 | 5.09 | 0.81 | 1442 | 0.18 | 0.00 | 0.00 | 3000 | 800-662-7447 |
| Van Kampen Municipal Inc A | VKMMX | 7.72 | 5.64 | 3.53 | 5.32 | 0.80 | 764 | 0.89 | 4.75 | 0.00 | 500 | 800-421-5666 |
| Schwab Long-Term Tax-Fr Bond | SWNTX | 8.00 | 6.23 | 4.03 | 4.80 | 0.78 | 63 | 0.49 | 0.00 | 0.00 | 1000 | 800-435-4000 |
| Safeco Municipal Bond NoLoad | SFCOX | 8.71 | 6.42 | 5.07 | 4.96 | 0.78 | 511 | 0.51 | 0.00 | 0.00 | 1000 | 800-426-6730 |
| Putnam Municipal Income A | PTFHX | 7.66 | 6.01 | 3.50 | 5.38 | 0.78 | 822 | 0.95 | 4.75 | 0.00 | 500 | 800-225-1581 |
| T. Rowe Price Tax-Fr Income | PRTAX | 7.74 | 6.05 | 3.84 | 5.06 | 0.74 | 1434 | 0.55 | 0.00 | 0.00 | 2500 | 800-638-5660 |

Source: Morningstar, Inc.

**TABLE B-22**

Municipal State Long-Term Funds

| Fund Name | Ticker | 3-Year Return | 5-Year Return | Standard Deviation | 12-Month Yield | Sharpe Ratio | Asset | Expense Ratio | Front Load | Back Load | Initial Purchase | Telephone No. |
|---|---|---|---|---|---|---|---|---|---|---|---|---|
| Alliance Muni Income II VA A | AVAAX | 10.33 | — | 3.54 | 5.02 | 1.64 | 10 | 0.67 | 4.25 | 0.00 | 250 | 800-227-4618 |
| Evergreen FL High-Inc Muni A | EFHAX | 8.69 | 7.37 | 2.49 | 5.17 | 1.58 | 274 | 0.87 | 4.75 | 0.00 | 1000 | 800-343-2898 |
| Alliance Muni Income II OH A | AOHAX | 8.99 | 6.27 | 3.16 | 5.14 | 1.35 | 14 | 0.75 | 4.25 | 0.00 | 250 | 800-227-4618 |
| Alliance Muni Income II MA A | AMAAX | 10.36 | — | 4.37 | 5.23 | 1.34 | 21 | 0.72 | 4.25 | 0.00 | 250 | 800-227-4618 |
| Delaware-Voyageur T/F AZ A | DVAAX | 9.33 | — | 3.60 | 4.93 | 1.30 | 12 | 0.46 | 3.75 | 0.00 | 1000 | 800-523-4640 |
| Sit MN Tax-Free Income | SMTFX | 7.35 | — | 1.88 | 5.15 | 1.27 | 188 | 0.80 | 0.00 | 0.00 | 2000 | 800-332-5580 |
| Delaware-Voyageur T/F FL A | DVFAX | 9.15 | — | 3.65 | 5.01 | 1.22 | 10 | 0.33 | 3.75 | 0.00 | 1000 | 800-523-4640 |
| Alliance Muni Income II FL A | AFLAX | 9.07 | 6.43 | 3.67 | 5.25 | 1.19 | 38 | 0.73 | 4.25 | 0.00 | 250 | 800-227-4618 |
| Alliance Muni Income II PA A | APAAX | 9.02 | 6.59 | 3.73 | 5.22 | 1.16 | 34 | 0.95 | 4.25 | 0.00 | 250 | 800-227-4618 |
| USAA TX Tax-Free Income | UTXTX | 9.47 | — | 4.29 | 5.03 | 1.13 | 24 | 0.50 | 0.00 | 0.00 | 3000 | 800-382-8722 |
| Delaware-Voyageur T/F CO A | VCTFX | 8.65 | 6.37 | 3.57 | 4.90 | 1.09 | 357 | 0.81 | 3.75 | 0.00 | 1000 | 800-523-4640 |
| Alliance Muni Income II AZ A | AAZAX | 8.85 | — | 3.76 | 5.09 | 1.09 | 21 | 0.78 | 4.25 | 0.00 | 250 | 800-227-4618 |
| Franklin AR Municipal Bond | FAKIX | 8.44 | — | 3.37 | 5.26 | 1.08 | 32 | 0.10 | 4.25 | 0.00 | 1000 | 800-342-5236 |
| Franklin WA Municipal Bond | FWMIX | 8.45 | 6.25 | 3.43 | 5.56 | 1.07 | 11 | 0.10 | 4.25 | 0.00 | 1000 | 800-342-5236 |

| Fund Name | Ticker | 3-Year Return | 5-Year Return | Standard Deviation | 12-Month Yield | Sharpe Ratio | Asset | Expense Ratio | Front Load | Back Load | Initial Purchase | Telephone No. |
|---|---|---|---|---|---|---|---|---|---|---|---|---|
| USAA FL Tax-Free Income | UFLTX | 8.85 | — | 3.89 | 5.01 | 1.06 | 153 | 0.50 | 0.00 | 0.00 | 3000 | 800-382-8722 |
| Dupree TN Tax-Free Income | TNTIX | 8.79 | — | 3.88 | 5.77 | 1.04 | 33 | 0.55 | 0.00 | 0.00 | 100 | 800-866-0614 |
| Delaware-Voyageur T/F NM A | VNMTX | 8.25 | 6.30 | 3.31 | 4.76 | 1.04 | 21 | 0.88 | 3.75 | 0.00 | 1000 | 800-523-4640 |
| Alliance Muni Income II MI A | AMIAX | 9.43 | — | 4.60 | 4.92 | 1.04 | 9 | 0.96 | 4.25 | 0.00 | 250 | 800-227-4618 |
| Federated PA Muni Income A | PAMFX | 8.27 | 6.37 | 3.34 | 4.85 | 1.03 | 238 | 0.75 | 4.50 | 0.00 | 500 | 800-341-7400 |
| Franklin TN Municipal Bond | FRTIX | 8.57 | — | 3.70 | 4.95 | 1.02 | 47 | 0.40 | 4.25 | 0.00 | 100 | 800-342-5236 |
| Smith Barney Muni PA A | SBPAX | 8.89 | — | 4.22 | 4.99 | 0.99 | 18 | 0.37 | 4.00 | 0.00 | 1000 | 800-451-2010 |
| Dreyfus Premier St Muni TX A | PTXBX | 8.44 | 6.74 | 3.66 | 4.61 | 0.99 | 60 | 0.72 | 4.50 | 0.00 | 1000 | 800-554-4611 |
| Smith Barney Muni GA A | SBGAX | 9.18 | — | 4.57 | 4.93 | 0.98 | 23 | 0.48 | 4.00 | 0.00 | 1000 | 800-451-2010 |
| Smith Barney Muni FL A | SBFLX | 8.11 | 6.51 | 3.34 | 5.15 | 0.98 | 147 | 0.85 | 4.00 | 0.00 | 1000 | 800-451-2010 |
| Nuveen Flagship CO Muni A | FCOTX | 8.88 | 6.79 | 4.32 | 4.76 | 0.96 | 38 | 1.00 | 4.20 | 0.00 | 3000 | 800-621-7227 |
| Lord Abbett T/F Income WA | LAWAX | 8.29 | 5.88 | 3.60 | 4.66 | 0.96 | 62 | 0.57 | 4.75 | 0.00 | 1000 | 800-874-3733 |
| Delaware-Voyageur T/F WAInsA | DVAWX | 8.42 | 6.44 | 3.78 | 4.91 | 0.96 | 2 | 0.44 | 3.75 | 0.00 | 1000 | 800-523-4640 |
| Franklin TX Tax-Free Inc I | FTXTX | 7.28 | 6.23 | 2.43 | 5.27 | 0.95 | 128 | 0.76 | 4.25 | 0.00 | 1000 | 800-342-5236 |
| Oppenheimer FL Municipal A | OFLAX | 7.74 | — | 3.02 | 4.91 | 0.94 | 36 | 0.53 | 4.75 | 0.00 | 1000 | 800-525-7048 |
| Lord Abbett T/F Income GA | LAGAX | 8.69 | — | 4.18 | 4.71 | 0.94 | 18 | 0.38 | 4.75 | 0.00 | 1000 | 800-874-3733 |

Source: Morningstar, Inc.

**TABLE B-23**

Municipal High-Yield Funds

| Fund Name | Ticker | 3-Year Return | 5-Year Return | Standard Deviation | 12-Month Yield | Sharpe Ratio | Asset | Expense Ratio | Front Load | Back Load | Initial Purchase | Telephone No. |
|---|---|---|---|---|---|---|---|---|---|---|---|---|
| United Municipal High-Inc A | UMUHX | 9.58 | 7.95 | 2.66 | 5.63 | 1.86 | 517 | 0.78 | 4.25 | 0.00 | 500 | 800-366-5465 |
| Delaware Natl Hi-Yld Muni A | CXHYX | 8.68 | 7.08 | 2.32 | 5.59 | 1.70 | 70 | 0.87 | 3.75 | 0.00 | 1000 | 800-523-4640 |
| Eaton Vance Hi-Yield Munis A | ETHYX | 11.37 | — | 4.16 | 5.79 | 1.69 | 120 | 0.95 | 4.75 | 0.00 | 1000 | 800-225-6265 |
| Evergreen FL High-Inc Muni A | EFHAX | 8.69 | 7.37 | 2.49 | 5.17 | 1.58 | 274 | 0.87 | 4.75 | 0.00 | 1000 | 800-343-2898 |
| American High-Income Muni Bd | AMHIX | 8.88 | — | 2.78 | 5.13 | 1.49 | 464 | 0.87 | 4.75 | 0.00 | 1000 | 800-421-4120 |
| Franklin High Yld T/F Inc I | FRHIX | 8.61 | 7.52 | 2.72 | 5.77 | 1.41 | 6001 | 0.61 | 4.25 | 0.00 | 1000 | 800-342-5236 |
| Strong High-Yield Muni Bond | SHYLX | 9.43 | — | 3.78 | 5.59 | 1.27 | 625 | 0.70 | 0.00 | 0.00 | 2500 | 800-368-1030 |
| Colonial High-Yield Muni A | CHYBX | 8.62 | — | 3.05 | 5.84 | 1.27 | 63 | 0.96 | 4.75 | 0.00 | 1000 | 800-426-3750 |
| PaineWebber Muni High-Inc A | PMHAX | 8.27 | 5.77 | 2.75 | 5.21 | 1.25 | 63 | 1.15 | 4.00 | 0.00 | 1000 | 800-647-1568 |

| Fund Name | Ticker | 3-Year Return | 5-Year Return | Standard Deviation | 12-Month Yield | Sharpe Ratio | Asset | Expense Ratio | Front Load | Back Load | Initial Purchase | Telephone No. |
|---|---|---|---|---|---|---|---|---|---|---|---|---|
| Franklin High Yld T/F Inc II | FHYIX | 8.02 | — | 2.70 | 5.17 | 1.17 | 515 | 1.18 | 1.00 | 1.00 | 1000 | 800-342-5236 |
| T. Rowe Price Tax-Fr Hi-Yld | PRFHX | 8.31 | 6.65 | 3.18 | 5.34 | 1.10 | 1295 | 0.72 | 0.00 | 0.00 | 2500 | 800-638-5660 |
| Stein Roe High-Yield Munis | SRMFX | 7.84 | 6.55 | 2.97 | 5.39 | 0.99 | 342 | 0.77 | 0.00 | 0.00 | 2500 | 800-338-2550 |
| Smith Barney Muni High Inc A | STXAX | 7.87 | 6.00 | 3.06 | 5.29 | 0.98 | 500 | 0.83 | 4.00 | 0.00 | 1000 | 800-451-2010 |
| Prudential Muni High-Inc A | PRHAX | 8.38 | 6.76 | 3.66 | 5.87 | 0.97 | 449 | 0.64 | 3.00 | 0.00 | 1000 | 800-225-1852 |
| Vanguard Muni High-Yield | VWAHX | 7.86 | 6.51 | 3.46 | 5.31 | 0.86 | 2627 | 0.19 | 0.00 | 0.00 | 3000 | 800-662-7447 |
| Van Kampen Tax-Free Hi-Inc A | VKMHX | 7.44 | 6.23 | 3.03 | 5.69 | 0.82 | 732 | 0.94 | 4.75 | 0.00 | 500 | 800-421-5666 |
| IDS High-Yield Tax-Exempt A | INHYX | 7.34 | 5.92 | 3.13 | 5.53 | 0.76 | 5736 | 0.70 | 5.00 | 0.00 | 2000 | 800-328-8300 |
| MFS Municipal High-Income A | MMHYX | 7.09 | 6.17 | 3.29 | 5.85 | 0.63 | 1136 | 0.89 | 4.75 | 0.00 | 1000 | 800-637-2929 |
| Hancock High-Yield Tax-Fr A | JHTFX | 6.91 | — | 3.70 | 5.58 | 0.51 | 40 | 1.06 | 4.50 | 0.00 | 1000 | 800-225-5291 |

Source: Morningstar, Inc.

**TABLE B-24**

Strategic/Multisector Bond Funds

| Fund Name | Ticker | 3-Year Return | 5-Year Return | Standard Deviation | 12-Month Yield | Sharpe Ratio | Asset | Expense Ratio | Front Load | Back Load | Initial Purchase | Telephone No. |
|---|---|---|---|---|---|---|---|---|---|---|---|---|
| Alliance Multi-Mkt Strat A | AMMSX | 10.33 | 4.02 | 3.04 | 9.68 | 1.91 | 97 | 1.57 | 4.25 | 0.00 | 250 | 800-227-4618 |
| Janus Flexible Income | JAFIX | 10.58 | 8.56 | 4.02 | 6.69 | 1.52 | 925 | 0.86 | 0.00 | 0.00 | 2500 | 800-525-8983 |
| Smith Barney Divr Str Inc A | SDSAX | 8.67 | 7.15 | 2.65 | 7.93 | 1.47 | 390 | 1.03 | 4.50 | 0.00 | 1000 | 800-451-2010 |
| Hancock Strategic Income A | JHFIX | 10.50 | 8.77 | 4.84 | 8.36 | 1.24 | 500 | 0.92 | 4.50 | 0.00 | 1000 | 800-225-5291 |
| Idex Flexible Income A | IDITX | 9.49 | 7.40 | 3.94 | 6.54 | 1.23 | 14 | 1.85 | 4.75 | 0.00 | 500 | 888-233-4339 |
| T. Rowe Price Spectrum Inc | RPSIX | 8.82 | 7.77 | 4.25 | 6.25 | 0.96 | 2472 | 0.00 | 0.00 | 0.00 | 2500 | 800-638-5660 |
| Eaton Vance Strategic Inc B | EVSGX | 9.94 | 6.76 | 5.98 | 8.68 | 0.90 | 136 | 2.08 | 0.00 | 5.00 | 1000 | 800-225-6265 |
| Dreyfus Strategic Income | DSINX | 8.45 | 6.48 | 4.37 | 7.03 | 0.83 | 289 | 1.03 | 0.00 | 0.00 | 2500 | 800-373-9387 |
| Colonial Strategic Income A | COSIX | 8.68 | 7.74 | 4.78 | 8.96 | 0.82 | 777 | 1.18 | 4.75 | 0.00 | 1000 | 800-426-3750 |
| Oppenheimer Strat Income A | OPSIX | 8.21 | 6.74 | 4.86 | 9.01 | 0.69 | 3930 | 0.93 | 4.75 | 0.00 | 1000 | 800-525-7048 |
| Salomon Bros Strategic Bd A | SSTAX | 8.98 | — | 6.31 | 8.98 | 0.67 | 22 | 1.24 | 4.75 | 0.00 | 500 | 800-725-6666 |
| North American Strat Inc A | NASIX | 9.14 | — | 6.69 | 7.42 | 0.66 | 17 | 1.50 | 4.75 | 0.00 | 1000 | 800-872-8037 |
| Evergreen Strategic Income A | EKSAX | 7.45 | 4.89 | 4.76 | 7.05 | 0.52 | 181 | 1.26 | 4.75 | 0.00 | 1000 | 800-343-2898 |
| Federated Strategic Income A | STIAX | 7.74 | — | 5.67 | 9.27 | 0.50 | 125 | 1.10 | 4.50 | 0.00 | 1500 | 800-341-7400 |
| Merriman Flexible Bond | MTGVX | 6.51 | 5.57 | 2.86 | 6.38 | 0.49 | 8 | 1.46 | 0.00 | 0.00 | 2000 | 800-423-4893 |
| Kemper Diversified Income A | KDIAX | 7.33 | 7.44 | 5.00 | 8.06 | 0.47 | 556 | 1.03 | 4.50 | 0.00 | 1000 | 800-621-1048 |
| Fidelity Adv Strat Income T | FSIAX | 7.87 | — | 6.68 | 7.23 | 0.45 | 174 | 1.19 | 3.50 | 0.00 | 2500 | 800-522-7297 |
| Franklin Strategic Income | FRSTX | 8.00 | — | 7.46 | 8.86 | 0.42 | 198 | 0.25 | 4.25 | 0.00 | 1000 | 800-342-5236 |
| Putnam Diversified Income A | PDINX | 6.42 | 5.70 | 5.71 | 7.38 | 0.23 | 2066 | 0.99 | 4.75 | 0.00 | 500 | 800-225-1581 |
| Van Kampen Strategic Inc A | VKSAX | 6.51 | — | 7.84 | 8.80 | 0.18 | 45 | 1.81 | 4.75 | 0.00 | 500 | 800-421-5666 |

Source: Morningstar, Inc.

**TABLE B-25**

Zero Coupon Bond Funds

| Fund Name | Ticker | 3-Year Return | 5-Year Return | Standard Deviation | 12-Month Yield | Sharpe Ratio | Asset | Expense Ratio | Front Load | Back Load | Initial Purchase | Telephone No. |
|---|---|---|---|---|---|---|---|---|---|---|---|---|
| American Cent-Ben TarMat2020 | BTTTX | 23.63 | 13.47 | 24.17 | 6.20 | 0.86 | 587 | 0.53 | 0.00 | 0.00 | 2500 | 800-345-2021 |
| American Cent-Ben TarMat2010 | BTTNX | 14.10 | 9.30 | 12.68 | 4.19 | 0.80 | 238 | 0.62 | 0.00 | 0.00 | 2500 | 800-345-2021 |
| American Cent-Ben TarMat2015 | BTFTX | 15.32 | 8.43 | 16.22 | 0.00 | 0.71 | 173 | 0.61 | 0.00 | 0.00 | 2500 | 800-345-2021 |
| American Cent-Ben TarMat2000 | BTMTX | 8.66 | 6.08 | 5.54 | 6.11 | 0.70 | 238 | 0.56 | 0.00 | 0.00 | 2500 | 800-345-2021 |
| American Cent-Ben TarMat2005 | BTFIX | 9.24 | 6.12 | 8.03 | 0.00 | 0.57 | 481 | 0.57 | 0.00 | 0.00 | 2500 | 800-345-2021 |
| Scudder Zero Coupon 2000 | SGZTX | 5.88 | 4.09 | 3.77 | 5.92 | 0.18 | 19 | 1.00 | 0.00 | 0.00 | 1000 | 800-225-2470 |

Source: Morningstar, Inc.

**TABLE B-26**

International Bond Funds

| Fund Name | Ticker | 3-Year Return | 5-Year Return | Standard Deviation | 12-Month Yield | Sharpe Ratio | Asset | Expense Ratio | Front Load | Back Load | Initial Purchase | Telephone No. |
|---|---|---|---|---|---|---|---|---|---|---|---|---|
| Goldman Sachs Global A | GSGIX | 10.92 | 8.22 | 3.24 | 6.66 | 2.00 | 201.7 | 1.17 | 4.50 | 0.00 | 1000 | 800-526-7384 |
| Dreyfus Global Bond | GDBDX | 8.97 | — | 4.27 | 6.36 | 0.99 | 15.7 | 1.35 | 0.00 | 0.00 | 2500 | 800-373-9387 |
| Smith Barney Global Govt A | SBGLX | 8.12 | 6.63 | 3.52 | 7.01 | 0.93 | 87.5 | 1.26 | 4.50 | 0.00 | 1000 | 800-451-2010 |
| MainStay Intl Bond A | MAIAX | 8.13 | — | 4.02 | 7.11 | 0.82 | 14.3 | 1.56 | 4.50 | 0.00 | 500 | 800-624-6782 |
| PaineWebber Global Income A | PGBAX | 6.82 | 5.56 | 2.54 | 6.3 | 0.69 | 404.1 | 1.21 | 4.00 | 0.00 | 1000 | 800-647-1568 |
| Warburg Pincus Glob Fix-Inc | CGFIX | 6.9 | 5.62 | 3.08 | 8.52 | 0.60 | 163.8 | 0.96 | 0.00 | 0.00 | 2500 | 800-927-2874 |
| Templeton Global Bond I | TPINX | 6.97 | 5.76 | 3.34 | 5.77 | 0.58 | 194.3 | 1.15 | 4.25 | 0.00 | 1000 | 800-292-9293 |
| AIM Global Govt Income A | GGINX | 7.16 | 3.73 | 4.02 | 5.84 | 0.54 | 140.5 | 1.34 | 4.75 | 0.00 | 500 | 800-347-4246 |
| Lord Abbett Global Income A | LAGIX | 7.17 | 5.94 | 4.18 | 6.23 | 0.52 | 121.1 | 1.10 | 4.75 | 0.00 | 1000 | 800-874-3733 |
| Merrill Lynch Global Bond A | MAGOX | 6.66 | 4.34 | 4.74 | 5.81 | 0.33 | 24.9 | 0.87 | 4.00 | 0.00 | 1000 | 800-637-3863 |
| IDS Global Bond A | IGBFX | 6.41 | 5.76 | 5.29 | 5.98 | 0.24 | 728.8 | 1.20 | 5.00 | 0.00 | 2000 | 800-328-8300 |
| Franklin Global Govt Inc I | FRGLX | 5.85 | 4.54 | 5.17 | 7.88 | 0.12 | 111.1 | 0.90 | 4.25 | 0.00 | 1000 | 800-342-5236 |
| T. Rowe Price Global Bond | RPGGX | 5.66 | 5.04 | 3.99 | 5.57 | 0.01 | 40.8 | 1.20 | 0.00 | 0.00 | 2500 | 800-638-5660 |
| Capital World Bond | CWBFX | 5.46 | 6.19 | 3.77 | 5.08 | 0.05 | 635.4 | 1.07 | 4.75 | 0.00 | 1000 | 800-421-4120 |
| Fidelity New Markets Income | FNMIX | 6.45 | 2.80 | 27.65 | 18.44 | 0.05 | 159.4 | 1.08 | 0.00 | 0.00 | 2500 | 800-544-8888 |

| Fund Name | Ticker | 3-Year Return | 5-Year Return | Standard Deviation | 12-Month Yield | Sharpe Ratio | Asset | Expense Ratio | Front Load | Back Load | Initial Purchase | Telephone No. |
|---|---|---|---|---|---|---|---|---|---|---|---|---|
| Managers Global Bond | MGGBX | 5.54 | — | 5.60 | 0.75 | 0.05 | 18.1 | 1.63 | 0.00 | 0.00 | 2000 | 800-835-3879 |
| Oppenheimer Intl Bond A | OIBAX | 5.59 | — | 8.52 | 12.08 | 0.04 | 97.8 | — | 4.75 | 0.00 | 1000 | 800-525-7048 |
| Federated Intl Income A | FTIIX | 5.38 | 5.25 | 5.67 | 4.95 | 0.02 | 146.0 | 1.30 | 4.50 | 0.00 | 1500 | 800-341-7400 |
| Kemper Global Income A | KGIAX | 5.29 | 6.15 | 3.72 | 5.94 | 0.00 | 69.9 | 1.32 | 4.50 | 0.00 | 1000 | 800-621-1048 |
| T. Rowe Price Emerg Mkts Bd | PREMX | 4.10 | — | 26.84 | 16.16 | −0.05 | 150.8 | 1.25 | 0.00 | 0.00 | 2500 | 800-638-5660 |
| American Cent-Ben Intl Bond | BEGBX | 4.88 | 7.21 | 6.90 | 0.31 | −0.07 | 157.0 | 0.84 | 0.00 | 0.00 | 2500 | 800-345-2021 |
| Scudder Emerging Mkts Income | SVEMX | 0.51 | — | 27.14 | 13.03 | −0.21 | 310.1 | 1.49 | 0.00 | 0.00 | 2500 | 800-225-2470 |
| Strong International Bond | SIBUX | 3.83 | — | 6.48 | 5.29 | −0.26 | 19.9 | 0.70 | 0.00 | 0.00 | 2500 | 800-368-1030 |
| T. Rowe Price Intl Bond | RPIBX | 4.07 | 5.18 | 5.50 | 5.57 | −0.26 | 840.6 | 0.86 | 0.00 | 0.00 | 2500 | 800-638-5660 |
| Legg Mason Global Govt Prim | LMGGX | 3.88 | 5.37 | 5.00 | 4.87 | −0.33 | 112.9 | 1.86 | 0.00 | 0.00 | 1000 | 800-577-8589 |
| Putnam Global Govtl Income A | PGGIX | 2.62 | 1.58 | 5.91 | 8.68 | −0.53 | 255.1 | 1.29 | 4.75 | 0.00 | 500 | 800-225-1581 |
| MFS World Governments A | MWGTX | 2.23 | 2.54 | 5.47 | 4.21 | −0.66 | 149.4 | 1.35 | 4.75 | 0.00 | 1000 | 800-637-2929 |
| Scudder Global Bond | SSTGX | 3.05 | 2.55 | 3.68 | 6.72 | −0.72 | 108.5 | 1.00 | 0.00 | 0.00 | 2500 | 800-225-2470 |
| Fidelity International Bond | FGBDX | 0.69 | −1.55 | 5.39 | 5.97 | −1.01 | 66.6 | 1.27 | 0.00 | 0.00 | 2500 | 800-544-8888 |
| Scudder International Bond | SCIBX | 1.27 | 0.12 | 4.51 | 6.26 | −1.05 | 145.4 | 1.36 | 0.00 | 0.00 | 2500 | 800-225-2470 |

Source: Morningstar, Inc.

# Internet Resources

## ASSOCIATIONS AND OTHER NONPROFIT ORGANIZATIONS

**Alliance for Investor Education:**
http://www.investoreducation.org

**American Association of Individual Investors:**
http://www.aaii.org

**American Association of Retired Persons:**
http://www.aarp.org

**American Savings Education Council:**
http://www.asec.org

**Bank Securities Association:**
http://www.bsanet.org

**The Bond Market Association:**
http://www.psa.com

**Electronic Traders Association:**
http://www.electronic-traders.org

**Institute of Certified Financial Planners:**
http://www.icfp.org

**International Association for Financial Planning, consumer services:**
http://www.iafp.org/ala.html

**Investors Alliance:**
http://www.freequote.com

**NASDAQ:**
http://www.nasdaq.com/

**National Association of Personal Financial Advisors:**
http://www.napfa.org

**National Association of Investors Corporation:**
http://www.better-investing.org

**National Association of Securities Dealers,**
**Office of Individual Investor Services:**
http://www.nasd.com/is_foyer.html

National Endowment for Financial Education:
http://www.nefe.org

National Investor Protection Trust:
http://www.investorprotection.org

National Investor Relations Institute:
http://www.niri.org

Savers and Investors League:
http://www.savers.org

## GOVERNMENT AGENCIES AND ORGANIZATIONS

Bureau of the Public Debt (info on savings bonds):
http://www.publicdebt.treas.gov/sav/savinvst.htm

Federal Reserve Board:
http://www.bog.frb.fed.us.

Federal Trade Commission:
http://www.ftc.gov

Investment Company Institute:
http://www.ici.org

Internal Revenue Service:
http://www.irs.ustreas.gov

North American Securities Administrators Association, Investor
education:
http://www.nasaa.org/investoredu/

Securities and Exchange Commission, Investor Assistance:
http://www.sec.gov/invkhome.htm

Social Security Administration:
http://www.ssa.gov

## COMMERCIAL INVESTOR SITES

Bloomberg Online: Mutual Funds:
http://www.bloomberg.com/fun/bbco/fndcol/fndcol1.html

Fundz:
http://www.fundz.com

**IBC Financial Data:**
http://www.IBCDATA.com

**Lipper Analytical Services, Inc.:**
http://www.lipperweb.com

**Morningstar, Inc.:**
http://www.morningstar.net

**Mutual Fund Investor's Center:**
http://www.mfea.com

**Mutual Fund Interactive:**
http://www.brill.com

**Quicken Financial Network**
http://www.qfn.com/

**Quote.Com:**
http://www.quote.com/

**S&P Micropal:**
http://www.micropal.com

**S&P Personal Wealth:**
http://www.personalwealth.com

**Yahoo:**
http://www.yahoo.com

# INDEX

Ralph G. Norton is currently the Chief Investment Officer of ING Funds. He is the former managing editor (and former popular columnist) for the Personal Wealth Internet Site of Standard & Poor's Consumer Markets. He is also a former member of the Standard & Poor's Investment Policy Committee and Mutual Fund Sub-Committee. Norton is a regular contributor to *Business Week, Barron's, The Wall Street Journal, The New York Times,* and *USA Today.* He is a guest on a weekly television show on KWHY in Los Angeles, and is also familiar to viewers of CNNfn, CNBC, CNN, and *Good Morning America.* A popular speaker, Norton regularly speaks to financial advisors and investors at conferences and seminars around the nation.